PRAISE FOR *Not for Sale*

"Batstone paints a picture of modern-day slavery that stretches across the whole world and includes our own neighborhoods. With clear language and moving stories, he highlights the impact of slavery on the most vulnerable: the children of developing nations. Batstone also tells the stories of the courageous modern-day abolitionists who are making a difference in the lives of children despite incredible odds. Batstone's message—and mine—is that we can end this egregious injustice."

> —Dean R. Hirsch, president, World Vision International

"Human trafficking is not an issue of the left or right, blue states or red states, but a great moral tragedy we can unite to stop. Batstone in the most compelling way tells the stories of those bound in slavery today and the modern-day abolitionists working tirelessly to end it. *Not for Sale* is a must-read to see how you can join the fight."

> —Jim Wallis, author of *God's Politics* and president, Sojourners/Call to Renewal

"In *Not for Sale,* Batstone exposes the alarming rise of one of the great moral crises of the day, human slavery. His well-written true-life accounts of victims and survivors will inspire you to join the growing twenty-first-century abolitionist movement."

> —Ambassador John Miller, former director of the U.S. State Department's Office to Monitor and Combat Trafficking in Persons

D0469623

NOT
for Sale

NOT
for Sale

*The Return of
the Global Slave Trade—
and How We Can Fight It*

REVISED AND UPDATED

David Batstone

HarperOne
An Imprint of HarperCollinsPublishers

HarperOne

HarperCollins books may be purchased for educational, business, or sales promotional use. For information, please write: Special Markets Department, Harper-Collins Publishers, 10 East 53rd Street, New York, NY 10022.

HarperCollins Web site: http://www.harpercollins.com

HarperCollins®, ⚒®, and HarperOne™ are trademarks of HarperCollins Publishers

FIRST EDITION PUBLISHED IN 2007
FIRST REVISED EDITION PUBLISHED IN 2010
Designed by Level C

Library of Congress Cataloging-in-Publication Data

Batstone, David B.
Not for sale : the return of the global slave trade—and how we can fight it /
by David Batstone. —Rev. ed.
p. cm.

ISBN 978–0–06–199883–6
1. Human trafficking. 2. Slavery. 3. Child slaves. 4. Forced labor. I. Title.
II. Title: Return of the global slave trade—and how we can fight it.
HQ281.B33 2010
306.3'62—dc22
2010014748

12 13 14 RRD (H) 10 9 8

To Wendy, Rusty, Ruth, Jade, Linda, and Loie
Your love surrounds me and your actions inspire me.

A little more matriarchy is what the world needs,
and I know it. Period. Paragraph.

—*Dorothy Thompson*

Contents

NOT
for Sale

Introduction

Finding Slavery in My Own Backyard

Trafficking thrives in the shadows. And it can
be easy to dismiss it as something that happens
to someone else, somewhere else. But that is not
the case. Trafficking is a crime that involves every
nation on earth, and that includes our own.

—*Hillary Rodham Clinton, U.S. Secretary of State*[1]

More than 30 million slaves live in our world today.[2] Girls
and boys, women and men of all ages are forced to toil in the
rug-loom sheds of Nepal, sell their bodies in the brothels of
Rome, break rocks in the quarries of Pakistan, fight wars in the
jungles of Africa, and sew clothes in the garment factories of
California.

Go behind the facade in any major town or city in the world
today, and you are likely to find a thriving commerce in human
beings. You may even find slavery in your own backyard.

For several years my wife and I dined regularly at an Indian
restaurant near our home in the San Francisco Bay area. Unbe-
knownst to us, the staff at Pasand Madras Indian Cuisine who
cooked our curries, delivered them to our table, and washed
our dishes were slaves.

It took a tragic accident to expose the slave-trafficking ring.
A young woman found her roommates, seventeen-year-old

Chanti Prattipati and her fifteen-year-old sister, Lalitha, unconscious in a Berkeley apartment. Carbon monoxide emitted from a blocked heating vent had poisoned them. The roommate called their landlord, Lakireddy Reddy, the owner of Pasand, where the girls worked. Reddy owned several restaurants and more than a thousand apartment units in northern California.

When Reddy arrived at the girls' apartment he declined to take them to a hospital. Instead, he and a few friends carried the incapacitated girls out of the apartment in a rolled-up carpet and put them into a waiting van. When Reddy and his cronies tried to force the roommate into the van as well, she put up a fierce fight. A local resident, Marcia Poole, happened to be passing by in her car at that moment and witnessed the bizarre scene of several men toting a sagging roll of carpet with a human leg hanging out the side. She slowed her car down to take a closer look and was horrified to see the men attempt to force a young girl into their van. Poole jumped out of her car and did everything in her power to stop the men. Unable to do so, she stopped another passing motorist and implored him to dial 911 and report a kidnapping in progress. The police arrived in time to arrest the abductors.

Chanti Prattipati never regained consciousness; she was pronounced dead at a local hospital. A subsequent investigation revealed that Reddy and several members of his family had used fake visas and false identities to traffic hundreds of adults and children into the United States from India. In many cases Reddy secured visas on the pretext that the applicants were highly skilled technology professionals who would be placed in a software company. In fact, they ended up working as waiters, cooks, and dishwashers at Pasand or at other businesses that Reddy owned. He forced the laborers to work long hours for minimal wages, money that they returned to him as rent to live in one of his apartments. Reddy threatened to turn them in to the authorities as illegal aliens if they tried to escape.

The Reddy case is not an anomaly. In fact, just as it happens in my community, it likely happens in your community, too. Well over one hundred thousand people live enslaved at this moment in the United States, and as many as seventeen thousand new victims are trafficked across our borders each year.[3] Attorneys from the U.S. Department of Justice have prosecuted slave-trade activity in cities across the United States and in nearly every state of the nation.

Like the slaves transported to America's shores two hundred years ago, today's slaves are not free to pursue their own destinies. They are coerced to perform work for the personal gain of those who subjugate them. If they try to escape the clutches of their masters, modern slaves risk personal violence or reprisals to their families.

Just how prominent a global crisis the slave trade has become was apparent when President George W. Bush took the podium before the United Nations General Assembly in September 2003. As expected, the president first addressed international concerns over the U.S. intervention in Iraq. As he neared the end of his speech, Bush shifted his attention to "another humanitarian crisis" of global proportions. "Each year eight hundred thousand to nine hundred thousand human beings are bought, sold, or forced across the world's borders," he said. "The trade in human beings for any purpose must not be allowed to thrive in our time."[4] Bush went on to underscore how the slave trade targets vulnerable women and children and fuels a thriving organized-crime syndicate that threatens global security.

President Bush did not exaggerate the crisis, which has grown at an alarming pace since he spoke those words in 2003. The commerce in human beings today rivals drug trafficking and the illegal arms trade as the top criminal activity on the planet. The International Labour Organization, the eighty-year-old nongovernmental agency tied to the United Nations, reports that forced-labor victims have been denied more than $20 billion in earned wages, and that figure does not include victims of sex trafficking.[5]

In recognition of the fact that human trafficking was spinning out of control, the U.S. Congress created a high-level position at the State Department specifically to combat the slave industry. President Bush first appointed former congressman John Miller to the post in March 2003 and promptly lifted his position to the ambassador level. Ambassador Luis CdeBaca, a former prosecutor in the Department of Justice, currently holds the post. The primary mission of the Office to Monitor and Combat Trafficking in Persons is to motivate and support governments to address their own participation in the global slave trade. To that end, one of its most potent tools is a report called the *Trafficking in Persons (TIP) Report,* published annually since 2001 as mandated by the U.S. Congress. When the *TIP Report* was first issued, only 82 countries were ranked according to their efforts to fight human trafficking on their home turf. In 2009, the State Department ranked 175 nations.[6]

No nation wants to be known as a haven for slaveholders and traffickers. Nonetheless, 145 countries are listed as Tier 2 or lower on the *2009 TIP Report* issued by the State Department. These nations may be source, transit, or destination countries for victims of human trafficking. In some cases, these countries serve as a base for all three activities. The exhaustive research that the State Department conducts makes it clear that slavery plagues every country, even the United States.

Many people bristle to hear the word *slavery* used to describe the modern practice of exploitation. Deeply ingrained in the collective psyche of Western culture is the notion that slavery ended in the nineteenth century. It is not unusual to read a newspaper account of "slavelike conditions" in a copper mine in, say, Bolivia. The laborers were kidnapped, coerced to work without pay, and prohibited from leaving the mine. So why would the writer refer to the laborers' condition as "slavelike"? Because the writer buys into the cultural myth that "real slavery" was vanquished long ago.

It certainly was a momentous day in 1833 when the British Parliament passed the Slavery Abolition Act, which gave freedom to all slaves held captive in the British Empire. Likewise, the Thirteenth Amendment to the U.S. Constitution, passed in 1865 at the conclusion of the Civil War, left no ambiguity about the legal standing of slavery in America: "Neither slavery nor involuntary servitude . . . shall exist within the United States, or any place subject to their jurisdiction."

The establishment of laws that criminalized the slave trade meant a major advancement in the cause for human freedom. Though slavery persisted for decades thereafter, legislation gave abolitionists an effective tool to hold slaveholders accountable for their inhumane activity. Abolition laws eventually spread to nearly every nation in the world.

In our own day, however, a thriving black market in human beings has emerged once again. It is a criminal enterprise involving both local scoundrels and sophisticated international syndicates. Corruption among law-enforcement agents and government officials plays a key role in its success. And it is not limited to one specific region of the world; human trafficking respects no borders. Hence, modern slavery cannot be eliminated with a single stroke of the pen like what Abraham Lincoln achieved when he signed the Emancipation Proclamation.

The European Union (EU), for example, cannot figure out how to stop the flood of 120,000 women and children trafficked each year into its member states. Most of these slaves are abducted in Africa or the beleaguered former republics of the Soviet Union and transported through porous borders. Ninety percent end up coerced into Europe's proliferating sex industry.[7]

The European ministers got serious about the slave trade in 2002 when they required all member states to implement the Palermo Protocol, a strong UN initiative that aims to nurture effective anti-trafficking measures across borders. Most western European countries subsequently created ambitious community-education campaigns and poured resources into law enforcement aimed at traffickers. All the same, traffickers somehow managed to maintain a steady flow of new sex slaves into the region. As Benita Ferrero-Waldner, then foreign minister for the EU, admitted in 2006, "Despite efforts to tackle this trade, the uncomfortable truth is that trafficking people is sometimes an even more profitable business than trafficking weapons."[8]

Indeed, more slaves live in bondage today than were bartered during four centuries of the transatlantic slave trade. No group has felt its impact more brutally than children in the underdeveloped nations. Slaveholders prey on the defenseless, and children so easily become vulnerable.

Ten Million Children Exploited for Domestic Labor—this title for a 2004 UN study on the exploitation of children internationally hardly needs explaining. UN surveys found 700,000 children forced into domestic labor in Indonesia alone, with staggering numbers as well in Brazil (559,000), Pakistan (264,000), Haiti (250,000), and Kenya (200,000). The UN report indicates that children remain in servitude for long stretches of time because no one identifies their enslavement: "These youngsters are usually 'invisible' to their communities, toiling for long hours with little or no pay and regularly deprived of the chance to play or go to school."[9]

That "invisible" tag often gets attached to descriptions of modern slavery. Just as I never suspected that my favorite restaurant had become a hub for a trafficking ring, slavery likely crosses our path on a regular basis without our awareness. We may pass a construction site and never think twice about whether the laborers there work of their own volition. Or we might drive along city streets at night, see young girls on a street corner peddling their bodies, and wonder how they could ever "choose" such a life.

That's the paradox: slavery is in reality not invisible. Except in rare circumstances, slaves toil in the public eye. The truth is that we do not expect to find it in "respectable" settings.

In 2009 in the sleepy suburban town of Walnut Creek, California, a real-estate agent and mother of three children was convicted in a federal court of domestic slavery. Mabelle de la Rosa Dann, forty-six, forced a young woman from Peru to cook, clean, and tend to her three young sons for nearly two years (between 2006 and 2008). Dann brought the young woman into the United States under false pretenses, confiscated her passport, and led her to believe she would be accused of theft if she tried to escape. The nanny worked fifteen hours a day, seven days a week, and slept at night on the living-room floor. Dann barred her from watching Spanish-language TV and severed all communication with her family in Peru.

To learn that slaveholders press children into forced labor in the cacao plantations of the Ivory Coast may not surprise us.[10] But we regard it as unthinkable that an otherwise upstanding citizen might be a slaveholder.

Kim Meston wishes that she had not been so invisible to her New England community. In a rural town near Worcester, Massachusetts, the minister of the local church used her as his domestic sex slave for five years without raising the slightest suspicion in the community.

Kim's parents were Tibetan exiles living in a refugee camp in northern India. When Kim was in her teens, her sister's husband introduced the family to a church minister visiting from the United States. The reverend offered to bring Kim to America, where he would provide a formal education and opportunities for a better life. "He told my parents that he would treat me as his own daughter," Kim recounts.[11]

Her brother-in-law lobbied the family persuasively to let Kim go. He even offered to accompany her to Delhi, where he could help her secure a visa to travel to the United States. In the ultimate betrayal, the brother-in-law made his own financial arrangement with the minister to traffic Kim.

At the age of sixteen, Kim began a double life in America. Everything would have appeared normal to the casual observer: she attended the local high school, ran on the track team, and attended church on Sundays. The minister even had a wife and a stepdaughter living in his home. But behind closed doors, she became the household servant, doing nearly all of the cooking, housecleaning, ironing, and even tending the church grounds.

Moreover, the minister sexually abused Kim frequently over a five-year period.

The minister threatened to have Kim's Tibetan family back in India thrown in jail if Kim told her school friends a word about her treatment. So she suffered in silence, and no one in the community thought to ask about how she might be faring. They simply assumed the best intentions of the minister and his family. "His deception was well constructed," notes Kim. "The minister was a pillar in the community, and I was viewed as the poor child from the third world who was the lucky beneficiary of his generosity."

Finally, at the age of twenty-one, Kim escaped her tormentor. She initially planned to run away and never turn back. Yet she received news from her family in India that the minister had trafficked two of her cousins into the United States to take her place inside his home. Kim mustered the courage to take her case to the local police. The minister was arrested, convicted, and sent to jail. Kim was able to start her own business, a retail store in the Boston area, and now volunteers her time to prevent more vulnerable women from falling into sexual exploitation and enslavement.

Elements of Kim's experience are disturbingly common in the modern slave trade. She was a young girl in a transient environment (a refugee camp). A trafficker (the minister) conspired with someone close to the family (the sister's husband) to extract her from the community and take control of her life. She was trafficked to another country, where she did not understand the culture or the laws, and was told that her family would be harmed if she did not fully cooperate. The slaveholder used her sexually and exploited her labor. Once she escaped, the slaveholder went out and quickly found two more girls to replace her.

To write this book, I conducted hundreds of interviews with trafficking victims from the United States, Mexico, China, Korea, the Philippines, Cambodia, Thailand, Peru, India, Uganda, South Africa, and many countries in eastern Europe. I encountered this essential story line time and time again. Of those individuals extracted out of impoverished countries and trafficked across international borders, 80 percent are female and 50 percent are children.[12] They are taken to unfamiliar destinations where, in the absence of legal protections and family networks, they can be kept in slavery. The consistency of the story line, in fact, suggests the overarching mechanisms of a global industry.

Like any other commercial market, the slave trade is driven by the dynamics of supply and demand. Criminal agents make handsome profits off unpaid labor: if you don't pay your workers, it is cheaper to produce goods or, in the case of sex slavery or domestic servitude, to offer valued human services. Due to these financial advantages, slaveholders can compete successfully in almost any market. The profit margins will rise as high as the demand will bear.

We may not even realize how each of us drives the demand during the course of a normal day. Kevin Bales expresses well those commercial connections: "Slaves in Pakistan may have made the shoes you are wearing and the carpet you stand on. Slaves in the Caribbean may have put sugar in your kitchen and toys in the hands of your children. In India they may have sewn the shirt on your back and polished the ring on your finger."[13]

To ensure a steady stream of recruits, slaveholders rely on slave traders to fulfill their supply. The slave trader may be a recruiter or a trafficker; often individuals will play both roles.

Their capacity to meet the demand for slaves becomes a problem only if one of two conditions comes into effect: there is a scarcity of new recruits, or engaging in illicit activity becomes a real risk. In most of the world today, neither condition presents itself as an obstacle. To the contrary, there exist a glut of potential recruits and a negligible threat of prosecution. Hence, the slave trade grows at a rapid pace.

Widespread poverty and social inequality ensure a pool of recruits as deep as the ocean. Parents in desperate straits may sell their children or at least be susceptible to scams that will allow the slave trader to take control of the lives of their sons and daughters. Young women in vulnerable communities are more likely to take a risk on a job offer in a faraway location. The poor are apt to accept a loan that the slave trader can later manipulate to steal their freedom. All of these paths carry unsuspecting recruits into the supply chains of slavery.

"The supply side of the equation is particularly bleak," says Senator Sam Brownback of Kansas. "Fifty million refugees and displaced persons exist worldwide today. This ready reservoir of the stateless presents an opportunity rife for exploitation by human traffickers."[14]

During the era of the American plantation economy, the slaveholder considered slave ownership an investment. The cost of extracting and transporting slaves and ensuring that they would be serviceable by the time they reached their destination was considerable. Though the slave owner usually treated the slave like a beast, the slave's treatment would be equal to that of a prized bull. The slave owner aimed to extract the value of his investment over the course of the slave's lifetime. Proof of legal ownership, therefore, served an important purpose.

In the modern slave trade, the glut of slaves and the capacity to move them great distances in a relatively short period of time drastically alters the economics of slave ownership. As relative costs plummet, slaves cease to be a long-term investment. The fact that slave ownership is illegal today in every country is of little consequence. The owner need not be too concerned about maintaining the health of the slave. The description of modern slaves as "disposable" profoundly fits; just like a used battery, once the slave exhausts his or her usefulness, another can be procured at no great expense.[15]

Notwithstanding these emerging trends in global markets, traditional modes of slavery also persist. Bonded labor has existed for centuries and continues to be the most common form of slavery in the world today. In a typical scenario an individual falls under the control of a wealthy patron after taking a small loan. The patron adds egregious rates of interest and inflated expenses to the original principal so that the laborer finds it impossible to repay. Debt slaves may spend their entire life in service to a single slaveholder, and their "obligation" may be passed on to their children.

The tale of Bonda, a slave I met during my travels in India, graphically illustrates the plight of a bonded laborer. The owner of a rice mill used small loans to enslave Bonda's entire village. The villagers labored eighteen hours daily and were banned from passing beyond the walls of the rice mill without supervision. After years of relentless oppression, Bonda's wife broke down one day and killed herself. Disconsolate over his loss, Bonda threw caution to the wind. He found a gate in the rice mill left open one day, and he bolted.

The owner did not treat insubordination lightly. He sent bounty hunters after Bonda, who was captured without much trouble. Once they brought Bonda back to the rice mill, the owner gathered all the slaves into an assembly in the center of the compound. For their edification he used a cane to beat Bonda within an inch of his life. The owner then chained the unconscious man to a wall in the slaves' living quarters. And that became his bed for the rest of his days at the rice mill. He did his daily chores and then was placed back in his chains.

Bonda's tale, I am pleased to report, ends on a happy note. An abolitionist organization called International Justice Mission (IJM) instigated a raid on the rice mill and emancipated Bonda along with his entire village. Local police arrested the owner and put him on trial for his crimes.

That, in fact, was the unexpected surprise of my journey to monitor the rise of modern-day slavery. I had steeled myself emotionally to end up in the depths of depression and despair. To be honest, I did make some unpleasant stops in my journey. The day I went undercover to investigate a brothel in Phnom Penh, Cambodia, for instance, broke my heart. A brothel owner invited me to take my pick of any one of the thirteen-year-old girls that crowded the sofas in front of me. A few extra bucks and I could have two of them for the night, he offered. I could not bear to think of these little girls passing through this ritual a dozen times each night.

But my journey did not end at the station of despair. The prime reason: I met a heroic ensemble of abolitionists who simply refuse to relent. I felt like I had gone back in time and had the great privilege of sharing a meal with a Harriet Tubman or a William Wilberforce or a Frederick Douglass. Like the abolitionists of old, these modern heroes do not expend their energy handicapping the odds stacked against the antislavery movement. They simply refuse to accept a world where one individual can be held as the property of another.

Lucy Borja is rescuing girls and boys off the streets of Lima, Peru. Padre Cesare Lodeserto is stealing trafficked girls and young women away from the mafiosi of eastern Europe. Anna Rodriguez is shutting down brothels and freeing forced laborers from the agricultural fields in Florida, and Susan Coppedge is ensuring that traffickers in Georgia arrive in federal jail cells with very long sentences to pay for their crimes.

Not one of these special characters, all of whom are featured in this book, went looking for slavery or set out to be abolitionists. Each simply reached out a compassionate hand to a refugee in need, a homeless street child, or a survivor seeking justice. That gesture exposed him or her to the ugly undercurrent of human trafficking. Their passage from one act of kindness to fighting for justice on a grander scale is the quintessential story of the abolitionist.

This book aims to be a handbook for the modern-day abolitionist. As such, it does not pretend to be an exhaustive study of slavery either in the United States or around the globe in the twenty-first century. It follows the trail of a select group of extraordinary abolitionists into their respective settings. We get a feel for the people around them who have fallen into captivity. We delve into the historical antecedents and social forces that frame their time and place. We learn how the slave traders they resist use power and violence to exploit the weak. And we gain an insight into the specific strategies these abolitionists deploy to bring about emancipation for the captives.

These stories make it clear that the modern-day abolitionists are not all cut from the same mold. The women who embrace the child soldiers of Uganda move in a different universe from those abolitionists in Los Angeles who confront forced labor in garment factories. A Thai painter provides outreach and shelter to children who are trafficked across the border from Burma, while an American-born lawyer uses the public justice system to free entire villages in other parts of South Asia. Some abolitionists rely on their faith in God, while a dedication to love or an abiding belief in justice inspires others.

Despite their unique bearings, these abolitionists do share a sense of their moment in history. They recognize that human freedom stands poised at a crucial crossroads in our time. Powerful forces aim to turn human beings into commodities that can be bought and sold like any other piece of property. To declare "Not for sale" affirms that every person has the inalienable right to be free, to pursue a God-given destiny.

To inspire others to declare "I am not for sale; you are not for sale; no one should be for sale" is my overriding purpose in writing this book. The abolitionists featured herein are truly extraordinary, but they cannot win the fight alone. They are overwhelmed and beleaguered. The size and scope of their initiatives are about the norm in the abolitionist movement, but these dedicated people sorely need reinforcements to help them. They need a new wave of abolitionists to join them in the struggle.

This new edition of *Not for Sale* provides more recent case studies and updated research. More important, I have the privilege of chronicling in this second edition the blossoming of an antislavery movement around the globe. The Not For Sale Campaign, which launched on the very same day that the first edition hit the bookstores, has played no small part in that story. You will read in the pages ahead how the Campaign has enabled key characters in the first edition to carry out heroic acts. We have achieved huge wins, such as partnering with Kru Nam to build a village for the more than 125 kids she freed in northern Thailand. We teamed up with Lucy Borja to provide shelter and new futures to hundreds of street kids in Lima, Peru. We have established over forty regional operational centers in North America to investigate and document trafficking cases and engage advocates on regional agendas.

In that respect, this second edition dramatically shows that the breath of freedom is uniting people internationally. No longer can we stand by while millions live in slavery. It is not enough to think about change. It is not enough to talk about change. It is time to shift gears—marrying movement with intelligent action.

My students at the University of San Francisco often remark that they feel as if they were born in the wrong era, after all the important issues of history have been decided. It's as if they were born in 1975 in Liverpool with a burning desire for pop music. They have a real passion for a craft, but it's already been done.

They could not be more wrong. We have arrived at a momentous stage in the struggle for human freedom. The curtain has gone up, and the future waits for what unfolds.

All of us wonder how we would have acted in the epic struggles of human history. Would we have stood up and been counted among the courageous and the just?

How would we have responded in 1942 when Nazi soldiers came to our door in pursuit of our Jewish neighbors? Would be have been the collaborator who reveals to the soldiers where the Jews on our block might be found? Would we have played the role of the spectator who pleads ignorance, minding our own business and watching the drama unfold from our front-room window? Or might we have dared to act as an advocate, giving our neighbors shelter in the attic or helping them escape across the border? Would we have stood up and been counted among the just?

Imagine that we lived in rural Tennessee in 1855 and Harriet Tubman came to our door. "We are smuggling fugitive slaves across an underground railroad, and we need safe houses where they can receive shelter, food, and rest," she might have said. "Contacts in the network say that you might be willing to open your home as a way station. Will you help us?" It's our moment of truth. If Harriet Tubman had come calling, would we have stood up and been counted among the just?

Or what if we were in the company of Jesuits who established a mission in the New World in 1624? The Spanish slave traders warn us to dismantle our mission, where the natives work and keep their tribal structure intact. "We control this territory," they would have said, "and you are undermining our lucrative trade in natives. End the missions now, or we will shut them down our own way." Would we have stood up and been counted among the just?

There are times to read history, and there are times to make history. We live right now at one of those epic moments in the fight for human freedom. We no longer have to wonder how we might respond to our moment of truth. It is we who are on the stage, and we can change the winds of history with our actions. Future generations will look back to judge our choices and be inspired or disappointed.

A bit overdramatic, you might think. Yet I do not know of any other way to express the urgency of rescuing the millions of children forced to sell their bodies to sexual exploiters or forced to toil in agricultural fields or factories. In a single country, Uganda, nearly forty thousand children have been kidnapped and violently turned into child soldiers or sex slaves.

The destinies of children around the globe hang in the balance, and those children are powerless to break free.

As Edmund Burke is oft quoted as having remarked two centuries ago: "All that is necessary for the triumph of evil is that good men [and women] do nothing."

One
Shining Light into the Darkness

Thailand

Chan was nine years old when his mother sold him to a factory owner in Mae Sai, Thailand. Mae Sai lies close to the border with Burma (Myanmar) and boasts a thriving black market in illicit goods. Chan and his sister fetched a price of twenty dollars each.

Following their sale, Chan and his sister joined eight other children in a factory, peeling small cloves of garlic. They worked in a single large room attached to a small office where the owner could sit and supervise his young laborers through a wall of glass. The kids worked long hours for no pay and scant meals. Peeling as many cloves as the owner demanded turned out to be almost impossible, and their punishment for coming up short was a sound beating.

They slept a few hours each night in a nearby apartment until the owner woke them up, shoved them into the back of a van, and brought them back to the factory. That became their entire existence: the factory, the van, and the second-story apartment. The children hardly had time to dream about their lives before they were sold—before they were slaves.

A RECIPE FOR MASS VULNERABILITY

The U.S. State Department rates Thailand as a Tier 2 country in its *2009 Trafficking in Persons Report,* citing rampant human trafficking in both its rural and urban regions. "Thailand is a source, transit, and destination country for men, women, and children trafficked for the purposes of forced labor and commercial sexual exploitation," the report explains.[1] Additional studies, including a *Time Asia* cover story, confirm the proliferation of slavery in Thailand: "The sordid traffic touches nearly every part of Asia. But Thailand and India in particular serve as hubs of the flesh trade: exporters and importers of children and adults on a massive scale."[2]

So why does slavery thrive in Thailand and throughout Southeast Asia? Four powerful forces collude to rip apart stable communities in the region: (1) rapid industrialization; (2) devastating poverty; (3) armed conflicts; and (4) exploding population growth. Though economists and political scientists may reach no definitive consensus about which of these four factors is paramount, they concur that Southeast Asia is passing through a period of radical transition. And whenever a social order undergoes seismic changes, the powerless suffer most.

Southeast Asia has made a dramatic leap toward industrialization in recent times. The region's base of production has shifted from subsistence farming to cash-crop agriculture and manufacturing (though not at the same pace in each country). Peasant families find it increasingly difficult to make a livelihood off the land. Often they head to urban areas in hopes of finding a job.

Though industrialization has the potential to stimulate growth in the overall economy, wealth is being distributed unevenly. An elite sector benefits from the concentration of land and capital and makes financial arrangements that do not take into account the needs of the poor masses. Students of history recall social inequalities that accompanied the process of industrialization in the Western world, of course. Although it is hoped that modernization in Southeast Asia will eventually bring economic progress to the many, in the short term the poor get tossed to and fro like flotsam on a raging sea.

For instance, Deena Dudzer documents in a study how the global financial crisis of 2008–9 fueled a significant rise in factory closings and a mushrooming in the number of Thais facing unemployment.[3] "Whether parents or children, both have to struggle to survive," a Bangkok aid worker laments to Dudzer.

The same economic forces hit Cambodia hard. At least one in every three of Cambodia's 15 million people live below the poverty line today. Cambodian women, above all, do not get the chance to study formally or learn vocational skills; and illiteracy rates among women far outpace those for men.[4] While finding a job in Cambodia or Thailand can be difficult under any circumstances, an uneducated and impoverished woman does not fit the profile of workers most legal employers seek to hire.

Southeast Asia has experienced more than its share of armed conflicts over the past fifty years, which adds to social instability. Sirirat Pusurinkham, an ordained minister who leads an orphanage and small church at Prattachisuk, Thailand, asserts that the "social turmoil in Thailand provoked by World War II was a seedbed for the growth of prostitution in the country [and] . . . spurred the first example of a sex entertainment center for international tourists in Thailand."[5] The industry quickly boomed and led to broad commercial sexual exploitation.

In like fashion, the Vietnam War had a traumatic effect on the Vietnamese people and impacted the people of Laos, Cambodia, and Thailand as well. Combatants are not the only casualties of war; communities take years to heal from the wounds. Many hill tribes in Laos, for instance, have yet to regain their mooring.

The present situation in Burma—or Myanmar, under the current regime—further demonstrates the far-reaching effect of armed conflict. A military dictatorship maintains a fragile hold over a bevy of tribal groups and warlords, each of whom fight for their autonomy. Violent conflicts can erupt at any given moment. A 2009 United Nations High Commissioner for Refugees (UNHCR) briefing verified that Burmese military groups force children as young as ten years old to serve as "porters" and child soldiers in the intense conflict taking place in the Karen region close to the border with northern Thailand.[6]

As if the foregoing trends do not bring enough of a challenge, a population boom puts added strain on the region. In many countries of Southeast Asia, more than half the population alive today falls under the age of fifteen. Confronted with a scarcity of jobs and food, local communities do not have sufficient resources to sustain their young people. As harsh as it sounds, the youth are the first to become expendable.

Amid all these disruptions to social stability, slavery emerges as a tempting financial solution. Human traffickers commonly target children in destitute rural villages. The owner of a brothel in Southeast Asia can buy a woman or child for as little as twenty dollars. Virgins fetch anywhere from five hundred to as much as a one thousand dollars. To put those figures in perspective, one thousand dollars corresponds to three and a half times the average annual income in Cambodia.[7]

The sale of a daughter or (less commonly) a son in moments of financial need usually does not raise an eyebrow in Southeast Asia. In times past, a poor family might sell a child to a wealthy household to serve as a house servant or a field worker. In more recent days, the sex trade has raised the demand for slave children, and the impoverished masses generate the supply.

The precise number of parents who sell their children to traffickers in Southeast Asia cannot be easily assessed. A 2003 article in the *UN Chronicle* clearly pointed to the participation of family members in the transactions: "Traffickers often use local people in a community or village to find young women and children, and target families who are poor and vulnerable. In some situations, family members sell children to middlemen or traffickers."[8]

A research study revealed that close to 35 percent of the Vietnamese families living in Cambodia sell a daughter into the sex trade, while another 25 to 30 percent seriously consider the option but do not follow through with the sale.[9] The Vietnamese exist as a marginalized minority in Cambodia, so one must be careful not to generalize from this set of data. Nonetheless, the numbers reflect how widespread and culturally acceptable the sale of daughters can be.

Why would a parent sell a child? For most of us, there is absolutely no circumstance under which we would consider such a transaction. (We should pause, however, to remember that U.S.-based anti-trafficking groups have documented cases of American parents selling their children into slavery. Check out www.SlaveryMap.org to review the range of trafficking cases inside the United States.)

One cannot ignore how the Thai cultural and religious environment places women in a vulnerable position. Buddhist religious traditions reinforce the relegation of females to second-class status. In Thai (Theravada) Buddhism women cannot even reach the highest levels of spiritual enlightenment. The best they can hope for in this lifetime is to build up enough good karma to be born male in their next life. The reverse logic also holds true: to be born female in this present embodiment suggests that a woman acted wrongfully in her previous existence.

Cultural racism also runs deep in Thailand, which further assists traffickers in "recruiting" children from indigenous groups that reside primarily in rural parts of the country and throwing them into the sex industry in Bangkok, Phuket, or Chiang Mai.[10]

Truthfully, refugees all over the world walk a perilous path. They become a minority in a new society, often without legal standing, and more powerful individuals seek to exploit that vulnerability. For example, Thai traffickers today view the Burmese population as a deep recruitment pool.[11]

Kru Nam: An Artist Turned Abolitionist

A painter with a university degree in art may not be the most likely candidate to be a child rescuer, yet Kru Nam operates on the front lines of the antislavery movement in Thailand.

She could not ignore the young street kids who lived along the aqueducts that surround Chiang Mai, the largest city in northern Thailand. One day she decided to take empty canvases, brushes, and tins of paints down to the riverfront and learn the kids' stories. Once she turned the children loose painting, they created a series of disturbing images that added up to a horror story.

Kru Nam discovered that most of the kids did not come from Thailand; many originated in Burma, with a sprinkling of Laotians, Vietnamese, and Cambodians tossed into the mix. The kids shared with her their tales of how they had arrived on the streets of Chiang Mai.

The Burmese boys spoke of a well-dressed Thai gentleman who had visited their village. Accompanying him was a fourteen-year-old boy who wore fine-tailored clothes and spoke Thai fluently. The man explained to their parents that he was offering scholarships for young boys to attend a fine school back in Thailand. He would pay their school fees and cover their living expenses. "Look how well this child from your region is doing," he said, pointing to his young Burmese companion. "If you let me take your son back to Chiang Mai, I will do the same for him."

Though the tribal people of Burma are reluctant to part with young girls, they give more license for sons to travel afar in search of a livelihood. Quite a few families, therefore, agreed to let their sons go with the Thai man. Once the boys reached Chiang Mai, the trafficker immediately sold them to owners of sex bars.

The kids who lived along the riverfront told Kru Nam that they were the lucky ones. They had escaped. Many of their friends remained captive in the sex bars. Her blood boiled. She could not stand by and do nothing.

Kru Nam did not exactly have a plan when she marched into the first sex bar she ran across that night. She did not even attempt to negotiate with the owner, assuming that would be a waste of time. Her mission was clear: rescue as many of the young kids as she might. In that first bar, several kids sat at tables entertaining male customers. One by one she approached each table where a child sat and calmly said, "Let's go." Moments later, she was leading six young kids out the door and to her shelter.

Though Kru Nam made several more impromptu raids on sex bars, she eventually had to tread with more caution. Owners put the word out that they would kill her if she walked into their bars. "She is stealing our property," they said in outrage to each other.

Chan: A Cruel Destiny

Chan did not comprehend why his father so often left their home to cross the border into Thailand. He was too young to realize that his father was a drug smuggler. His dad would depart early in the morning and rendezvous with his Thai supplier. Then he would return to Burma and deliver the drugs to the dealer. As the middleman in the exchange, he received a tiny share of the profits yet faced the most serious risks. The military regime that rules Burma does not deal lightly with freelance drug smugglers.

Chan's life changed irrevocably one evening when Burmese soldiers burst into his home yelling his father's name. The soldiers shot Chan's father at point-blank range as Chan and his family, screaming, huddled together on their sleeping mats. The family waited for the guns to be turned on them, but the soldiers ignored their screams, turned on their heels, and marched out the front door, leaving them unharmed.

During the ensuing three-day mourning period, Chan recalls neighbors bringing small bits of food, which was all that they could afford to share. His father's body was cremated at the temple on the third day, according to Buddhist custom. The family returned home destitute.

Chan's mother quickly realized that she could not feed her family and went to the streets as a beggar. It did not take long for a trafficker to locate his fresh prey. Noting that this woman had two children, no husband, and zero source of steady income, the garlic-factory owner persuaded her to sell Chan and his sister. Only a month passed between his mother's arrival on the streets as a beggar and the transaction that turned Chan from a little boy to a forced laborer.

CHILDREN AS A LABOR FORCE

In its 2009 *State of the World's Children* report, UNICEF estimated that around the globe more than 150 million children aged five to fourteen are working each day. The report indicates that 45 percent of Cambodia's children are working. The numbers are lower for other countries in the Southeast Asia region but remain nonetheless alarming: Vietnam has 16 percent of its children laboring; Laos, 11 percent; and Thailand, 8 percent. The report offers no figures for Burma, largely due to the difficulty of obtaining accurate data from such a closed society.[12]

The International Labour Organization (ILO) also has consistently documented child labor and its detrimental impact. In its study *Give Girls a Chance: Tackling Child Labour*, the ILO estimates that 100 million girls around the world labor in dangerous working conditions that harm their health and development and reduce their educational opportunities.[13] "Trafficking for labour is closely linked to work in agriculture, domestic work, construction and unregulated sectors," explains the publication. "However some 43 percent of all those trafficked for forced labour are trafficked for commercial sexual exploitation."[14] In sum, trafficked children often are subjected to extreme violence, HIV/AIDS, and psychological trauma.

The ILO offers several remedies to child slavery: "One of the priorities identified in the study is prevention, through vigorous enforcement of national laws and regulations. . . . Raising awareness of forced labour is important both for the population at large and for the police and judiciary and other responsible authorities."[15]

Like most every other country in the world, Thailand has passed laws prohibiting sex trafficking, slavery, child labor, forced marriage, the sexual exploitation of children, and the deprivation of liberty.[16] The solution, therefore, relies on consistent enforcement of the law, as the ILO proposes. The U.S. State Department's *2009 Trafficking in Persons Report* reveals that although the royal Thai government passed a new trafficking law in 2008 and trained its law-enforcement officials on its enforcement, prosecutions are rare. The Thai government "did not . . . achieve a conviction for a labor trafficking offense during [2008],"[17] the *TIP Report* bluntly states.

Chan: A Painful Flight to Freedom

Chan was sick of the smell of garlic, emotionally drained by the fear of the guard dogs that ensured the children did not escape the house, and sore from the frequent beatings. Above all, Chan could no longer bear to watch his little sister grow ill and emaciated. He could not help her; he could not help himself.

Although other children already had attempted to run away—and carried the dog bites to demonstrate the futility of their act—Chan planned his escape. One night he gathered up all the courage he could muster in his ten-year-old frame, waited for the dogs to turn the corner, and leaped from a second-story window to the paved street below. Despite the shock of intense pain running through his limbs, he quickly realized two things: (1) his frail sister would never survive the jump; and (2) he must get away from the house as fast as his legs would carry him. He made the heart-rending decision to leave his sister behind and fled through the streets of Mae Sai.

Chan never seriously considered returning home to his mother in Burma. He guessed that, just like the factory owner, she would beat him for his lack of obedience. Worse yet, she might send him back to the factory. He felt alone, hurt, and scared, yet he was determined to survive.

Kru Nam: A Buddy in a Time of Need

Kru Nam knew that running into sex bars and rescuing kids did not represent a long-term strategy. She was placing her own safety and that of the children at risk. Shifting tactics, she organized street teams to roam the night market of Chiang Mai and locate unaccompanied kids that were fresh off the bus from the Thai–Burmese border. Recruiters for the sex bars also trolled the streets on the hunt for vulnerable kids. Kru Nam placed herself in direct competition with the traffickers to find the vulnerable children first.

Kru Nam then realized that if she moved upstream before the kids hit Chiang Mai, she would have an edge over the traffickers. So she moved about 150 miles north to the border town of Mae Sai. She initially set up a drop-in center and shelter in the town, which at first took in twenty-five kids but grew to support nearly sixty survivors rather quickly.

One evening on the streets of Mai Sai, Kru Nam bumped into Chan. The boy was knee-deep in a dumpster, hoping to find anything to eat or sell. Street kids in Mae Sai often eke out an existence by selling recyclables from the garbage. When she looked at Chan, Kru Nam saw a boy in crisis. He told her that he was eleven years old, but his body was so disfigured by severe burns (the factory owner's torture of choice) and his frame so small due to malnourishment that Kru Nam could not really pinpoint his age.

Chan had seen Kru Nam previously. She reached out to every street kid, encouraging them to participate in the activities offered by her agency, Volunteers for Children's Development Foundation (VCDF). Whenever she spoke to him, however, he had been wary. He did not trust adults. Maybe he did get into street fights, pass a day or two without food, and spent too much time bombed out of his brain from sniffing industrial glue. But at least he was free.

One day Chan made a surprise visit to the urban drop-in center. Entering the three-story facility, he heard children practicing their language skills, watched women in small groups learning how to sew, and noted both young and old visitors engaged in painting and drawing. The scuff marks on the floors and crayon scribbles on the walls—and the sheer amount of noise—told him that this center was a comfortable place. Chan became a frequent visitor, taking advantage of free meals, medicine, and bathing facilities. Before he realized it, Chan was developing friendships with the center's staff. They taught him how to read and write and cheered him on when he played his favorite sport, badminton.

Yet the dreams—or more accurately, the nightmares—

persisted. Even as Chan grew stronger emotionally and physically, thoughts of his sister haunted him. Was she still alive? Was she still trapped in the factory? He opened up to Kru Nam, sharing bits and pieces of his history with her. He was reluctant to divulge most of the details, and Kru Nam sensed his deep fears; he literally would jump at the slightest unexpected sound. Eventually, Kru Nam persuaded Chan to move to her home for rescued children, Buddies Along the Roadside, located in the countryside outside Mae Sai. Chan now slept in a safe, secure bed for the first time in years—not under a bridge or on the floor of a slaveholder's apartment.

Chan slowly evolved from an isolated, scared child to one who made friends, enjoyed school, and played the guitar. About five months after his move to Buddies, Chan finally broke down and told Kru Nam about the nightmares. He shared the brutal tale of his days as a slave. Though now free, every single night he imagined his sister trapped in the factory, dying, and no one rushing to save her. Tears streamed down the cheeks of the boy who never dared to cry.

Annie Dieselberg: A Light in the Darkness

Fortunately for those enslaved in Thailand, Kru Nam is not the only abolitionist operating on the front lines. Annie Dieselberg also embraces freedom as her life calling. She named her Bangkok-based project NightLight International, playing off the image of a light that brings safety to people who are lost in the darkness. The creativity that fuels her project matches the compassion that brought it into existence.

When Annie launched NightLight in 2005, she ambitiously hoped to provide an alternative for young girls working in commercial sex bars. For more than a decade, Annie and her husband had worked with trafficking victims in Bangkok. Having watched so many women locked into demeaning sexual exploitation drove Annie to dream in full color. She could continue to help broken individuals once predators had disposed of them, or she could confront the problem head-on. She chose the steep path.

Annie is accustomed to taking the road less traveled. She spent most of her childhood in Zaire, the daughter of parents devoted to Christian ministry. The family relocated to Thailand when Annie was in her teens. She spent one year living with her parents in Thailand before attending boarding school in India. Then, after high school graduation, she showed up at the University of West Virginia wrapped in a *salwar kameez* and sporting bangles on her wrist. "The other students did not know what to make of this strange white girl with blond hair who dressed and acted like a total foreigner," Annie says with a laugh as she reminiscences. "I may have looked like any other American, but I sure brought some unusual ideas to the classroom."

Even today her appearance can be deceiving. She does not cut an imposing figure—in her forties, a mother of four children, and of slight build and stature. She could be a soccer mom in any American suburban community.

Fire in the belly—no better description fits Annie's persona. She speaks and acts with the intensity of a Hebrew prophet of old. "Women on the streets may look like they are free when you tour Bangkok, but they are not!" Thus Annie begins her orientation to the sex trade. "Trafficked women are often moved around, and many of them do not know the language or the monetary currency. They feel alone, isolated from friends or family who might give them a helping hand."

So Annie decided to step in and be that helping hand. In early 2005, she took a visiting American church group to a sex bar. While the men in the delegation remained outside praying, Annie led a small team of women inside. "We sat with a young woman who was only twenty-two years old, with two children of her own," Annie says, recounting the episode. "She told us how much she hated working at the bar. When I asked her where she would like to be, she told me that she would like to be home with her kids."

So Annie and her spiritual sisters paid the bar owner six hundred baht (roughly fifteen dollars) to "rent" the woman for the night—the standard price a customer pays for a full evening of "entertainment." The payment unexpectedly turned into a redemption fee.

Annie only recently had taught herself how to make jewelry. So she spontaneously offered the bar girl a job to work alongside her producing jewelry for commercial sale. The young woman accepted and became NightLight's first employee.

Annie did not have a work studio at that moment. So she told her new employee to meet her at a McDonald's restaurant in central Bangkok. With the waft of burgers and fries deep in their nostrils, Annie delivered her first training session in jewelry production. Annie then sent her first employee off home with a suitcase full of beads and stones under her arm.

SHAME AS A WEAPON

Shame is a club that beats enslaved women at practically every turn. It starts when young girls from impoverished families are blamed for the destitution of their parents. "Good" daughters manage the health and welfare of their mother and father. Their suffering translates into her shame, so she is willing to make any sacrifice to change their condition.

The community's perception of sexual purity also plays a major role in a young girl's shame. Once an unmarried girl has lost her virginity, she is considered despoiled. It does not matter whether a family member sexually abused her or a stranger raped her. Purity is all or nothing: either she has it or she doesn't. Her family will treat her as a blight to its honor, and no "respectable" man will want to marry her. The girl might as well be sold into a life of prostitution, for she has lost her innocence. So strikes the club of shame.

Traffickers and brothel owners alike also use this cultural value to manipulate girls. If a new recruit resists the idea of having sex with a paying customer, the slaveholder might rape her himself. "Now you are used goods," he snorts triumphantly. "You might as well give it up for other men." Tragically, the girl is apt to understand the logic of this brutal indoctrination and resign herself to life in the brothel. She has lost everything: her family will reject her, and her neighbors will treat her as a pariah. And each day she stays, the possibility of rejoining respectable community life diminishes. She lives in exile.

Brothel owners, paying clients, and at times even government officials benefit from her acquiescence. The ILO reports that sex tourism contributes close to 15 percent of the gross domestic product of countries such as Malaysia, Thailand, Indonesia, and the Philippines.[18]

Annie Dieselberg: Designing a Future

Programs that encourage girls to escape the sex trade but leave them poor and jobless do not yield long-term success stories. The girls remain vulnerable to being trafficked once again. Annie Dieselberg, therefore, created her project to equip young women for life beyond the sex trade.

Like a prism, NightLight may be viewed from a number of angles. For starters, it is a for-profit business that trains women in how to make and sell jewelry. The products are made today in NightLight's humble factory in central Bangkok and sold primarily through niche markets in Thailand and the United States. The jewelry is of high quality, and the designs range from classic to trendy.

"Everyone makes money off these women: the recruiter, the trafficker, the owner of the bar—you name it," says Annie. "But the woman herself stays mired in poverty." Just naming the injustice has gotten Annie fired up, and she cuts loose with a searing social critique: "Society won't pay a poor woman a decent wage, but men will shell out big bucks just so they can abuse her body for a few minutes!"

Despite a limited budget, NightLight pays twice the minimum wage established by Thai law. Obviously, the workers do not get rich off this pay, but the compensation does offer a sustainable livelihood. In order to be considered for employment, the women must agree to leave the sex industry completely. They also must commit to a forty-hour week, working Monday through Friday during normal business hours.

The policy of paying a salary rather than a fee per produced item facilitates NightLight's other mission: to develop healthy women. During the course of a normal workday, women engage in workshops on health care, HIV/AIDS prevention, personal financial management, spiritual formation, and the English language.

NightLight employs 80 women, although Annie reports that more than 130 have been a part of the business since its launch. Building-code regulations limit the number of employees to its present size, so NightLight keeps a long waiting list. Financial resources present the biggest hurdle to expansion to a new factory. Frankly, Annie never intended NightLight to grow as fast as it has. The project took on a life of its own as word spread throughout the sex bars that escape was possible. And Annie, understandably, finds it hard to put on the brakes.

"At one point early on, I felt like we had to halt our progress," she said. "But then one young woman for whom I had been praying for six years called and asked if I would help her leave the sex trade. I took it as a sign from God to move forward."

Sean Litton: Busting a Trafficking Ring

"Imagine yourself in a dark room. You stick out your hand to grab what you believe to be a snake, but you realize that you are actually holding the tail of an elephant."

That's how Sean Litton, the International Justice Mission's vice president of interventions, describes the serendipity involved in the investigation of sex trafficking. A routine lead may result at any moment in a major bust.

IJM deploys a corps of seasoned public justice professionals— criminal investigators, prosecutors, political analysts, and diplomats—to confront slavery wherever it exists in the world. Its staff gathers detailed evidence of illegal bondage and encourages local police authorities to free the slaves. The agency then collaborates with local prosecutors to build a case against slaveholders or traffickers that might stick in a court of law.

Litton points to the relatively innocuous alert that he received from a Thai-based nongovernmental organization (NGO) in late 2004. A Thai man had approached the NGO after he had been forced to pay fifteen hundred dollars to buy his niece out of bondage. Pressed for details, the man explained that Siri, his niece, had called him from Malaysia, pleading for help. A heavily armed group of men were holding her captive in a brothel and were demanding a ransom for her release. Siri's captors released her upon receipt of the money, and she was now safely back home. But Siri's uncle wanted justice done to the men who had forced his niece into prostitution.

The NGO committed to assisting the family but sensed that it was out of its depth dealing with heavily armed sex traffickers, so it called IJM for assistance. IJM strongly discourages the practice of paying traffickers a redemption fee to release slaves. Siri, however, was able to provide IJM with a few financial and personal details concerning the traffickers, and this created an opportunity to pursue an investigative trail.

An IJM investigator met with Siri to recover everything she knew about this trafficker. She identified a man called Johnny as the leader of the syndicate that had trafficked her into the brothel. Siri had been working as a tailor in the city of Mae Sai. Her income of $75 a month was fairly decent by Thai standards, especially for a woman in her twenties. But one of Johnny's recruiters had promised her a job in a restaurant in Malaysia with a starting salary of $250 a month. "You are only

twenty-one years old and single," said the recruiter, herself a
woman, in a crafty ploy to persuade Siri. "You're likely to meet
a wealthy Chinese man who will marry you."

Once the young tailor had agreed to the proposal, the
recruiter helped her apply for a passport and made travel arrangements. On the appointed day of departure, she put Siri
in a minibus along with several other young women "lucky" to
have landed a restaurant job. As soon as they had crossed the
southern border of Thailand and passed into the destination
city, Johnny met them.

To their dismay, he informed the women that his "investment" to bring them to this destination bound them to a six-
month contract to work in his "entertainment business." To
reinforce his control, Johnny demanded they turn over their
passports for "safekeeping."

Siri provided the IJM investigator with enough clues to indicate that Johnny was not operating alone but as part of an
organized crime syndicate. During the few weeks she stayed in
Malaysia, Siri was forced to work in a variety of brothels, each
exploiting two hundred or more women. Siri reported that she
was constantly under surveillance; armed guards kept a close
watch over her.

The criminals did not want the slaves to build any meaningful relationships out of which an escape plan might hatch, so
they regularly moved the sex slaves from house to house and
brothel to brothel. Siri did not have enough conversations with
the other victims to learn that the majority had been trafficked
from throughout Southeast Asia.

After several weeks of living a nightmare, Siri begged Johnny
to send her back to Thailand. He told her that what she was
asking was impossible because she owed him fifteen hundred

dollars; he listed costs for transportation, a passport, housing, food, and a finder's fee for the recruiter. Siri told Johnny that she could raise the "reimbursement" if he would allow her to make a phone call to her family. He consented, and she called the one person she hoped might take action: her uncle.

Hearing Siri's testimony, the IJM staff based in Thailand started to piece together the reach of this crime ring. "The case touched on every element of human trafficking," says Litton. "Fraud, bonded labor, sex slavery, violations of immigration law, and kidnapping—all woven seamlessly into a single network."

Given the risks of confronting a sophisticated Mafia, Litton decided to call in reinforcements from IJM headquarters in Washington, D.C. The organization's top-drawer investigator, whom Litton refers to simply as "the Genius"—in large part because he doesn't want to disclose the man's identity for the sake of future cases—was sent to the target city to go undercover.

As the IJM investigator made the rounds of the city's high-profile brothels, he confirmed that Siri had not exaggerated the fortresslike security that the trafficking ring deployed. Armed security guards equipped with walkie-talkies monitored the perimeter of the buildings. Steel doors blocked the front entrance of the brothels. A guard checked out potential clients through a small porthole that slid open and shut.

The Genius was able to pass the careful eye of scrutiny at the front door of the brothel, where a pimp ushered him into a lounge where he could review the women available for his pleasure.

The investigator now reached a crucial moment, when he earned his reputation as the Genius. He evaluated on the spot which of the candidates would be most likely to cooperate in his investigation. Given the constant threat of violence, some women are too frightened to betray their captors. Others may want to win favor with a cruel master by exposing the investigator. So the Genius had to run the women through his own personality profile; how he does it remains a mystery even to Litton.

Over the ensuing several days, the Genius interviewed a batch of women who were pleased to share their tale of abduction and captivity. He carefully recorded their stories and, cautious not to raise the suspicions of the brothel owners, instructed the women to follow their normal protocol. While he conducted interviews, a team of IJM lawyers toiled around the clock to turn the material into a compelling report that would be strong enough to stand up in court once it came to prosecuting the criminals.

The investigation turned up a great deal about the trafficking syndicate. The women originated in countries throughout Asia—above all Cambodia, Vietnam, Burma, Laos, Thailand, and southern China. Every girl interviewed had been trafficked without her consent. The youngest female interviewed was fourteen years old, though most of the women fell between the age of sixteen and twenty-five. The women had to complete anywhere from seven to ten tricks a night, with an average charge of forty dollars per visit. When the women were not working, the trafficking ring distributed them in groups of twenty to homes across the city to make it more difficult for the police to track them. An Asian-based Mafia was at the hub of the syndicate, which operated vibrant cells throughout Southeast Asia. The clients driving the demand were mostly wealthy Asian businessmen.

Once the IJM team felt that it had gathered sufficient evidence, it took on the ambitious task of engineering collaboration among the appropriate police bodies in Thailand and the other countries involved. Up to that point, these agencies had never collaborated on a trafficking case.

Most critical of all, IJM presented a report of its investigation to senior law-enforcement officers in Malaysia. Once they had reviewed the evidence that IJM had gathered, the police officers were enthusiastic about bringing down the syndicate. Wary of the vacuum in the local law, IJM sought an agreement from them that the police raid would follow two essential conditions: (1) the trafficked women would be treated as victims and not as criminals; and (2) the traffickers would be not only arrested but also prosecuted.

In early April 2005, a large police force raided some of the largest brothels operating in the target city. Unfortunately, the traffickers were tipped off, and the police did not arrest a single syndicate member on the day of the raid. On the rosy side, the police rescued ninety-five women from the brothels.

The case turned out to be a revelation for IJM. Up until that point, it had focused its efforts on internal trafficking within Thailand and Cambodia. Now that the agency had exposed the broader regional trafficking, it needed to reassess its operations to address the sophisticated networks that were growing in Asia.

Subsequent IJM and police investigations helped the local police arrest one of the key agents of this trafficking ring along with seven accomplices. The Thai recruiter who had ensnared Siri was among those arrested. IJM lawyers worked to secure successful prosecutions of all eight perpetrators, proving that there can be criminal-justice consequences using the laws on the books in Southeast Asia.

Annie Dieselberg: "It's Just His Girl"

Annie's friends back in the United States often innocently ask why she doesn't simply go to the police and report the coercion of women in the Thai sex industry. Whenever that question arises, a vivid memory pops into her mind.

She was strolling down a major thoroughfare in Bangkok one afternoon when a female's shrieks drew Annie's attention to an assault in progress on the opposite side of the street. The woman had been fleeing a man twice her size, and the man had just caught up to her. With his right hand, he held a sharp shining object against her neck. He used his other hand to drag her back toward an open car door parked along the sidewalk.

Highly agitated by the woman's predicament, Annie turned her head in all directions to see if she could find help. To her relief, a Thai policeman dressed in full uniform stood a few feet behind her. He, too, was watching the scene unfold across the street, but he gave no sign that he might intervene.

Annie does not accept injustice silently. She marched up to the policeman and asked him politely if he could go across the street and help the woman. He gave her a dismissive shrug and muttered, "It's just his girl; they'll work it out."

By now the man was forcing the woman into the backseat of his car. The woman continued to scream for help as the man jumped into the driver's seat and screeched his wheels as he passed down the street. Annie looked up at the policeman incredulously for a moment and spilled out her righteous anger: "Officer, sir, why are you wearing that uniform?!"

THE MEN WHO DRIVE THE DEMAND

Every night the streets of Bangkok are filled with middle-aged men who walk hand-in-hand with teenage girls. These sex tourists have traveled from all over the world to be here and play out their own private fantasy. Some men pay for quick sex, but more prefer to buy a "girlfriend" for an entire night or even several days. The johns behave like young adolescents, publicly pawing their "dates," squeezing their buttocks and breasts with little shame.

Specialized travel agencies around the globe promote "exotic sexual adventures" with Asian women "who know how to please a man." After sex tourists experience firsthand how easy it is to buy young girls, they frequently make their own arrangements for return visits.

Thailand, in particular, has been branded internationally as a Disneyland for sexual escapades. A Bangkok-based children's-rights group tracked the country's boom in sex tourism for two decades. Its research shows that 2 million foreigners visited the country in 1984, 4 million in 1988, and more than 11 million in 2003.[19] Out of the total number of foreign visitors, roughly two-thirds entering Thailand were unaccompanied men. In other words, about 7.3 million unaccompanied men visited the country in 2003. Certainly, not all of these men came as sex tourists, but it's a good bet that a significant percentage did. In fact, according to a survey of travel agents conducted by international aid agency World Vision, 65 percent of all tourists to Cambodia are men, and one-fifth of them travel with the express purpose of having sex.[20]

Male clients from Japan, China, Korea, and Taiwan drive the demand for young girls who are virgins. In these Asian cultures, sex with a virgin is thought to bring good luck to a new business venture. Moreover, virgin girls pose less threat of exposure to sexually transmitted diseases. Incredible as it may seem, Nicholas Kristof, Pulitzer Prize–winning journalist for the *New York Times,* explained in a 2009 column that girls are stitched up to be resold as virgins. The girl he profiled, Pross, was sold as a virgin four times.[21]

The growing demand for virgins has created a niche market outside the usual channels for commercial sex—the bars, karaoke clubs, and brothels. A growing number of parents market their daughters' virginity as if they were independent talent agents, selling the girls to the highest bidder at the age of twelve or thirteen. Though the practice is much less common, Japanese and Chinese men are known to pay parents years in advance to "sponsor" a young child. The families receive a regular payment to raise a healthy daughter, and when the sponsor is ready, he will come and use her for sex.

Western sex tourists, on the other hand, tend to frequent the bars and brothels in major cities like Bangkok. Though some specifically request sex with children, most act in an opportunistic way; that is to say, they react spontaneously to what happens once they arrive at a sex bar or a karaoke club. Some men may not even initially plan to engage in commercial sex on their journeys to Southeast Asia but find it easy to do once they are there.

Sex tourism clearly feeds the demand for sexual slavery. Nonetheless, its contribution to the sex trade in Southeast Asia is vastly overrated in the global media. By far the largest proportion of johns comes from the local population. "Foreigners are not the only ones who exploit our children," confirms Cambodia's former minister for women's affairs. "The real disease comes from within."[22] A 2008 *Economist* piece confirmed the problem: "South-East Asian governments still sometimes talk as if there were no home-grown pedophiles. Often, as used to be the case in the West, the powerful are used to being above the law."[23]

Particularly in Cambodia and Thailand, men will visit a brothel together during a night of partying; it's simply a part of the evening's entertainment. A number of studies conducted in both Cambodia and Thailand show that approximately 40 to 50 percent of local men pay for commercial sex during the course of a year.[24] Married women quietly accept that their husbands will pay to have sex on a night out with the boys. Men have sexual needs, the wives reason, and at least they will not be in pursuit of eligible single women who could displace them.

Paying for sex has become embedded in many social rituals. Businessmen use paid sex as a courtesy in the arrangements of commercial deals; if a firm does not offer its clients sex, it may risk losing them to competitors who will. Working-class men buy sex for their friends on birthdays and other special occasions. Doting fathers pay for their sons to have their first sexual experiences at a brothel.

Annie Dieselberg: Breaking the Control

Annie and her team visit the sex bars in Bangkok a couple of times each week so they can foster relationships with the young women who work there. As long as they keep buying drinks at a reasonable pace, the owner typically does not mind. Now that NightLight has earned its reputation as "an alternative to the sex club," though, a few bar owners have warned their girls not to talk to Annie.

It disturbs Annie that so many of the women feel trapped, without an exit. The bar managers have intimidated them thoroughly with random acts of violence and threats to their families. The abuse runs the gamut, beyond physical beatings: the bar owners aim to control them emotionally and spiritually as well.

Some managers perform spiritual rituals inside the bar, usually early in the evening before the bar girls have left on "dates." On several occasions, Annie has been present to witness the drama and describes a very bizarre scene. The manager arranges the women in a circle and then presents a large wood totem that has the distinct shape of a male penis. The owner sprinkles water on the totem and then passes it around for each woman to fondle. Once it has moved around the circle, he moves around the bar touching the end of the totem onto each table where customers will be sitting that evening. Finally, he selects a couple of bar girls to finish the ritual. They move to the front door of the bar, place the totem between their legs, and then throw water through their legs out into the street.

The spiritualism deeply affects the women, especially those raised in rural settings, where it is widely assumed that spirits can enter a person and take over one's body. Women who have left the sex trade frequently ask Annie how they can break free from these spirits. Even if they escape the bar owner, they can never outrun a spirit.

Annie makes it clear that resisting the criminal networks that make money off the sex trade must go beyond the humble efforts of abolitionist groups like NightLight. "We badly need a movement of the Spirit in the global church," she says.

Pressed as to whether churches actually can make a dent in

the global slave trade, Annie becomes resolute: "I spent most of my childhood in Zaire and in Thailand, and I saw a great deal of injustice. But when I watch the darkness that destroys the lives of women and young children in the sex trade, I feel that I am confronting a profoundly evil force."

For that reason, Annie looks to religious communities to deploy prayer and action against sex trafficking in their own local region and to link those efforts to international movements. "The world badly needs the love for family and bonds of community that the church teaches," she says. "Now we have to go out into the society and live it."

Kru Nam: Mother to Over One Hundred

Kru Nam frequently asked Chan if he wanted to return to his home to check whether his sister had been released from the factory. Chan shook his head each time. The last time she asked, he nodded no emphatically. Then he told her that about a year earlier, he had sneaked back home to Burma. Even in the darkness of the night, he had been able to see that his mother no longer lived there. A different family occupied the house.

Had he ever been able to find the factory again, Chan probably would have found that its owner had changed as well. Businesses are transient in Mae Sai, and traffickers are mobile.

Eight years after he and his sister were sold into slavery, Chan still does not know whether she is alive. Nor does he know the whereabouts of his mother. Chan does cherish his freedom, though, and is grateful that he is one of more than 120 children who are free from slavery because an artist decided that rescuing children was her greatest talent.

THE CAMPAIGN: HELPING KRU
NAM AND ANNIE DIESELBERG

As the conclusion of this book describes at greater length, Kru Nam's extraordinary courage to rescue children inspired me to move from author to activist.

It seems only fitting, then, that some of the Not For Sale Campaign's international efforts have focused on Thailand. By the time the initial edition of the book was finished and heading to the publisher, Kru Nam had rescued more than sixty children. She had secured land in the Golden Triangle region, where the borders of Laos, Burma, and Thailand intersect, but she and the children were sleeping in tents and makeshift shelters. I promised to build her permanent housing, and we successfully raised the funds to do just that in 2007. Since then, we have helped Kru Nam enlarge her children's village to numerous structures. In late 2009 we built a health clinic and delivered $2 million worth of medical equipment and supplies to equip it, which serves not only Kru Nam's rescued children but the surrounding community as well.

The Campaign also launched its commercial Freedom Store in 2007 and proudly carries NightLight jewelry. Each necklace, bracelet, or pair of earrings sold through the Freedom Store's Web site, at a freedom party, or by one of our Freedom Store retail "outposts" provides support to Annie Dieselberg's team.

I view these two initiatives in Thailand as two sides of a coin. Kru Nam rescues children, while Annie rescues women. Kru Nam provides education and therapy to promote long-term health and well-being for children; Annie provides emotional fortitude and economic sustainability to women who have never had the option to support themselves and their families with an honest, living wage. Kru Nam works for the betterment of the next generation of Thais, while Annie works to save the current generation. The Not For Sale Campaign is committed to remaining a vital partner to these brave women, both of whom show the world that abolitionists are needed in all shapes and sizes as a prism to shine light into the darkness.

Two

Breaking the Chains of Bonded Laborers

India

Gary Haugen gives lawyers a good name.

His pedigree could land him a corporate-counsel post at a Fortune 500 company or secure a coveted appointment in the judicial system. Blue-chip education? Check that box. He graduated from Harvard and then earned a law degree at the University of Chicago. Stellar career path? Check that box too. He served a six-year tenure as a trial attorney in the civil rights division of the U.S. Department of Justice (DOJ). The DOJ even loaned him to the United Nations to direct a high-profile war-crimes investigation. In short, Gary moves as a professional at the top of his game.

How fortunate for those trapped in slavery that he exercises his talents as an abolitionist. In 1997 he founded International Justice Mission (IJM)—the organization that emancipated Bonda and the rest of his village from the rice mill—and developed it into an extraordinarily effective operation.

Gary is a pragmatic idealist. Like a general immersed in the heat of battle, he can rattle off a detailed strategy. The next moment he can wax philosophical on the nature of good and evil or expound his concept of the state in a civil society. It's a rare mix of talents—driven by big ideas, yet acting with surgeonlike precision.

His IJM office, located on the outskirts of Washington, D.C., offers more clues to what makes him tick. Positioned on his bookshelf rest two stones, one stacked atop the other. Ask Gary what IJM aims to accomplish, and he turns to the bookshelf. He picks up the stones and tells how troubled he was to discover an entire village in South Asia enslaved, toiling in a rock quarry. A cold and callous owner forced young and old alike to break boulders down to a size suitable for construction. He recounts how IJM helped to liberate these slaves. Out of gratitude, one young boy handed Gary these stones as a memento.

Whenever setbacks bog him down, the stones give Gary a tangible reminder of the high stakes at play in IJM's work.

Narayan: The First Deception

Karma never ceases to confound Narayan. How could a kind favor result in such a terrible curse?

Narayan had visited Mr. Vasu with the best of intentions. The last words his sister Maya had spoken to him bore the weight of desperation: "Narayan, we have no money; please do what you can to find us work."

Narayan already had a job in a brick kiln. He had taken a loan from its owner so that he could buy a cow. His uncle Amar and cousin Bishnu had taken a cash advance from the same man. Though they had labored together at the kiln for more than a year, none of them had made as much as a dent in their pile of debt.

Most of Narayan's kin lived in the same village where he was born. During religious festivals, the owner let Narayan, Amar, and Bishnu visit them. Not that their family celebrated the festivals in a lavish way. They survived on the bare essentials; ending a day with a full stomach was sufficient cause for celebration.

Family solidarity proved to be their best defense against the ravages of poverty. So when the brick-kiln owner asked Narayan if he knew of workers looking for jobs, he immediately thought of his sister Maya.

"My friend operates his own brick kiln," the owner told Narayan. "He will provide housing and food on the property."

Narayan and his uncle Amar paid a visit to Mr. Vasu the following day. He showered them with honor far beyond what they might expect as members of a low caste. The men could not recall the last time they had eaten so well: he served them a curry with rice and substantial pieces of chicken mixed into the dish.

Immediately after the meal, Mr. Vasu got down to business. "I need about a dozen workers who can start immediately," he told them.

Narayan was equally direct: "My sister and her husband will come, and I am confident that another handful of our relatives will work as well. But they would need a total of $650 up front so that they can take care of some urgent needs."

"Those terms are acceptable," Mr. Vasu replied. "But they will work for me, and solely me, until they pay back every bit of the $650." He paused long enough for Narayan and Amar to nod their heads in assent. Then he added another condition: "And if they run off without repaying my money, I will hold the two of you responsible. You will serve as their guarantors."

Narayan and Amar left the property on an emotional high. Six hundred and fifty dollars spread across the family would provide sweet relief. Moreover, Mr. Vasu seemed like a kind man who would look after their relatives well. Narayan could not wait to tell his sister the good news.

Gary Haugen: "I Would Want Someone To Get Me Out!"

Gary has had a wealth of experience in hot spots around the globe. In 1989, as he was completing his law degree, he spent four months in the Philippines investigating atrocities that soldiers and police had committed against the civilian population. During his stay in Manila, he made contact with people who worked in poor Filipino neighborhoods, providing health care, literacy training, economic development, and emergency shelter.

As the years passed, Gary stayed in contact with these friends, who told him of the obstacles they faced in their aid and development work. First, they shared how the powerful exploit the poor. When the poor resist, the violent bear them away. Even though laws to protect citizens' rights exist, the police and the courts do not enforce justice consistently. Gary's friends confessed that they felt powerless to act once violence erupted. "So, what should we do," they asked Gary, "when the powerful take advantage of the weak?"

A second daunting obstacle facing them involved the abduction of children. Young girls between the ages of ten and fourteen frequently vanished from their aid projects. They asked the kids at their street shelter, "Hey, I haven't seen Rosa around for a while. Do you know what happened to her?" The kids would just shrug their shoulders. The next day brought more disappearances: "Hey, where's Maria? Has anyone seen Flora?" More silent shrugs.

Eventually, they discovered the truth. The girls were being kidnapped and forced to sell their bodies in brothels. When Gary's friends investigated further, they discovered that the police often played a prominent role in running the brothels.

"What are my nice friends who are trying to serve the poor to do?" Gary asks sympathetically. "They can't just write off the girls as casualties of a corrupt system; that doesn't feel right. But they don't have a lot of experience working with the police."

Gary realized that his friends had stumbled into areas of his own expertise. He had to admit that he could tackle these problems without feeling overwhelmed. To take apart a social problem and design a viable strategy—wasn't that in fact what he had been trained to do?

Blessed with a gift in a moment of critical need, Gary established an agency to rescue victims of violence, sexual exploitation, slavery, and oppression. He became employee number one in a small office in Washington, D.C. Today IJM has almost three hundred full-time staff in fourteen different offices in the developing world and in its Washington, D.C., headquarters.

Grounded in a deep religious faith, Gary interprets IJM's mission as an expression of the Golden Rule: "Do to others as you would have them do to you" (Matt. 7:12).

"If I were trapped in a brothel, what would I want?" Gary asks rhetorically as he launches into a sermon. "I would want someone to get me out! If I were enslaved in a brick factory, I would want someone to end my bondage! If I were being trafficked, I would want to be rescued. That's our work: to love our neighbors and set them free."

Maya: Firing Up the Kiln

Five couples—all related in one way or another—committed to work in the brick kiln. Narayan and Amar had made the opportunity sound very appealing. "Mr. Vasu treated us far better than our own boss does," they reported enthusiastically. "He's also a holy man. He used his own money to build a temple in the local village and devotes himself to its care. You could not ask for a better employer!"

Maya had not expected Narayan to find them a job so soon. Financial crises have a propensity to linger. The last drought had wiped out every bit of the cushion that she and her husband, Ajay, had worked so hard to save. Their small plot of mustard greens had dried up. Large farms in the region had also experienced the decimation of their crops and no longer had use for day laborers. Maya watched both sources for her family's meager income vanish overnight.

Yet the number of mouths she and Ajay had to fill did not change. Ajay had an obligation to support his parents. Maya and Ajay had an eight-year-old son of their own as well. All three generations crowded into one tiny hut.

Despite their pressing needs, Maya and Ajay approached Mr. Vasu's cash advance with caution. The drought would not last forever; once the rains returned, they could stand on their own feet. So when the family sat down to divvy up the loan, Maya and Ajay requested only thirty dollars as their share. That amount could sustain Ajay's parents and their son for some time. Surely it would not take too long to earn back such a small sum, they reasoned.

A week later, twelve aspiring brick-kiln laborers, including Maya and Ajay, said their good-byes to the rest of the village.

One couple brought along their ten-year-old daughter; another member of the family brought along a five-year-old daughter. The other parents left their young children in the care of relatives. The laborers promised to visit during the religious festivals if not sooner. Based on Narayan's experience, they had no reason to assume otherwise.

It took half a day, and three bus rides, to reach Mr. Vasu's property. Upon arrival, the laborers meekly approached the tall iron gate positioned at the front of the compound. Following fifteen minutes of passive deliberation, they rattled the bars with a stick. A young man emerged around an inside wall to greet them. As he removed the padlock and motioned for them to enter, he introduced himself as Mr. Vasu's son. His father had gone to town to run errands and would return soon, he explained. In his absence he, the eighteen-year-old heir, would orient them to the facility.

Maya took stock of the fact that the son reset the padlock on the gate once they moved inside. She also noted the high cement wall that surrounded the front half of the property. It connected to a wire fence that ran around the back end of the compound. Beyond the fence, as far as her eyes could see, lay rows of freshly planted rice.

The son guided them first to their living quarters—a small, rectangular building located in the middle of the property. Along the way, he pointed to a house situated along the left fence. "That's where my father and I stay," he said, "but most of the time we live with my mother in the village." As if carefully mulling over his next choice of words, he paused, and then said, "You are not to approach the house; it's off-limits to you."

The "living quarters" where the family would be staying turned out to be a single room. Wood lattices jutted out from multiple points along the back wall, somewhat resembling stalls in a horse stable. (In fact, from that day forward, the family referred to their shelter as "the stable.") The dirt floor had been swept recently, and the mud walls and thatched roof kept the room markedly cooler than the sweltering heat outdoors.

Maya and her kin placed their meager belongings in the room and then rejoined the guided tour. A chimney stretched high into the sky about fifteen feet from the stable. At its base an open mouth gaped, but no fire burned inside. "It will take a while to get the fire to a heat needed to dry the bricks," the son remarked.

Just then a voice behind them boomed, "And I trust it will be the last time that any of us will see a cold kiln!"

Startled, Maya and her relatives jerked their necks around to see a portly man standing no more than five feet behind them. He was clothed in saffron-colored pants and shirt, a common dress for holy men.

"Hello, I am Mr. Vasu," he began, "and you are now in my service." As he slowly enunciated these words, the man held up a set of papers in his right hand. "This contract formalizes the terms of our arrangement."

The owner then strutted like a peacock over to Ajay and handed him the papers. Ajay accepted them awkwardly. Being completely illiterate, a failing he shared with all his kin, Ajay simply held the documents to his side.

"As you will read," Mr. Vasu went on as if he were oblivious to the humiliation he produced, "you will be expected to pay back the money that you borrowed, plus interest. I will provide food and add its cost to the amount that you owe. For every thousand bricks you produce, you will earn $4.50. I will deduct what you earn from your debt. Once you have canceled your debt, I will compensate you for your labor in cash, or you may choose to look for other employment. Until that day arrives, you will work only at this kiln. Any questions?"

The laborers stood mute. His presentation mirrored more or less what Narayan had explained to them, though they admittedly did not comprehend what "interest" might mean. No matter, they were happy to be in a position to earn some wages.

"It's all written down for you to read," Mr. Vasu repeated, as if he were delighted to be tossing salt into a fresh wound. "I will come back in half an hour, and each of you will sign the contract. Meanwhile, I want you to get started on firing up the kiln."

As he spoke, Maya thought her imagination must be playing tricks on her. She could swear that a hot flame seared through her body.

Work at the kiln began the next day at 6 A.M. The family worked collectively. Moving the brick molds in and out of the kiln required tremendous strength, so the men generally assumed that task. Pretty much everyone else manufactured the bricks.

Maya passed most of the day packing wet clay and straw into row after row of wood forms. Once the sun rose high in the midmorning sky, she would start carrying the clay molds atop her head into an open space where direct rays could reach them. For the molds to dry into a stable form usually took a couple of hours in the sun. In midafternoon, the family took an hour's break and grabbed a bite to eat. After lunch, some continued packing the molds, others moved them into the sunlight to dry, and yet others brought the dried molds to the kiln to bake the bricks into their final form. They strove to have all the bricks completely baked by sunset.

The men rotated the job of stoking the kiln. Working outdoors means facing sweltering heat in normal conditions; standing next to a glowing charcoal furnace can be downright unbearable. The skin, glistening with sweat, becomes an inviting haven for clay dust and soot. Reaching deep into the pores, the dust dries with the heat, causing the skin to crack. At day's end, the man working the kiln looks like a walking briquette of charcoal.

Mr. Vasu drove the work crew with capricious demands. If they produced fewer than a thousand bricks in a day, he would yell, "You lazy dogs! Why were you so slack today?" If they worked at a faster pace and produced twelve hundred bricks, he would scream, "You manipulative cheats! Don't expect to be paid for more than a thousand bricks." When reviewing the day's production, he always found a reason to complain. He would pull out bricks with the slightest flaw and decry their "faulty workmanship."

The verbal abuse began the day they arrived. By the end of the first week, it had turned to physical violence. The men he whacked with sticks; the women he struck with an open palm. One day Maya got slapped to the ground as she was walking to the well for a drink of water.

"Why aren't you working?" Mr. Vasu asked gruffly. "The heat is unbearable today," Maya replied honestly, "and I am dying of thirst."

She did not see the blow coming. His hand struck her hard on her right ear and sent her sprawling. "Maybe that will help you forget about your thirst!" he muttered and walked away.

Power reserves for itself the right to act capriciously. Clay molds could tumble accidentally off a woman's head, and Mr. Vasu would laugh as if watching a slapstick comedy. The same mishap could occur a few days later, and he would lash out ferociously.

One afternoon he clubbed Ajay brutally for overheating the fire, a mistake that caused an entire pallet of bricks to crack. To their utter surprise, the following day Mr. Vasu gave the family a chicken to cook "as a reward for doing such good work."

That day lingered in their memories, for eating chicken was not common at the compound. Three times daily they poured porridge and mustard greens into their bowls. On rare occasions they supplemented their diet with vegetables, though both meat and vegetables cost far beyond their tiny food budget.

Mr. Vasu usually gave them money to buy food on his own schedule, yet some days the workers would go a day without eating because he failed to provide funds. The first time that occurred, Maya's cousin reminded Mr. Vasu that a week had passed since their last trip to the market. The owner gave him a scowl and walked off. He returned a few minutes later with his stick and struck her cousin forcefully several times. "I will tell you when it's time to go to the market!" he yelled out as he wielded the club.

Mr. Vasu permitted only a few individuals to go to the market, and he always forced the children to stay behind and work. "If you do not come back," he would warn those going off to the market, "I will make this place a living hell for those who are left behind."

Maya initially assumed that greed motivated his restrictions on their movement: he wanted to keep as many of them working as possible. But her mind changed when Mr. Vasu flatly refused to let them travel to a religious festival back at their home village. "Because you dogs have been so lazy, I cannot fulfill my brick orders," he snarled. "You must stay and work."

Slowly it dawned on Maya that they had not landed a job. They had joined a prison labor camp.

Gary Haugen: Anatomy of a Rescue

Early in the existence of IJM, Gary and his team conducted an extensive needs survey. Their focus group targeted nearly seventy organizations operating relief and development programs around the globe. Collectively, these groups supported tens of thousands of workers in more than a hundred countries.

Every single agency reported back to IJM that their workers encountered serious cases of abuse. They witnessed forced labor, sex trafficking, corrupt seizure of land, and corruption in the public justice system. When the agencies tried to address the injustice, they received minimal support from the police or the courts.

The survey results confirmed what Gary had experienced in his previous human rights investigations: oppressors use violence to commit acts of injustice and to discourage potential rescuers from coming to the aid of the victims.

The absence of an effective public justice system blocks every step the poor take to change their social condition. For example, the staff of a renowned aid and relief agency reported to IJM that coercive labor was undermining its efforts in South Asia to enroll kids in school. Young children were being forced to roll cigarettes for seventy to eighty hours per week or to weave carpets in makeshift factories. Though these practices are illegal throughout the region, the guardians of the law look the other way. If they refuse to stop the slave owners, to whom can the children turn for help? Even their advocates in this top-tier international aid agency feel powerless.

Another aid agency working in India reported to the IJM survey an even more alarming crisis. Its health clinic encountered a fresh wave of kids who had contracted AIDS. The children were coming to the clinic straight out of the city's red-light district. Though the agency gave assistance to those afflicted, it realized that more preventive work would be needed to address the problem. But rescuing those kids already embedded in the brothels meant confronting both criminal elements and an ineffective police bureaucracy.

IJM has gained most of its notoriety for rescuing victims. To some degree, its skewed public image can be attributed to the media. Many Americans became acquainted with the agency for the first time after watching a *Dateline* television show about an IJM-led raid on the Svay Pak brothels in Cambodia. The intervention, which took place in 2004, rescued thirty-seven girls between the ages of five and seventeen and led to the arrests of several brothel owners as well as the dismissal of a few corrupt police officers.

Rescuing victims can be dangerous, dramatic, and glitzy. Sadly, a television producer will not give equal airtime to a successful microenterprise project that reduces a community's vulnerability to sex traffickers.

Frankly, the fascination with rescuing victims goes beyond entertainment. It is a natural response to want to save individuals who fall into captivity. When people first embrace the abolitionist cause, they often imagine themselves storming a labor camp to rescue individuals in captivity. More modest dreamers might ponder how they could buy a young girl out of a brothel and give her a new life.

Due to this romanticism, IJM's rescue work can be misunderstood. The agency does not run cowboy posse operations.

To the contrary, its interventions are linked carefully to a broader agenda to sustain communities and to strengthen the public justice system.

In that regard, IJM's efforts should be distinguished from the well-intentioned efforts of some Western agencies to buy victims out of slavery. Redemption purchases have been deployed "successfully" in the Sudan and among a handful of international groups that free women from brothels.

Certainly, extreme cases may arise when slave redemption might be necessary. But buying a slave's freedom can lead to several unintended consequences. For starters, it may create an even more dynamic market in the trade of human beings. Slave traders treat humans like any other commodity with financial value. If the demand increases and there is no shortage of supply, purchases generate recurring revenue. Slave traders will simply go out and recruit other vulnerable people and force them into labor until a Western agency comes along and pays for their redemption.

Buying back slaves also diminishes the prospect of prosecuting slave traders. Police agents rarely show a willingness to get involved in the investigation of a crime that has already been "resolved." If the victim is rescued without the involvement of the police, most court systems are also reluctant to pursue a criminal case.

Gary Haugen recognizes the effort to buy back slaves for what it actually is: an end run around the real problem. The concept of paying off criminals would not arise if the public justice system functioned properly. Moreover, slave redemption becomes a self-defeating strategy. If we presume the power of those who act outside of the justice system, playing the game by their rules, they will win every time. "If you do not have the rule of law," Gary argues, "you have the rule of those who wield power at their own whim."

IJM uses a method it calls the "power-actor analysis" to identify law-enforcement agents with whom it might work to bring about justice. The procedure presents questions like these: How does the legal structure currently operate in the community? How do matters of public justice get resolved in informal ways? Who is the person formally responsible for executing justice? Who within the IJM network would be the best person to interact with our best law-enforcement candidate?

In most cases, IJM does not approach members of the police agency at the bottom of the chain of command. The beat officers are more likely to be socially connected to the perpetrator and likely to have a family or financial tie. Ideally, IJM finds a senior officer who has the capacity to make things happen without a supervisor's approval.

Once the right "power actor" has been identified, IJM presents its evidence and gives him or her the opportunity to do the right thing and get credit for it. "The best leverage is the truth," Gary stresses, and in most cases that is sufficient motivation for the power actor to apply the law.

The fact that an international legal agency has presented the evidence may serve as useful leverage. Few law-enforcement officials will take the risk of being publicly exposed for sitting on evidence and refusing to act. Playing the foreign card could also backfire, however. The official might consider it a matter of pride to snub his nose at the "foreign agency" despite the fact that most IJM staff members are, in fact, from the region. All of these considerations must be weighed in the power-actor analysis.

"Intervention takes a tremendous amount of prep work," Gary admits. IJM's job is much easier when it already has a history in a region and has built relationships with highly committed magistrates. When it starts from scratch in a new area, IJM has to perform a lot of meticulous groundwork.

Maya: One Violation Leads to Another

Though Mr. Vasu regularly made reference to their debt, Maya had no clue how much she and her relatives actually owed. It took her almost six months to build up the courage to ask him for a financial accounting.

He once had claimed that they would earn $4.50 for every thousand bricks they produced; in essence, that quantity of bricks represented a day's labor. Spread out over five families, the wage would not be significant. But Maya figured it would at least enable them to chip away at their debt.

So when Mr. Vasu informed her that her debt had actually doubled, she was confounded. "That's impossible," she boldly blurted. "We have labored here for six months."

Almost as if he expected this response, Mr. Vasu pulled out a sheet of paper filled with lines and numbers. "As you can see," he began with a sickly smile, "you have incurred interest on your initial loan. I also have given you a substantial amount of money to pay for your food."

Maya stared at the paper, but the numbers made no more sense than erratic scribbles. Certain that she would offer no protest, he offered some advice: "It looks like you are just going to have to work harder."

When she reported back to the family what she had learned, they grumbled in disbelief. One of her cousins voiced what everyone was thinking: "How are we ever going to work ourselves out of this prison?"

It was humanly impossible to, say, double their daily production. Regardless, whenever they did surpass the benchmark of a thousand bricks in a day, Mr. Vasu did not give them credit for their surplus.

To make matters worse, the kiln would shut down for weeks at a time. On those occasions, Mr. Vasu explained that they had caught up with outside orders. During these waiting periods, he pressed the men to labor around the compound—scouring the kiln, sweeping up the straw, mending the fence, and so on. For performing these chores they received no compensation.

The owner, likewise, entreated the women to clean the temple that he had built for the local village. On the first such occasion, he transported to the temple only three women—Maya and two of her cousins. Beginning early in the morning, they scrubbed the floors and polished the statues of divine figures. By midafternoon, they had finished their assigned chores, so they waited for Mr. Vasu to return and take them back to the compound.

When he arrived, he did not come alone. Maya assumed that the five men who accompanied him had temple responsibilities. They held no such holy ambition.

"Maya, I have a chore for you in the back room," Mr. Vasu said, and then barked loudly, "Come!"

She dutifully followed behind the owner and one of his cronies. Once they had passed into the back room, her owner shut the door and calmly ordered her to take off her clothes.

It took Maya a few moments to absorb the shock of his command: could a "holy man" so brazenly act with evil in his own temple? Realizing the vulnerability of her situation, she turned to flee. Her owner's friend already had positioned himself to cut off her retreat and hit her to the ground. He held tightly onto her arms while Mr. Vasu tore off her clothes and raped her. He then switched positions to assist in his friend's own act of violation.

"Get dressed. We will return to the compound in ten minutes," Mr. Vasu said once they had finished their assault. He spoke in such a casual tone that she wondered why she felt so awash in shame while he apparently felt none.

Once dressed again, she returned to the main temple and understood immediately that her cousins had undergone the same torment. The women did not say a word to each other, nor did they speak of their violation once they returned to the compound. Fearful of further humiliation, they held on to their secret.

DIGNITY BEYOND CAPTIVITY

Rescuing slaves does not end the moment they are freed from captivity. To abandon the rescued and expect them to fend for themselves leaves them vulnerable to falling back into a forced-labor relationship with a different owner. Abolitionists, therefore, must answer the question "What next?" before they rush into a rescue plan.

That solution probably will not be as simple as sending them back home. In some cases, enslaved individuals are trafficked across borders, perhaps from an ocean away. Survivors may be ongoing targets for the original traffickers who extracted them from their home village.

Though social workers throw around terms like *reintegration* and *restoration,* the process of aftercare often turns out to be far more complicated. Teenage girls freed from a brothel may decide that a pattern of shame and abuse awaits them in their home village, so they elect to build a new life elsewhere in a supportive environment free of recrimination.

That complexity was revealed during my interviews with workers rescued from a rice mill in India. Among the rescued, twenty-five of the laborers were related by family. When I asked the matriarch of the family where she came from originally, she offered a puzzled look and replied, "The rice mill." She explained that her father had been pressed into labor when he was in his twenties, so she had worked in the rice mill her entire life. She raised her own children as laborers in the same mill.

As the matriarch recounted the saga of four generations of servitude that began with a ten-dollar loan, her thirty-five-year-old daughter offered pieces of her own story. She, too, had met her husband at the rice mill. They were raising three children, aged eleven, thirteen, and eighteen, who had a long future of boiling and drying rice ahead of them. IJM and a local magistrate had teamed up to alter the destiny of this extended family overnight. What would "sending them back home" mean to this family and to millions of forced laborers with similar histories?

IJM today helps more than two thousand people in South Asia, all former slaves and their families, in a broad array of aftercare programs. For the period immediately following a rescue, IJM collaborates with a network of relief partners to provide ex-slaves with shelter, food, emotional counseling, and protection from vindictive owners. Except in extreme circumstances of imminent violence, the agency will delay executing a rescue plan until it has a long-term support structure in place. IJM assists former slaves in obtaining loans or grants from local authorities and available government land for houses.

Additionally, IJM helps former slaves enroll their children in public school—often the most important tangible right that those in slavery so desperately want.

How critical is effective aftercare? Monitoring the results of its own programs, IJM learned that 94 percent of the former slaves it places in a supportive environment do not return to bondage.

Maya: The Bold Escape

Like jackals that have tasted blood and return to their prey, Mr. Vasu and his friends sexually assaulted the females at every opportunity, acts that included beating and burning their bodies. Usually, the owner and his son acted alone. With increasing frequency, Mr. Vasu announced to the women, "It's time to clean the temple." He said it in front of their husbands in a hushed tone, as if they were joining him in a sacred duty.

Though the women maintained their shame in secret, they did hatch a plan for a mass escape. Their husbands rejected out of hand such "desperate measures." The consequences of a failed escape frightened them far more than the daily mistreatment they received at the hands of Mr. Vasu. If they were to run away, he would leave no stone unturned to find them.

Then one evening, Mr. Vasu brought his temple friends back to the compound after a wild drinking spree at a local tavern. The rowdy gang burst into the laborers' living quarters and started dragging the females outside. When their husbands put up a fierce resistance, the gang beat them mercilessly with sticks and tied them up to prevent their interference. Writhing in pain on the dirt floor of the stable, the men could only listen to the ribald chatter of the marauding herd as they violated their wives.

The pieces of the puzzle finally fell into place; sunk deep in humiliation, they now understood why their wives so desperately wanted to escape. Once the horrible ordeal drew to an end, the bruised women stumbled back into the stable. Out of respect, their husbands did not say a word. But the next morning, as the entire family stood at the table throwing clay and straw into wood forms, they mapped out a plan.

Ajay had overheard the owner telling his son about a festival they would attend in the local town. The Vasu men set off one afternoon several days later, and that evening the family scaled the iron gate. Though negotiating the spikes at the top of the gate was no easy feat, they helped one another make it to the other side safely.

Knowing that Mr. Vasu would interrogate local residents, the fugitives used the cover of darkness to get as far away from the compound as they could without being seen. Then, at the first hint of dawn, they jumped on a bus that would take them toward their home village.

The fugitives received a hearty welcome from their village kin, who had wondered whether they had vanished off the face of the earth. "Why didn't you ever visit us?" they asked innocently. To a horrified audience, Maya and the others shared the tale of their days in captivity.

The fugitives soaked in the familiar warmth of their homes, but they realized that this would be the first place that Mr. Vasu would send bounty hunters to look for them. Distant relatives lived on the other side of their province. They all agreed that it would be best to hide out there. They would do whatever was necessary to avoid capture and a return to the brick kiln.

IS THIS SLAVERY? TRUE OR FALSE

When slave owners become subject to criminal prosecution, they typically cloak their acts in a number of falsehoods. IJM created a handout for use in South Asia that aims to straighten out the record. It lists the most common rationalizations that slave owners have used and counters those falsehoods with the truth. The following list is paraphrased from the handout:

Falsehood: "My loan helped these people in an emergency."
Truth: Although the initial loan may have brought immediate relief, forced labor puts the victims in a far more vulnerable position. Because they are paid very low wages and are often charged high interest rates, they are never able to repay the lender and may suffer a lifetime for a single loan.

Falsehood: "The worker asked me for the advance."
Truth: Whether or not workers wanted an advance, the employer cannot legally take away their freedom.

Falsehood: "If it weren't for me, these people would be homeless."
Truth: The provision of housing, which is often substandard, does not mitigate the injustice of enslaving victims. Moreover, relevant law states that freed laborers are not to be evicted from their homes.

Falsehood: "If you release these people, they'll be jobless."

Truth: In addition to the rehabilitation to which victims are entitled by law upon release, they are freed from debt, removed from an abusive labor situation, and allowed to find a better source of income.

Falsehood: "If I'm not repaid for the loans I gave, I'll lose a substantial amount of money."
Truth: Because the loan was illegal in the first place, it is null and void. To accept payment on such a loan is to be subject to criminal penalty. Regardless, in most cases victims have repaid the loans multiple times over and the owner has already made astounding profits on the loan.

Falsehood: "The industry would fail if it couldn't use forced labor."
Truth: Fair labor practices are necessary for legal, moral, and economic reasons. It is true that the cost of eradicating slavery might be borne largely by the wealthy classes. But eradicating slavery will also lead to the modernization of industry practices and may boost a country's economic progress.

Falsehood: "The workers are free to go if they pay the advance first."
Truth: Relevant law specifically prohibits employers from preventing individuals from pursuing employment elsewhere. An inability or unwillingness to repay an advance does not abrogate that right.

Falsehood: "You are just picking on my operation. Every other business in the industry does the same thing."

Truth: The law is binding. An industry's failure to follow the law does not give any employer the license to deny workers their fundamental rights.

Falsehood: "Brokers brought me these people. I didn't know how they were paid or what freedoms they had."
Truth: The law assumes that those in charge of a company know its operations. On that basis, the law deems those in charge of a company guilty when an offense occurs, regardless of their personal knowledge.

Falsehood: "No one will work if I don't give them cash advances."
Truth: Advances are not illegal. The issue is whether or not the laborers are forced to work.

Falsehood: "Even if the law says the advance must be canceled, the workers still have a moral obligation to repay the debt."
Truth: As well as having no legal obligation to pay the debt, laborers have no moral obligation. A moral obligation cannot arise from an immoral act.

Narayan: Temple Hostages

Narayan thought it strange that his sister and Ajay did not return home for religious festivals. He knew that Maya disliked being under anyone's obligation. Maybe she and Ajay had decided to work extra hard to cancel their debt. Narayan made a silent pledge to visit them at their brick kiln soon.

Then early one morning Narayan caught a glimpse of Mr. Vasu as he passed through the gate of the brick kiln. Within the hour, Narayan's boss emerged from his office and told him that Mr. Vasu wanted to speak with him alone. Narayan's curiosity turned to dread; surely the man had not come to report good news.

Mr. Vasu was pacing across the middle of the office when Narayan entered. He rushed toward Narayan and thrust his head forward so that only inches separated their faces. "Your family has failed to fulfill their obligation!" he screamed. "They have run away. If you know what's good for you, you will tell me where they have gone."

Narayan could not believe that his sister would behave so rashly. "I am sure that they will return," he offered. "They probably went on a brief visit to our home village."

"I didn't think you would cooperate," Mr. Vasu replied. "I warned you and your uncle that I would hold you responsible for their actions. Go fetch your uncle and your cousin—you will be leaving with me now."

Mr. Vasu spat his words out with such venom that Narayan reckoned it was useless to argue. He nodded his head and walked out the door.

Outside the office Narayan's boss awaited him. "Don't worry, Narayan," he whispered. "You can come back in a few days. Mr. Vasu will turn over every rock until he tracks down your family."

A chill ran up Narayan's spine, yet he held his composure and gave his boss a polite nod. He headed directly to where Amar and Bishnu were working and explained to them the troubling circumstances. A few moments later, they shuffled out of the gate behind the determined strides of Mr. Vasu. The man pointed to the rear bed of his pickup truck, and they jumped in.

As the pickup barreled along the highway, the men went over likely scenarios. Where else would their relatives go but back to their home village? And why would they act so outrageously against the wishes of their boss?

They took a break from their earnest conversation to figure out why the truck had come to a halt in front of a village temple. They presumed that Mr. Vasu would transport them back to his compound.

Half a dozen men emerged from the temple as soon as they arrived. Two of the larger men leaned over, gruffly jerked Amar out of the flatbed, and carried him toward the temple. The remainder of the men moved Narayan and Bishnu in like manner.

The brutes made a circle around the laborers and beat them brutally with sticks, clenched fists, and boots. Narayan passed out after a fist knocked him square in the nose. When he regained consciousness, both his relatives were lying next to him, passed out in a sea of red.

It was just turning dusk when Mr. Vasu returned with his thugs. "Are you ready to talk now?" he asked in menacing tone.

"As I've said all along, we didn't even know that they had left your property until you came to the brick kiln this morning," Narayan said with his head down, not daring to look at his tormentor directly. "I would guess they went to our home village."

"Wrong!" Mr. Vasu screamed as he gave Narayan a hard kick in the ribs. "I already sent some of my men to the village this morning, and they weren't there. No one there will admit to having seen them. So where else could they be?"

The captives had run out of answers. So the thugs tore off their clothes, pinned them down, and shaved their scalps bald. Then Mr. Vasu instructed his men to hold each one upright while he took a photo to capture their humiliation.

The men slept that night naked on the concrete floor of the temple. Narayan twisted to find a part of his body that did not feel tender so that he might be able to rest comfortably. As he struggled to fall asleep, his eyes scanned the temple. Since he was a young boy he had attended a temple ceremony every week. He now wondered: Did the gods who watched over this sacred place not see his distress? Why didn't they intervene now and offer him protection?

Gary Haugen: Pursuing Justice

Gary discovers time and time again that the perpetrators of injustice deploy two tools to get their way: coercion and deception. Coercion, forcing an individual to perform an act against his or her will, usually involves the threat or act of physical violence. Perpetrators use deception to mask their true intention and to cover up their crimes. The combination of coercion and deception makes it difficult to bring slave owners and other violators of human rights to justice.

Gary's previous work as a human-rights investigator prepared him well for his abolitionist work. In 1989 the Lawyers Committee for Human Rights commissioned Gary to spend four months in the Philippines investigating abuses. The country had recently emerged from the long shadow of dictatorial rule. A new populist leader had assumed control of the government, and the Filipino people had high hopes for a new era of justice. Unfortunately, violations against the poor had not ended, and the perpetrators were going unpunished.

Once Gary had settled in the Philippines, he elected to focus first on a high-profile massacre that had taken place in the village of Lupao. Soldiers from the Filipino army had been charged with the murder of seventeen unarmed villagers; among the victims were six children. Most of the evidence that Gary reviewed, including the testimonies of seven survivors, indicated that the soldiers had, indeed, executed the unarmed civilians. Despite the preponderance of evidence, a military court had acquitted all of the accused soldiers. Immediately following the acquittal, the new democratic president of the country tried to justify the results to the public, announcing that witnesses to the event had chosen not to cooperate with the court. Her justification matched the story of military prosecutors and the presiding judge of the court trial, who all reported that without the help of witnesses, they could not prove the guilt of the accused soldiers.

As he studied the case review, Gary smelled a rat. In his experience, individuals who witness the murder of a loved one deeply desire to testify against the perpetrators and bring them to justice. So why didn't they show up for their court date?

Rather than rely on court documents, Gary elected to take a nine-hour bus ride to Lupao and get to the bottom of the mystery. There he met with a number of the witnesses and learned that all seven survivors actually had testified at the court-martial and had clearly identified four of the defendants. As Gary suspected, the official reports of the trial had been an outright lie.

Though the faces and places change, Gary experiences the same dynamics in his IJM work today. The powerful everywhere use coercion and deception to abuse the rights of the poor. They deploy their own security forces and resolve disputes in their own way. The poor and the weak, on the other hand, cannot provide their own security or execute their own justice. The rule of law, properly executed, is their only source of security and the only place where they might find justice. The powerful can work around a corrupt system; the poor cannot.

Narayan: Family Obligations

Mr. Vasu interrogated the laborers at the temple for two days. Though they never altered their story, the torture continued unabated.

On the third day, Mr. Vasu moved them to his compound and changed tactics. He gave them ill-fitting clothes and forced them to perform meaningless tasks of hard labor. For an entire day, they shoveled sand out of a dump truck and piled it high on the ground. The next day they shoveled the sand off the ground and filled up the dump truck. The purpose behind these chores only Mr. Vasu knew, for he continued to take photos of their activities.

On day six of captivity, Mr. Vasu woke Amar early and ordered him to jump into the back of the truck. He drove him back to the temple. Amar feared that he was entering a renewed phase of torture. Instead, Mr. Vasu told Amar that he was to go and search for the runaway slaves. Mr. Vasu said that he would continue to torture Narayan and Bishnu until Amar returned.

"But I honestly do not know where to look for them," Amar complained. He was sure that he was being set up for failure.

"You will call me by phone each day to let me know what progress you are making," Mr. Vasu replied, unmoved by his protest. "And Amar, if I do not hear from you on a given day, I will take your punishment out on your poor relatives. And if you attempt to run away, I will kill both of them."

The owner gave Amar a small sum of money to cover the cost of bus fares and phone calls and sent him forth on his mission.

Mr. Vasu did not receive a call from Amar that day, nor the next day, nor any day after. When it came to threats, he was a man of real integrity, always following through. Each night he beat Narayan and Bishnu harshly. "Where is your Amar?" he would taunt them as he brought down his stick. "Your entire family is making you pay for their failure to keep promises."

Gary Haugen: Structural Prevention

In late 1994, the U.S. Department of Justice put Gary on loan to serve as the director of the UN genocide investigation in Rwanda. Only months before his appointment, tribal Hutus had butchered complete villages of Tutsi women and children as a senseless hysteria swept the country.

Gary started his investigation with a list of one hundred mass graves where witnesses and UN military intelligence personnel indicated that a massacre might have taken place. It's hard to imagine a more gruesome task. At each site, he and his team sorted through the bodies and looked for evidence that might lead them to the perpetrators. They would learn that no fewer than eight hundred thousand Tutsis were killed in an eight-week span.

Gary and his team found one mass grave situated behind a Roman Catholic church in the town of Kibuye. In April 1994, nearly 450 people sought shelter in the church after they heard reports of hostile militia activity in the region. When the troops arrived, they killed every person they could find, including those who prayed for mercy in church pews.

As Gary's feet sank in the mud of the mass grave and his nostrils filled with the stench of rotting bodies, he was tempted to sink into despair. What could justice mean here? And what good would it do to convict the perpetrators now that the violence had ended?

He came to a profound conclusion: the pursuit of justice creates a social legacy. It did mean something that the International Tribunal for Rwanda used the evidence his team documented to indict the leaders of the Kibuye massacre—the governor of the region, the mayor of the town, and their accomplices. Holding perpetrators accountable for their crimes against humanity not only dignifies the suffering of the victims; it instills in the survivors a confidence in the rule of law. Moreover, the criminal convictions sent a strong message to the next generation of Rwandans that abuses do not go unpunished. "Never again" must be the motto that guides future generations, and it begins with enforcing justice today.

This dogged pursuit of justice has informed Gary's work at IJM. Not that he hasn't faced his share of legal disappointments: despite the fact that IJM has pressed hard with local prosecutors in India to convict slave owners for their crimes, not a single perpetrator has spent a night in jail due to a forced-labor conviction.

So he is not surprised when social "realists" tell him to give up his quest for public justice in countries where the rule of law is anemic. "They are just way too corrupt," they say. "It's just the way those people are, and they'll never change."

Gary does not accept that argument. When he reads political history, he appreciates that Western democratic societies are the result of a long experiment to restrain violent behavior. Our public justice systems aim to ensure that citizens do not sort out their disputes through the exercise of brute physical power. That should not imply that people in democratic societies are inherently nicer or more reasonable. We enjoy civil rights and freedom of movement because we have a functioning public justice system. Though far from perfect, it offers a better solution for violence.

Gary recalls an episode when he went undercover in an investigation of child sex trafficking in Cambodia. A pimp led him to a room where he presented a dozen girls between the ages of five and ten. For a few dollars, these children would perform any sexual act requested by customers.

"Keep in mind that the sexual exploitation of minors is completely against the law in Cambodia," Gary says, shaking his head. "But here I am, very openly engaging in a negotiation to violate these young girls!" He adds, with frustration, "This transaction could happen because the law is not enforced. Slavery flourishes in the world because it is tolerated by law enforcement!"

For that reason, Gary believes that pursuing the conviction of criminals is one of the most effective tools to deter future crimes. Only then will individuals who are trafficking or abusing people get the message that they must stop or face the consequences.

In that respect, the agenda for modern-day abolitionists stands apart from that of the nineteenth-century abolitionists who confronted the transatlantic African slave trade. At that time, the slave trade was state sanctioned and intricately tied to the financial interests of the state. Abolitionists like William Wilberforce and Frederick Douglass appropriately channeled their energies to make slavery illegal.

Today, however, there is not a country in the world where slavery could be considered legal. Yet slavery still thrives. If the laws that already appear on the books were enforced, the slave trade would end tomorrow. But the laws are not enforced, and slave owners know they can rely on a broken public justice system to escape prosecution. They count on the apathy of local authorities; they create delays in the courts; and they leverage family ties and social influence.

"At the moment, slave owners and sex traffickers are not afraid," Gary laments. "Victims of sex trafficking, on the other hand, are afraid. Families trapped in forced labor are afraid. Our challenge is to reverse the equation. In that sense, our work has only just begun."

Maya: Family Reunion

Maya saw the strange man with the shaved head heading across the field toward her hut. As he drew closer, she suspected that the man had been in a bad accident: black and blue bruises discolored almost every inch of his swollen face.

"Peace to you, Maya," his familiar voice said when he reached the hut. He noticed her confusion, so he gently added, "I am your uncle Amar."

Maya gasped, then rushed to give him a hug. "Oh, my dear uncle! Whatever happened to you?"

"It is not a pretty story, my niece," he said in a sad voice. "Could you bring Ajay and your cousins? A single telling of this tale may be all that I have the strength to do."

Maya left him to rest at the hut while she ran out to a rice field where most of the family labored. They debated among themselves whether Amar had come by himself or whether

Mr. Vasu might be using him to lure them into a trap. They decided to send a team around the perimeter of the village to make sure that no bounty hunters were lying in wait. By midafternoon, the family had gathered back at Maya's house.

A ghastly silence gripped the family as Amar painfully recounted what had happened to him, Narayan, and Bishnu over the past few days and passed around the photos that Mr. Vasu had sent with him. It was awkward for the family to bear witness to the humiliation—and worse still that their escape set these events in motion.

Just when it felt as if the air could no longer hold the tension, Amar spoke: "We do not hold you responsible for what has happened to us. In many ways, we are responsible. Who could have imagined that Mr. Vasu would turn out to be such a tyrant?"

As everyone murmured agreement, Amar continued: "But now we have a real dilemma. Mr. Vasu pledges to kill Narayan and Bishnu if we do not return, and we all know not to hold his threats lightly."

Amar paused to see whether anyone wanted to speak, but everyone in the circle remained silent, eyes cast down to the ground. He decided to press forward: "As badly as I feel for Narayan and Bishnu, I cannot return. My guess is that you will refuse to go back as well. But we cannot abandon our relatives. We must do something."

"Yes, we wholeheartedly agree, Amar," Ajay said softly. "Here in this province the people are fortunate to have very good leaders. Yesterday I met with one of them and recounted to him our experience. He told me about an agency called International Justice Mission that protects enslaved people like us. I think we should ask him to connect us right away. Maybe the agency has the means to fight Mr. Vasu. Acting alone, I know that we cannot."

Maya Meets IJM: Operation Rescue

Once Maya and Ajay went to the village leader to plead for help, events moved swiftly. They visited the leader's home in the morning, and by early afternoon the man offered them a solution. It involved eight members of the family traveling to a secure location where they would give their testimonies to IJM. The village leader was confident that the hostages would be set free as long as the family members did their part.

"You can fully trust the people in this organization," he told the couple. "In the past, they have freed many laborers in my district, even from some of the most violent owners."

IJM used undercover investigation to confirm that they were dealing with a hostage situation. In normal circumstances, the agency would give itself several months to gather evidence on a slave owner: a more thorough case increases the chances for a successful conviction.

Despite the rush in this case, one factor worked in IJM's favor: only a dozen or so laborers appeared to be involved. Some of the slavery cases they investigate involve anywhere from 100 to 150 laborers.

The family did not need much convincing to cooperate. Surely Narayan and Bishnu were living on borrowed time. Moreover, they knew that Mr. Vasu would never surrender his claim on their own lives. If they did not stop him now, they would always be looking over their shoulder.

In her testimony to IJM, Maya did not have to rehearse a single detail; every painful moment of the past ten months was as fresh in her mind as if it had happened yesterday. She had initially not planned to mention the sexual assaults. But when the lawyer asked if she had been violated sexually, she surprised herself when she answered, "Yes, many times on the floor of the temple."

Within forty-eight hours, IJM staff accompanied local police on a raid of the kiln. They had difficulty finding the hostages at first; a search of the living quarters turned up nothing. An IJM backup team monitoring the raid from afar with binoculars, however, observed one of Mr. Vasu's cronies moving toward a small shed in an adjoining field. They radioed the ground team and alerted them to the suspicious activity. When the IJM team members approached the shed, they heard muffled cries. They forced open the locked door and found Narayan and Bishnu crouched on the floor, too terrified to speak.

IJM brought all of the freed slaves to the office of the district magistrate the next day. He issued to each of them a document stating that they owed no obligation to Mr. Vasu and were free to pursue their own destiny. The magistrate's office explained to them that the certification made them eligible for many benefits, including a lump sum of cash. The family happily returned to their home village that very afternoon.

Despite the evidence against Mr. Vasu, the police who conducted the raid declined to take him into custody. IJM persisted and presented to the police a list of criminal offenses that the owner of the brick kiln had committed, including wrongful confinement, physical abuse and torture, rape, and forced labor. Despite thorough documentation and credible testimonies from multiple victims, the authorities would not file charges. After two years of efforts by the staff at IJM, Mr.

Vasu was finally arrested. Released on bail, he now awaits trial. He has not spent a full day in jail for his crimes.

Maya and Ajay today work hard to make ends meet. When they are lucky, they both find fieldwork at one of the local farms. They have been able to buy a few cows and sheep. Though they cannot save much money, they make enough to feed and clothe their family and have some savings. They vow never to take another loan.

Despite a much better life, Maya admits that she still feels unsafe. Mr. Vasu could pop back into her life at any moment and take her back to the brick kiln. For that reason, she stays close to home. Who knows who might see her if she visits one of the larger towns in the region? Maybe one of Mr. Vasu's cronies will spot her at the market. Though the government recognizes her freedom, she still lives in fear.

Three

Rescuing Child Soldiers

Uganda

For more than two decades, a rebel army in East Africa has been enslaving children. The children, some as young as seven, are forced to perform as soldiers, sex slaves, and baggage porters. Human-rights groups estimate that as many as sixty-six thousand children have been taken captive.[1]

It is called "the forgotten war." Most westerners know next to nothing about it, and our governments do little to stop it. Frankly, the region holds no strategic geopolitical interest for us. We treat it as just another story of Africans killing Africans in endless guerrilla warfare—a Rwanda in slow motion. Perhaps if the rebels were stealing oil rather than children, the world would pay more attention.

The prime perpetrator of this atrocity is the Lord's Resistance Army (LRA), a guerrilla militia that, since its inception in 1986, has terrorized the northern region of Uganda. What began as a rebellion against the ruling government has turned into a messianic military cult. Its commander, Joseph Kony, claims that he will create a society based on the Ten Commandments. Ironically, he and his troops seem hell-bent on violating every one of them. Kony, a former Catholic altar boy, mixes verses from the Old Testament and the Koran together with traditional tribal rituals to create a bizarre religious cocktail. As the years pass, Kony's political objectives become less clear and his tactics more brutal.

Child abductees make up as much as 90 percent of the LRA's ranks.[2] Senior commanders coerce the children to raid villages, execute unwanted prisoners, and square off against the Ugandan national army. Former child soldiers and other eyewitnesses report that senior commanders regularly placed the children on the front lines of the battlefield.

Jan Egeland, the UN undersecretary-general for humanitarian affairs, visited northern Uganda and declared that the situation there must become a top priority for international action: "It's a moral outrage, frankly, to see thousands of children that have been abducted, that have been maltreated, that are going through the most horrendous torture by the rebel movement. . . . I cannot find any other part of the world having an emergency on the scale of Uganda with so little international attention."[3]

Charles: The Abduction

News reached the Achana household that a detachment of the Lord's Resistance Army was circulating in the province. The previous evening, LRA rebels had attacked a village nearby, no more than a twenty-minute walk away.

Betty Achana would not take any chances. When malaria had stolen two of her daughters as infants, she felt totally powerless. She would not let fate steal the destiny of her two sons as well.

She instructed her older son, Charles, to lead his younger brother out to the bush that night and sleep a safe distance from the village. She shared her plan with neighbors, and they saw its wisdom. So at the first hint of dusk, the village boys, each toting a blanket and a schoolbag, headed off to a familiar hiding spot.

Charles felt like any other ten-year-old child might in his situation: he was embarking on an adventure. Sleeping under the stars did not trouble him. On hot, dry nights he regularly ventured outside the family hut. He loved to lie still and identify the creatures by their night calls. This night, however, he chatted with his friends until his eyelids turned heavy.

Morning arrived without warning. Charles initially rolled over and turned his back to the sun, but then he recalled that it was a school day. Aware that the other boys did not share his enthusiasm for study, he did not stir them. He quietly rolled up his blanket and headed off in the direction of the school.

Charles strolled along the path, lost in his thoughts. He was practically on top of the soldiers before he noticed their presence. They sat casually around a smoldering fire, eating a simple porridge. Charles was not terribly alarmed; he often encountered national army troops as they made their rounds in the province. Skirting to the side of the soldiers, he kept his pace.

"Hey, you! Stop right there!"

Halting in his tracks, Charles turned and took his first good look at the soldiers. Something was amiss: they did not dress smartly, like national army soldiers. Though some wore army shirts, none had pants to match. And now that he had a closer look, he noticed that some of the soldiers were about his age. A wave of nausea swept over him.

"Where are you going, boy?" asked one of the men who cradled a gun in his right arm. Most of the younger boys, he noted, held a machete in their hands.

"I asked you why you were in such a rush!" the man screamed.

Charles realized he had failed to answer. "I'm headed to school," he said, almost in a whisper.

"Not anymore you aren't," said the commander with a hearty laugh. "Boy, you just joined the Lord's Resistance Army."

Florence Lacor: The Painful Road to Abolition

When discussing the crisis in northern Uganda, it is hard not to focus exclusively on the child slaves of the LRA. Once you meet Florence Lacor, you can no longer overlook the pain of the parents.

Florence tries to help the parents deal with their loss. She knows their pain. Her own daughter was missing for more than eight years, enslaved by the LRA, and Florence knew little of her whereabouts. It is the uncertainty, she realized, that leads to madness:

> Parents suffer so much when their children are abducted and held in captivity. When it's night, you know your child is out in the cold. When a thunderstorm comes, you can feel your child getting soaked. When you hear bombing, you think of the bombs dropping on your child. When your child dies, at least you can mourn. But when she is abducted, you always wonder what is happening. You can never forget.[4]

Florence's daughter was kidnapped in one of the most infamous LRA raids ever conducted. In October 1996, the rebels attacked Saint Mary's College, a private girls' boarding school located in Aboke, in northern Uganda. The assault became a public sensation, in part because 139 girls were abducted in one fell swoop. These girls were regarded as among the best and brightest in northern Uganda. If the girls of Aboke town could be taken, no one was safe.

On the night of the abduction, the director of the school, Sister Rachelle Fassera, heroically trailed the rebels into the bush and refused to relent. She begged them to release the girls, offering medicine, money, and even her own life. "Take me and release the girls, or kill me and release the children," one of the abducted girls recalls the nun telling the commanding officer of the raid.[5]

Incredibly, the LRA officer appeased her. He sat all the girls down and directed the senior commanders to carefully select the thirty most beautiful girls. Some of the girls tried cutting their faces with rocks or any other sharp objects they could find. Others posed as if they were crippled—anything to avoid selection.

Once they had completed their selection, the senior officer released the remainder of the girls into the nun's care and bade her leave quickly before he changed his mind. He then warned the chosen thirty that if any one of them escaped, he would summarily execute her twenty-nine peers.

Once news of the abduction reached Florence, she rushed to the school. She waited anxiously for Sister Rachelle's return; along with the other parents, she prayed that her daughter had been released. Alas, her daughter had the misfortune of being among those schoolgirls selected to become sex slaves for the senior commanders.

Although Florence had read newspaper accounts of abducted children in the rural areas, she never imagined that her daughter would be a target in a private school. "I frantically wanted to do something, anything, to rescue my daughter," she says, "but every action I could think of seemed futile."

In an effort to educate herself about the LRA and what it does with abducted children, she visited the children-of-war camp run by World Vision, a Christian relief and development organization that helps children and their communities worldwide. World Vision operates transitional camps for freed slaves in Gulu, the largest town in northern Uganda. One of its camps attends to females and young boys, and the other focuses on young men over the age of eighteen. At both camps, victims receive medical care, counseling, and vocational training. Since its launch in 1995, World Vision has helped more than fifteen thousand freed slaves put their lives back together.

After only an hour at the World Vision camp, Florence had heard enough. "I couldn't bear to imagine my daughter living through the experiences that I heard the former child soldiers relate," she recalls. "So I walked out and vowed that I would never return."

For months Florence alternatively grieved, prayed, got angry, and generally felt sorry for herself. She constructed her own internal prison, where any happiness would be soundly punished with lashes of guilt and shame.

Then one day she had an inspiration. She had learned at the World Vision camp that when the LRA abducts children, they frequently force the kids to kill their own parents. "Maybe I can't save my own daughter," she heard herself saying, "but I can be an advocate for those child slaves who are now orphans."

Florence returned to the World Vision camp and joined in its abolitionist efforts.

Margaret: Marching Orders

Two o'clock on a sunny afternoon in November.

How strange that she can recall the exact time. Afterward, Margaret spent eight and a half long years in the bush, where time had no meaning. But the moment of her capture stands frozen as a monument to her innocence.

When the rebels raided the village, she was nine years old. No one stood watch: rebels do not attack during the day. But here they were, announcing their arrival with gunshots and hollers.

Margaret scampered into her family hut, praying that the grass walls might offer miraculous protection. She heard a ruckus at the vocational training center that an international aid agency had built in the village; of course, the rebels would covet its equipment. The melee shifted to a neighbor's home. She hardly had time to hold her breath before a shaft of light crashed through the door.

A boy about her age stood in the passageway, slowly scanning the hut as if he were looking for something in particular. Then his eyes fixed on her. He lifted the machete that hung down his right side and pointed its end to punctuate an order: "Get up and follow me. Now!"

He escorted Margaret to the middle of the village. Her heart sank when she saw her brother captured along with almost every neighbor child. The soldiers guarding them carried crude clubs—actually, no more than slightly whittled tree branches. Margaret shuffled to a spot alongside the other prisoners.

Satisfied that they had gathered every item of value in the village, the rebels piled their booty into a single heap. They then ushered most of the adults into the training center. A handful of the village men were pulled out of the crowd and ordered to sit back-to-back next to the children.

The commander in charge yelled through the door to the prisoners inside the training center. "If I hear even a whisper coming out of this place, I personally will set it on fire," he warned. "And I assure you that no one will make it out alive."

Once the troops had sealed the door, the commander made his way to the children. He stopped abruptly several yards from where they huddled, and cast a hard look. "You no longer belong to this village; you belong to the Lord's Resistance Army!" he shouted.

He then fell into a speech that sounded well rehearsed: "If today, tomorrow, or any other day in the future you try to escape, we will hunt you down and kill you. Know that we will also return to this village and eliminate every last person. Neither the young nor the old will receive mercy."

The commander then ordered the children to divide into two camps, boys and girls. As soon as the boys had shifted to one side, a soldier pulled out several lengths of rope and tied their hands together tightly behind their backs.

The commander instructed the girls to walk in a line past the pile of loot. Soldiers distributed to each girl a load commensurate with her size. A teenage rebel wearing a tattered army shirt handed Margaret a set of cooking pans bound together with string. Margaret slung the pans over her shoulder and shuffled forward quickly, not giving the rebel a chance to add to her load.

The sun still hung high in the sky when they departed the village. The captives marched in a single file, with watchful soldiers ambling up and down the line. The column stayed on the move through daybreak. Margaret felt sharp stones and ragged elephant grass cut into her bare soles. A rebel rewarded those who paused along the path with a swift jab from his club.

Finally, at four o'clock the next afternoon, the commander halted the march. Margaret joined the other captives in a collective collapse to the ground. Suddenly released of body weight, her feet pounded. Despite the ache, she desired only to sink into a deep sleep.

"Hey, you lazy misfits, get up!" the commander's voice blared, ending her brief respite. "You've got work to do!"

He threw bright-colored jerricans at three of the girls, Margaret among them. "There's a well down that path a few minutes," he said, pointing a finger toward a clearing. "Go fill these jerries." Once the water crew had risen, he turned to the other girls: "The rest of you gather small sticks and build a fire for cooking."

Margaret moved slowly down the path. Ahead she saw what appeared to be an abandoned homestead. The roofs of the main huts were missing; the tops of the walls bore the charred scars of a recent burning. She made her way to the well, situated just beyond the ring of huts. Testing the pump, she was a bit surprised that it worked. It did not take her long to fill the jerrican.

She had not figured on the challenge of getting the water-laden container back to the camp. At first she tried holding it to her side, but after a few steps her light frame nearly tipped over. She next tried lifting the can up so that it rested on her right shoulder. That technique worked for a few steps, but her limbs, already weary from the long march, did not cooperate. As she entered the thick brush, her feet stumbled over a tree root. The jerry went flying off the path into the brush, and her body followed close behind.

For several seconds she lay on the ground, stunned. The stream of water poured from the upturned jerry and worked its way beneath her. Once she realized that the flow was soaking her clothes, she jumped up on her knees and stretched out her hands to right the can.

It was in that position that the child soldier found her. "Come back here on the path," he said with a whistle, as if scolding a disobedient dog.

Margaret quickly grabbed the jerry and scurried to stand alongside the boy. He guided her back to the camp and directly to the commander, who at that moment rested against a tree, chatting with a few senior soldiers.

"I caught this girl attempting to escape," said the boy rebel, "but she didn't get far."

Margaret wanted to defend herself, but fear had captured her tongue. It was as if she were standing outside herself, a bystander curious to find out what would happen next.

"Well done, Samuel," said the commander with an approving smile. Once his eyes shifted to Margaret, his face lost its warmth. "So, you don't like your new family, is that it?" he asked.

Margaret kept her gaze to the ground, not daring to face her tormenter. He grasped her arm with a tight squeeze and dragged her forward. "Let's show your friends what happens when you try to escape the Lord's Resistance Army," he said. "Samuel, go get Taylor and Walter, and bring your machetes with you," he yelled over his shoulder to the boy.

The commander shoved Margaret toward the girls who were trying to coax a band of tiny twigs to ignite into a respectable fire. The village boys sat bound with rope some fifteen feet from the stone ring that the girls had fashioned into a fire pit.

"It's time for a reckoning," the commander barked. The startled girls jumped back from the fire and spun around to give the commander their full attention. His audience secured, the commander threw Margaret roughly to the ground.

"You will learn that we do not tolerate betrayal," he began in an even tone. "When you try to escape our camp, we consider you traitors." He spoke the last word as if he had swallowed venom. "This foolish girl was caught trying to run away with one of our jerricans," he went on, looking directly at Margaret as she lay facedown on the ground. "She is lucky that we did not have to work hard to capture her; otherwise, she would be dead."

He paused for a few seconds to let the message soak in. He then swung around and addressed the child soldiers who stood with their machetes poised for action. "Samuel, you captured this stupid girl, so you get the honor of the first strike."

The boy walked proudly forward until his feet nearly touched the top of Margaret's head. He raised his arm high and, with the flat side of the machete, delivered a slap against her back.

The blow gave Margaret such a horrific shock that she forgot to scream. Hot coals placed along the length of her spine could not have caused such pain. She found her yell once the other young rebels joined in raining down machete slaps on every part of her body.

Margaret blacked out long before they stopped beating her.

THE NIGHT COMMUTERS

Thanks to improved security in northern Uganda, the children once known as the "night commuters" are safe in their home villages.

Before President Museveni increased the numbers of his soldiers in the north, many families living in northern Uganda would send their children off to seek safety in city centers before nightfall. Nighttime was a treacherous time, because the LRA preferred to raid under the cover of darkness. As many as thirty thousand night commuters would journey on foot— some for five to ten miles—to reach a shelter near a national army garrison. Not all of the children were fortunate enough to find a formal shelter. Many slept in bus terminals, in parks, under shop verandas, or in abandoned buildings. The kids would then walk back to their home village at dawn.

The flow of night commuters rose and fell in response to rebel attacks. By 2007, most international observers noted that the night commutes had ceased. Still, back in early 2006 when I first visited Uganda, it was not unusual to see children streaming into the city centers just to find a safe place to sleep.

Charles: The Initiation

After the rebels captured Charles, they seemed in no rush to break camp. Their resting spot, situated at the crossroads of several paths commonly used by local villagers, served as the perfect trap. They merely had to wait patiently for their prey to come to them.

By midmorning, they had snared half a dozen boys and three grown men. The prisoners dared not speak to each other; they sat quietly by the fire, staring blankly at the dying flames. One of the boys appeared to be around ten, the same age as Charles, and the rest a couple of years older. Charles did not know the boys, but he knew two of the men from his village.

Once the rebels started to pack up their camp, the man with the gun—who gave most of the orders—told the adult captives to move to an open space about ten yards from the fire. The men obediently shuffled to the spot where he pointed his gun. The commander then ordered the men to kneel in a straight line.

With a surly bark, the commander let the men know that they had positioned themselves too closely together. After arranging them more to his liking, he addressed the boys: "You pups, listen closely to me, because what I have to say is a matter of life and death."

He pointed to a pile of tree branches that had been cut into approximately six-foot lengths. "Each of you will grab a club, and you will use it to beat these ignorant men to their death," he announced. Then, as if further explanation might be warranted, he added, "They are traitors to the Acholi people."

One by one the boys got to their feet and walked over to the woodpile. After selecting a club, they moved behind the men, who stayed silent in a praying position, like lambs before the slaughter.

"Now strike these traitors over the head," yelled the commander. When not a single boy moved, the rebel leader snatched the club out of Charles's hand, swung it back, and whacked one of the older boys square in the back. The boy let out a blood-curdling scream and thudded to the ground. Cocking his club back for another swing, the commander glared at the next boy in line. He needed no further urging. The boy raised the club and brought it down hard on the man kneeling directly in front of him. Blood came pouring out of the man's head as he crumpled sideways. The unthinkable breached, the other boys immediately joined in the slaughter. The commander put the borrowed club back into Charles's hand and gave a satisfied smile as Charles put it to work.

In a matter of minutes, the three bodies lay lifeless at the boys' feet. Charles felt numb, like he wanted to cry but could not pull out the tears.

"That's it, boys, but there's still one thing left to do before you are worthy to be LRA soldiers," the commander announced. "To gain the strength of a warrior, you must lick your victims' blood so that it will run through your bodies."

After what the boys had just done, this request seemed simple. At least Charles thought so until he tasted the blood on his tongue. The sensation made the whole episode turn suddenly real; he could no longer pretend that this was a bad dream. His stomach lurched as if to vomit.

"Well done, boys. Welcome to the LRA," the commander said after each boy had completed the gruesome task.

In case they might overlook the full meaning of their initiation ceremony, he added, "There is now no going back to your home village. You are murderers; the families of the men you killed will seek revenge. You would be foolish to attempt escape. Where would you go?"

Florence Lacor: An Unexpected Joy

Florence is a "presence"—there is no better way to describe her. The actor Morgan Freeman has a knack for conveying a similar kind of gravitas in his films. Maybe it's the quiet confidence or the regal elegance or even the way her eyes seem to look straight into your soul. Whatever it is, Florence uses it powerfully to give comfort to the rescued children who come to the center in emotional tatters.

When she first started working at the rescue center, she found it tough going to hear former child soldiers describe how they had raided villages and abducted other children. They could be talking about her daughter! "I felt my blood boil," she confesses. "But then I realized that I had to get beyond my anger. These kids were innocent; they had been forced to assume the role of a soldier."

Florence eventually turned that corner. In many respects, she serves as a surrogate mother to boys and girls of all ages at the camp. They look to her for advice, for scolding, and for love.

She never stopped hoping that one day she might find her own daughter, of course. Whenever the national army alerted World Vision that they would be delivering a new batch of escapees, Florence asked if her daughter might be among them. Over an eight-year period she received the same reply: "No, Florence. She's not here."

Occasionally an ex-slave would acknowledge having seen her daughter, so at least Florence knew that she was alive. Such reports came irregularly, however, and Florence could not help wondering if her daughter might have fallen victim in the meantime.

One morning, early in 2004, as she was deep in prayer, Florence felt a wave of joy. "I was puzzled because nothing special had happened to warrant my happiness," she recalls, "but the feeling stayed with me all morning."

Once she arrived at work, she got the word that a number of children had been rescued. She journeyed out to the military airport in Gulu to meet them. A couple of the escapees informed Florence that her daughter was in the rebel camp with them when the national army attacked. They did not see where her daughter had run, and she was not with them when the national army captured them.

"After I helped get the kids settled at the rehabilitation center, I went home and continued praying," she says, recounting each detail of the day. "The feeling of joy had not left me, which was very strange, because usually any bit of bad news about my daughter broke my heart."

The next day she received a call at home from a friend in the national army. The troops had picked up her daughter in southern Sudan, and she was alive and well. Over the phone that evening Florence talked to her daughter for the first time in more than eight years. They were reunited in Gulu two days later.

Florence's long, dark night was over. Despite her personal celebration, she grieves for the mothers whose children will never return from the bush. "The pain a mother feels for her lost child never stops burning deep in her soul," she says, her eyes welling with tears.

NORTHERN UGANDA AND WAR: HISTORICAL BACKGROUND

Violent coups and armed rebellions have been all too common in Uganda's postcolonial history. To most westerners, the name of former dictator Idi Amin elicits images of torture, extrajudicial killings, and mass murders. The military general led a coup in January 1971 and, for the next eight years, ran Uganda like a military garrison. In a short span of time, he quadrupled the size of the military and manipulated ethnic divisions within the ranks as a means to maintain control. During his reign, an estimated three hundred thousand people were murdered, most of them civilians.[6]

Idi Amin, unfortunately, represents a succession of regimes that have ruled Uganda with an iron fist. The pattern is tragic: after a violent overthrow, the new regime takes revenge on the soldiers and civilians (or tribes) that provided the support base for the ousted regime. They carry out these crimes against their own people with impunity.

When it formed in 1987, the Lord's Resistance Army seemed like another armed rebellion acting on behalf of its tribal interests. The year before, a militant strongman from the western region of Uganda, Yoweri Museveni, had led a bloody overthrow of the regime of General Tito Okello Lutwa.

No event in Uganda transcends tribal politics. Okello was an ethnic Acholi, a tribe that is most prevalent in the country's three northernmost districts—Kitgum, Gulu, and Pader. The Acholi people have long felt abused by the more prosperous tribes in the south and west of Uganda. It's a legacy that goes back to nineteenth-century British colonial social policies that unevenly disadvantaged northern tribes. So when Museveni rose to power and his troops carried out violent raids against northern villages (or so the Acholi charge), the embers of old tribal grievances reignited.

Surviving members of Okello's armed forces and civilian dissidents from the north rallied around the leadership of Alice Auma (a.k.a. Lakwena), a spiritualist with political ambitions. Alice claimed that a spirit named Lakwena had possessed her. In the Acholi language, *lakwena* literally means "messenger." Lakwena gave Alice a message ordering her to cleanse the Acholi of their "sins" and to mobilize a military rebellion against the Museveni regime. The spiritualist assumed the name Alice Lakwena and called her militia the Holy Spirit Movement. As bizarre as the whole story sounds, the Holy Spirit Movement marshaled a stiff military challenge to Museveni's forces before retreating into Kenya. Alice Lakwena died in January 2007 while living in exile in a Kenyan refugee camp.

After the defeat of the Holy Spirit Movement, Joseph Kony, claiming to be Alice's first cousin although no blood tie has ever been authoritatively established, assumed the mantle to finish her divine mission. He fully expected the Acholi people to rise up behind his leadership, but that did not happen. He felt rejected by his own people and blamed it on their sinful nature. He turned his wrath on the Acholi people and undertook a campaign to "purify" them. If adults would not join his movement, he would raise up the Acholi children himself and teach them the meaning of liberation. The new generation would be faithful and would not betray him.

Margaret: The Sacrifice

Once the commander ordered Margaret to be beaten, every one of the rebels scurried to watch. They neither cheered nor laughed, yet they drew close to the violence like moths to light.

In Uganda, freedom usually costs the suffering of another. The village boys did not waste Margaret's sacrifice. With the rebels distracted, they worked as a team to loosen the knots binding their hands. Within moments, Margaret's brother and five of his friends slinked quietly off into the brush. Another dozen boys dared not move a muscle, even though the ropes no longer bound them. The severity of Margaret's punishment had made a solid impression.

Perhaps they chose wisely. Once the commander realized that the boys had escaped, he sent his best hunters in pursuit. They captured four of the boys and killed them on the spot.

Margaret's brother and one other boy made it safely all the way back home. The adults at their village doubted they would ever see their children again, so the sight of two of the abducted boys emerging from the bush became cause for great celebration.

Their happiness was short-lived. The boys relayed the commander's dire threat and told the adults that they had no doubt that rebel soldiers would soon descend upon the village and murder every living soul they found. The villagers immediately ran to their huts, grabbed a few valuables, and made haste for the provincial capital.

Within the hour, the rebel hunters crept quietly around the outskirts of the village. Their stealth proved unnecessary. They found the huts completely abandoned. The rebels freely spent their fury all the same. By day's end, only smoking embers remained of the village.

THE BUMPY ROAD TO FREEDOM

On a sunny afternoon in June 2006, three girls, all around sixteen years old, walked into World Vision's children-of-war camp in Gulu. The girls looked like skeletons, and a hollow gaze flattened their eyes. Friends they had known in captivity within the LRA gave them an animated greeting, and the girls responded with hardly a flicker of emotion.

The three arrived with their heads completely shaved, and one had a terrible burn on the top of her head that exposed part of her skull. When the national army had launched its attack on the LRA, the rebel camp was preparing its dinner. A commander forced this girl, in retreat, to pick up a boiling pot and carry it on her head. When she tripped and fell, the commander kept running and left her behind. Shortly thereafter, the national army captured her.

One further peculiarity stood out about these three girls. The majority of the teenage girls at the camp are young mothers. Not one of them held a baby in her arms.

The LRA does force some girls to fight as soldiers, but the senior commanders divide up the majority of the girls to be their sex slaves. It is not unusual for a commander to maintain four or five concubines; witnesses report that Joseph Kony surrounds himself with a harem of sixty young sex slaves.

Sometimes child slaves successfully escape LRA captivity using their own ingenuity, while others are rescued during a national army offensive. In recognition of the fact that the child soldiers did not join the rebels voluntarily, the Ugandan government passed an amnesty law in 1999. The amnesty safeguards from prosecution any LRA fighter—even Kony and his senior commanders—who surrenders to the government.

Once the national army takes child soldiers into custody, it brings them to a "child-protection unit" that it houses in its garrison in Gulu. The army holds them there for several days of questioning in an effort to gain intelligence on the rebels. National army officers urge the older boys to join the fight against the LRA, and a good number accept.

Some human-rights groups have criticized the length of some detentions and the coercive recruitment of older boys. The national army does not permit civilians to participate in the unit—a move that would offer better protection for children's rights.

The national army eventually releases the prisoners to a rehabilitation center. Aware of this protocol for processing rescued child slaves, parents regularly visit the World Vision camps, desperate to find their abducted children. Their happiness may turn to distress when they see sons and daughters without limbs or daughters holding their own babies.

Most of the child slaves already know the name World Vision. To dissuade their ranks from attempting an escape, LRA commanders (mis)inform them that World Vision will feed them poison or give them potatoes laced with shards of glass.

To ease the fears of new arrivals, the World Vision staff organizes a welcome celebration. When they walk into the camp, the freed child soldiers encounter a sea of open arms ready to give them an embrace. Often they find old friends, also rescued from the LRA, singing and dancing.

Immediately after the welcome party, a World Vision healthcare professional assesses the health of each child. Some children manifest serious injuries and require medical attention in a hospital. Nearly all are malnourished and suffer from scabies, worms, and damaged feet.

As the days pass and newly freed slaves become more comfortable in their new surroundings, they enter into rehabilitative counseling. The majority of children do not want to talk at first. To help them express painful memories, counselors at the camp will use drama, dance, song, and art. Most kids will draw the odious acts they participated in before they will talk about them.

Margaret: Becoming a Child Soldier

Until she turned eleven, Margaret could join the boys in military training. They learned how to assemble an automatic weapon and then take it apart; how to hold a gun, aim it, and shoulder its kickback. The commanders also taught them battle tactics and the art of retreat. Slowly but surely, the abducted children evolved into child soldiers.

The LRA uses the adult men they capture, on the other hand, as pack mules. The adults carry large weapons, the tents used by commanders, and other weighty items. How these porters could shoulder their burden day in and day out never ceased to amaze Margaret.

Early one morning, one of the porters made a break for it. The night security team had returned to camp and was focused on grabbing a bit of breakfast. The porter crawled for nearly the length of a football field, then jumped to his feet and sprinted. A child soldier who was out collecting twigs for the morning fire saw the man running and sounded an alert.

The sleepy camp transformed into a whirl of commotion. As commanders barked out orders, waves of child soldiers scampered out of the camp in pursuit. One of the girls—whom Margaret recognized from her school—took advantage of the chaos to bolt in the opposite direction.

Neither the porter nor the girl enjoyed more than ten minutes of freedom. The child soldiers quickly tracked them down and dragged them back to camp.

A slave could commit no greater crime than betrayal, a senior commander announced. Several junior commanders then commenced to pierce the porter in the buttocks with their bayonets. They treated it like a game; the man's yelps only enhanced the entertainment. Several sharp kicks flipped the man over, and the young men sliced off the man's penis. Finally, apparently tired of his squealing, one of the soldiers brought his bayonet down hard into the man's chest.

The torture shifted next to the girl. The young commanders stabbed her breasts repeatedly. As they prepared to expand the scope of their torture, the senior officer stopped them. "She must be punished by one of her own," he declared with authority.

He scanned the newly abducted girls and selected two to approach him. Then, as if an idea had just popped into his head, he looked directly at Margaret, saying, "You, come here. I trust you have learned a few lessons from your own beating."

He ordered boy soldiers to lend their clubs to his handpicked assassins. At first, the girls aimed blows at their victim's body, but it only prolonged her suffering. So one by one they crashed their clubs down on the girl's skull until she breathed no more.

Florence Lacor: The Burning Ritual

Within hours of their arrival, just freed from the LRA, Florence gives the children a set of new clothes. She gathers the clothes they arrived in—along with knapsacks, bandanas, hats, and anything else they wore as soldiers in the LRA—and stores them away for safekeeping. Often the children "won" the old clothes off a body they had killed. Surprisingly, they show some reluctance to give up these clothes to Florence. They had meager belongings in the bush, so these clothes had turned into a security blanket of sorts.

About once a month Florence presides over a very symbolic ritual. She gathers the children into a circle and places into the center a bundle. She asks the children if they recognize any-thing in the pile. One by one, they yell out in recognition of a personal item that had been part of their uniform in captivity.

Florence lets them know that they do not have to be bound to the past. "No one had the right to force you to do so many awful things," she tells them with compassion. "And now that you are free, you can make choices that will lead you on a different path."

After finishing this short homily, she asks one of the young girls to pour kerosene over the pile. She hands a set of matches to the young boys, who gleefully set the clothes on fire.

Charles: The Controller Ritual

Supreme commander Kony took away their fears. Shortly after their abduction, Charles and the other new recruits were taken to Kony's camp. He prayed over them and performed a ritual involving the oil that comes from the shea nut.

"When you cover yourself with this oil, the bullets of the enemy cannot pierce your body," he said. As he smeared on the oil, he added, "My spirit now is part of your spirit, and I know all of your thoughts. If during a battle you consider escape, or your thoughts turn to your family at home, my spirit will no longer protect you, and you will be killed by our enemies."

Kony also revealed to the children that they had been chosen for a special purpose—to purify Uganda and usher in a new kingdom. God had cursed Museveni and his troops; it was only a matter of time before they would fall. "We are fighting to bring peace to the Acholi people," he declared, a slogan that Charles would hear often during his captivity.

Mystical rites and spells infused almost every aspect of rebel activity. Charles was placed under the charge of a "controller." The controller took his "spiritual children" to the river and poured a solution of water and leafy herbs over their heads. As he did so, he prayed that the children would be "cleansed of impure thoughts of disobedience."

SUDAN AND THE UGANDAN CONFLICT

Sudan. The same government that foments war in Darfur has played a heavy hand in the conflict in northern Uganda.

The LRA agreed to help the Sudanese government fight its civil war against the Sudan People's Liberation Army (SPLA) in exchange for a steady supply of weapons and food. By the mid-1990s, the Ugandan national army had improved its capacity to track down rebel forces. The LRA was constantly on the run in the Ugandan countryside, so it decided to move its base into southern Sudan.

Sudan's involvement in the Ugandan conflict made the war more relevant to Western nations in some respects. The most significant shift occurred after September 11, 2001, when the United States stepped up its campaign against terrorism. President George W. Bush declared the LRA a terrorist organization. Pressed to demonstrate that it did not support terrorism, the Sudanese government claimed that it had cut off supplies to the LRA. If that did, in fact, happen, the weapons and food started flowing again in 2002 after the LRA helped Sudan take over the strategically important town of Torit from the SPLA.

Also in 2002, President Museveni of Uganda unleashed a major offensive, code-named Operation Iron Fist, against LRA bases located in southern Sudan. The national army geared up to completely wipe out the LRA. Instead, the campaign stirred up a hornet's nest.

The Ugandan army's attack on LRA bases in Sudan became so intense that the rebels divided into small operational units and infiltrated back into northern Uganda. Over the next eighteen months, the LRA abducted ten thousand children and wreaked havoc on the civilian population. It was not until the end of 2004 that the national army regained some semblance of military control in Uganda, and LRA bands trickled back into southern Sudan.

Then, in August 2006, the Ugandan government and the LRA signed a truce to the war. Under the terms of the truce, the rebels would leave their bases throughout Sudan and the Congo and establish bases at two sites in southern Sudan. The government of southern Sudan pledged to protect the LRA, and the Ugandan government promised that it would not attack the rebels. In less than a month, both sides had violated the terms of the truce.[7]

The International Criminal Court (ICC) further complicated the political situation in Uganda when it issued warrants for the arrest of the LRA leadership. The court would make Kony and his top four commanders liable for war crimes. Some political bodies argue that ICC indictments need to be kept in place in order for justice to be done. Others argue that they deny LRA leaders any incentive for giving up their fight and only prolong the war. Joseph Kony says that he will not surrender as long as he and his top commanders risk prosecution by the ICC.

Another glimpse at peace came in 2008 when it appeared Kony would come out of the bush and sign a peace deal. The

United Nations negotiators and others waited for days, but Kony never emerged. Instead, the LRA attacked a village in the Congo on Christmas Day 2008, abducting children and killing civilians. It seems the LRA is taking its rulebook from northern Uganda and applying it to parts of the Congo.

Margaret: The LRA "Wife"

Once she turned eleven, Margaret could no longer join the boys in combat. "It's time for you to become a wife," a senior commander informed her.

She had no precise idea what it meant to be a wife. Observing the older girls, she supposed it involved doing a commander's cooking and laundry.

The next day she was given to Michael, a twenty-year-old commander who had served in the LRA for almost nine years. He already had one "wife," and she gave Margaret a brief orientation to her domestic duties.

That first evening, Michael told his first wife, "Leave, and don't come back for an hour." He then ordered Margaret to come into the tent. As soon as she entered, he grabbed her by the back of the neck and pulled up her shirt. Margaret squirmed away from his hold, stumbled backward, and ran out of the tent. He did not pursue her, so she stayed out in the bush and slept on the ground that night.

In the morning, she returned cautiously to the tent. Michael's first wife, who was busy washing pans, did not look up from her chores. Margaret sat down next to her and picked up a dirty pan. Neither spoke.

Margaret was relieved that she could not see Michael's boots outside the tent. He must have departed already, she thought.

A few hours later, a senior commander strolled into their campsite and told Margaret that she had "need of instruction."

"Michael has taken a group of boys to check out rumors of enemy movements on the other side of the river," he began. "I do not expect him to return until tomorrow evening."

Margaret shook her head dutifully, but inside she felt a wave of joy: one more day of reprieve had just been granted to her.

"Michael told me what happened last night," the man continued. "Your behavior was unacceptable; no one refuses sex to an LRA commander."

He spoke this last sentence with such force that Margaret dared not give any response other than a nod. "You will do anything that pleases your husband," he declared. "Do I make myself clear?"

Though Margaret offered another nod, the officer did not leave the door open for further rebellion. "You will not eat again until you have slept with your husband," he said. "If I hear that you have violated my order, your punishment will be worse than you can imagine."

Margaret went hungry for the rest of that day and the day that followed. On the evening of Michael's return, she entered his tent, and without any words being exchanged, he raped her.

She quickly came to understand what "wife" meant in the LRA. For the next six years, she was a slave to Michael's every whim.

Florence Lacor: A Community of Survivors

Seventy-five young women performed a traditional dance in the main courtyard of the World Vision center. Each woman had in her hand a ceremonial wood hatchet, and they moved their feet and hands in collectively coordinated motion. At the front of the formation, two women squatted low on their haunches and fervently banged drums with the base of their palms.

Florence stood in the middle between the two drummers, her body swaying back and forth slightly. Though she is of average height, at that moment she looked eight feet tall. She periodically yelled out an Acholi word, and the women changed the direction of their stance. Slowly and in rhythm, Florence shuffled to the front of the new configuration.

The dance continued in this fashion for about an hour. Their endurance was astounding, especially given that the temperature boiled above one hundred degrees and the dusty courtyard offered zero shade.

The young women performing the dance have "graduated" from the center and now live an independent life in Gulu. They return one day a week for assistance with food, clothing, and emotional support. Activities like the dance remind the women that they are not alone. They belong to a spiritual clan of survivors.

The women are sixteen to twenty-four years old, and maybe 80 percent carry an infant or have a toddler running around their feet. At one time these young women were sex slaves to the senior commanders of the LRA.

The LRA educates males to view women as creatures that exist to serve their pleasures. When women do not submit to the authority of the men, they are handled violently.

The testimony of one ex-slave dramatically illustrated this dynamic. She witnessed Joseph Kony order the death of two young commanders simply because they showed too much kindness to their concubines. The supreme commander declared that their "poor example" would be a cancer that would destroy "natural relations" in the camp. Following the execution of the two commanders, Kony redistributed their property (their concubines) to "more worthy" officers.

The rebels assert that sex is a man's right, and they practice neither birth control nor protected sex. As might be expected, most girls in the LRA face pregnancy at some point. The commanders do worry about contracting HIV, which makes enslaving young virgin girls all the more appealing.

At the World Vision camp, the women receive education about HIV/AIDS and safe sex. All the same, many women refuse HIV testing. Revealing to anyone that you have contracted the virus is simply not done in rural Uganda. The women would feel far too much shame to admit it.

Young mothers stay in Gulu because they find it very difficult to reintegrate into their home communities. The stigma of being defiled—a victim of constant rape—carries enough shame. The assumption that the absent father is a commander of the hated LRA adds to a young woman's isolation. When ex–sex slaves do meet a man who expresses romantic interest, the potential suitor fears that an LRA commander will one day return to claim his "wife."

Florence does not sugarcoat the rough road these women have to navigate after liberation. She reports that as many as one out of every three of the young women will return to the father of her children—yes, the very LRA commander who raped and enslaved her—once he has been captured and granted amnesty. These women would rather live with the devil they know than confront alone the twin demons of poverty and social isolation.

The LRA commanders in turn are apt to consider the sex slaves their rightful property. One captured commander arrived at the World Vision camp and demanded to be reunited with three of his "wives" who had taken up residence there. When the women said they would have nothing to do with their tormentor, he became belligerent. Florence had a hard time getting him to understand that abduction does not translate into ownership.

Charles: The Young Corporal

Murder and pillage replaced reading and arithmetic in Charles's life. He learned how to shoot a gun, follow military commands, scout enemy movements, and obliterate a civilian target.

Raids on defenseless villages had two priorities: bringing back food and kidnapping new child recruits. When the rebels approached the village, they stretched out in a long line to prevent any civilian from escaping. Returning to camp without food was the only failure that would give a child soldier cause for trepidation; the murder and mayhem that accompanied the attack merely came with the territory. Charles and his companions became killers without a conscience.

It was hunger and thirst that preoccupied Charles. Even after a successful village looting, the commanders reserved for themselves the bulk of the food. They would apportion a single serving to a group of twelve child soldiers. The kids sat in a circle and took turns taking a bite. Anyone who took more than his fair share got tossed out of the group and missed the rest of that meal.

The scarcity of water made for even more desperate straits. At least in Uganda, the rebels could find running streams. In Sudan, Charles would sometimes go three days on a single gulp of water. On more than a few occasions, the child soldiers had to drink their own urine. The weakest literally died of thirst in the Sudanese desert.

Over time LRA commanders began to take note of Charles's prowess as a soldier. When he was only thirteen years old, a senior officer rewarded him for "strong leadership in the field" and promoted him to the rank of corporal. Charles began leading raids on smaller villages. He could even select the boys whom he wanted to accompany him.

Whenever high-ranking commanders spent the night in a camp, the rebels enacted a sophisticated defense. The child soldiers dug trenches in concentric rings around an inner circle where the commanders' tent had been pitched. The newest abductees slept in open-air trenches in the outer rings, while those boys with longer service positioned themselves in the inner rings. Following his promotion to corporal, Charles moved to an inner ring. On occasion, he even joined the security detail for chief commander Kony.

It filled him with pride to be leading boys far more senior in age. He even had authority over the porters; it did take a while to get used to ordering adult men around. The day would come, he was confident, when he would become a commander and be given wives to cook his meals and wash his clothes.

As Charles saw it, you stayed weak and got beaten, or you became strong and did the beating. He knew which path he planned to take.

Idan Lagum Lumoro: Breaking the Slave Mentality

Sadly, the constant physical and psychological abuse that the LRA uses against child slaves yields results. Most current LRA commanders were once abducted boys in whom a devotion to Joseph Kony was nurtured.

After their capture and release to a World Vision camp, the LRA officers usually attempt to reestablish a chain of command and order younger boys and girls to perform chores for them. Likewise, when they meet women at the camp who had once served as their concubines, the ex-commanders expect the relationship to continue.

Hence in 2003, World Vision created a separate rehabilitation camp for young men who had reached eighteen years of age. Idan Lagum Lumoro serves as its director. Not many individuals could be called "a force of nature," but Idan merits the title. She does not ask for respect; she commands it. Placing Idan in charge of these young men who have been trained to disrespect women was an ingenious choice.

Idan's role surpasses administrative tasks. She holds a weekly counseling session with each ex–child soldier. In these sessions, she walks a tightrope between compassion and accountability. The LRA abducted these young men as boys and rewarded them for brutality. They cannot be blamed for that legacy. But if they do not accept responsibility for their behavior in the camp, Idan delivers a stiff rebuke. "The past happened to you," she instructs, "but you happen now."

In early June 2006, Idan gathered all the residents at the center to discuss the prospects for ending the war. To appreciate their comments, you have to keep four factors in mind: (1) most of the young men had emerged from the LRA within the previous two months; (2) most had spent more than five years in captivity; (3) most had become ranking officers; and (4) most believe Kony has a vast spiritual power and that if they speak poorly of him, he will know it and will punish them.

"Slave mentality" is an inability to think outside of the box into which an individual has been forcibly packed. After years of strict LRA discipline, it was hard for any of these young men to escape their indoctrination.

One young man expressed his conviction that only Kony could interpret God's plan for Uganda. Others blamed President Museveni for prolonging the conflict, claiming that on each occasion on which Kony agreed to peace talks, Museveni violated the cease-fire and attempted to destroy the rebel movement. All wholeheartedly agreed that Kony would never accept unconditional surrender or subject himself to judicial prosecution. Because "Museveni cannot be trusted," the young men indicated, only international intervention could resolve the conflict.

Their slave mentality also became apparent when the discussion turned to their experiences in the LRA. Yes, it was horrible to be ripped away from their family at a tender age. Yes, they lamented the travesties they were forced to commit against their own people. But many admitted that if given the chance, they would return to the LRA. At least they felt they belonged in the rebel world. Now they felt like a lost piece of a puzzle. They fit nowhere.

Margaret: Playing the Numbers

Margaret's "husband" continued to find favor with the senior officers. They gave him two additional wives. To own a total of four girls, as he did, enhanced a commander's status significantly in the LRA.

Margaret privately celebrated Michael's advancement in the ranks for her own reasons. With four concubines to choose from, Michael called her into the tent at night far less often. And though he treated all his wives cruelly, he vented his aggression on one girl at a time. The sheer weight of numbers worked in Margaret's favor.

Her chores did increase once the older wives in Michael's harem started to bear children. All the girls shared the responsibility for child rearing. While it was always difficult to shift camps every couple of days, doing so with toddlers became much more complicated.

For nearly a year Margaret's rebel detachment had settled in southern Sudan. Beyond occasional skirmishes with the Sudanese guerrillas, life passed without too much drama. Thirst and hunger became their principal enemies. They could pass two days without a meal. They chewed on leaves and dry cassava in an attempt to satisfy their grumbling stomachs.

Hunger at times drove Margaret's detachment to desperate measures. They would ambush vehicles; on one occasion they scored a crate of beans by surprising an SPLA truck on a road near the border. They became so desperately hungry at one point that they attempted to raid a heavily armed Sudanese village. Many child soldiers were killed, and the raid yielded no bounty.

Then the Ugandan national army unleashed Operation Iron Fist, and Margaret's detachment infiltrated back into northern Uganda. For the next two years, her band was constantly on the move. The commanders kept their wives and children close by their side. They were paranoid that the girls would try to escape otherwise, and they were right.

Margaret did try to escape once during a raid on a village. Michael had tasked her with looting the homes during the attack. When she entered the first home, she found a young woman in her twenties cowering in the corner. Acting spontaneously, Margaret told the woman that she would not be harmed if she would help her escape. The grateful woman hid Margaret under a blanket on the floor and anxiously waited out the raid. For nearly fifteen minutes they heard no noises in the vicinity of the hut, and they thought they were home free.

Their illusion was shattered when Michael and two child soldiers burst into the hut. They came on a mission, and they soon found what they were looking for hidden under a blanket. Michael pulled Margaret up with such force that she thought her arms would be torn off. He shoved her roughly out the door of the hut. She could hear the woman inside the hut scream as the boys hacked her to death with their machetes.

Once they returned to their camp, Michael beat Margaret within an inch of her life. It would be the last time she tried to escape.

THE RUINS OF WAR

Child slavery should give the international community sufficient cause to intervene and put an end to the war in northern Uganda. The effect of the war on the entire population reinforces the moral obligation to do so without delay.

According to the United Nations, more than 1.7 million people—roughly 85 percent of the population of northern Uganda—were driven from their homes and into camps for internally displaced persons (IDPs). Recently, however, information from the Internal Displacement Monitoring Centre (IDMC) shows that nearly two-thirds of those individuals have returned to their homes. Children account for more than half the residents of these IDP camps.[8]

The Pabbo camp, located just outside of Gulu, is still home to more than forty-five thousand displaced persons, making it one of the largest IDP camps in all of East Africa. At Pabbo, a single source for drinking water exists for thousands of people. People wait in a line the length of several city blocks just to get fresh water. The huts at Pabbo are stacked extremely close together, which makes it a ticking time bomb. These dire social conditions yield high rates of epidemic illness and AIDS. Of more immediate concern, a fire in one hut spreads to the others almost instantly. In early 2004, a fire at this IDP camp destroyed three thousand homes.[9]

The elected leaders of the Pabbo camp do the best they can to cope with a hopeless situation. But until the LRA and the Ugandan government reach a final settlement, they admit that little can be done to alleviate misery at the camp. "We have almost forgotten what it feels like to be human," remarked the camp's senior leader.

Charles: Burying the Rifle

Once Charles became a corporal, more opportunities to escape presented themselves. He and his fellow combatants were often separated in the middle of a battle. The commanders taught them how to regroup once the fighting ended. It would have been just as easy, however, to walk the other way.

Charles had lots of reasons to feel cautious about attempting an escape. The commanders had warned repeatedly that the national army slices captured child soldiers up into small pieces. At times boys had disappeared, and they were never heard of again.

Even if he were willing to risk those consequences, Charles did not know where he would go. Before his abduction, he had not known a life beyond his home—and because he had participated in the murder of two men from his village, he could not go back there. He would be an alien no matter where he landed. So he stayed and endured his misery.

Then one afternoon, at age fourteen, he just snapped. The faces of those whom he had killed—especially the defenseless civilians—flashed before his eyes. He wanted to erase the acts and to return to the innocent village boy he once had been. Yes, he would go back. Maybe his old neighbors would kill him, but at least they would give him a decent burial. As it stood, if he died in an armed conflict, only the vultures would value his bones.

Charles hid his knapsack in the brush, slung his rifle over his shoulder, and walked briskly away from the rebel camp. He kept moving until nightfall and then lay down for a rest under the open sky. Rain came down in heavy sheets throughout the night. He made no effort to find shelter, but let the cleansing water pour over him and bless his journey.

At dawn the rain clouds passed, and he resumed walking. He did not encounter a soul in the bush until about midday. He heard the high-pitched voices of women off the path ahead. Hiding carefully behind some brush, he crawled forward to assess the danger. He saw three women bringing their hoes down hard on a patch of garden.

Aware that he might frighten them, Charles buried his rifle and sauntered out into the open casually. The women greeted him warmly, though they could not hide their puzzled expressions. Why would an unfamiliar young boy be out here in a remote region alone? He did not prolong the mystery.

"Could you take me to one of your village leaders?" he asked politely. "I have escaped the LRA, and I want to turn myself in."

At the very mention of the LRA, terror struck the women. Then one of them spoke up, her voice shaking. "I don't know how we could help you," she told him.

"I don't want to hurt anyone," Charles said, reassuring her. "I want to put an end to it."

"Okay, I will take you to my husband," the woman said. "Maybe he will know what to do."

Charles jogged back to the brush and uncovered his rifle. Throwing it back over his shoulder, he returned to the spot where the woman he had spoken to was waiting. Though the sight of the gun made her all the more nervous, she forged ahead.

They found her husband digging a well on the outer edge of a circle of huts. Alarmed to see an armed child walking behind his wife, he tightened his grip on the shovel. A shovel may not be the best weapon, but at least the boy appeared to be alone.

His wife quickly defused the tension, explaining to him Charles's mission. The man narrowed his eyes and gave Charles a long look while he pondered the best course of action.

"Well, before we go anywhere, you need to get rid of that gun," the man said matter-of-factly. "Just about anyone who gets a glance at you carrying that rifle will run the other way, and the ones who don't run . . . well, who knows what they are apt to do?"

Though he was reluctant to part with the rifle, Charles agreed to hand it over. The man received it, then immediately threw it down behind a pile of dirt that he had spent the morning building.

"All right, I think it's best to take you to the head of our village council," he said. "He lives no more than a ten minutes' walk from here."

Now that it was clear in his mind what he needed to do, the man moved swiftly to a narrow path that ran past the huts. Charles practically needed to run to keep pace.

They did not get far. After having traveled no more than a quarter mile, they met two national army soldiers on patrol coming the other way. The man let Charles offer his own surrender.

The soldiers did not speak much as they led him back to their local garrison. Charles had braced himself for torture, so he did not expect joviality. But once they arrived at the army base, a senior officer extended him a warm welcome. "Congratulations on having the courage to leave the ranks of the LRA," he said, shaking Charles's hand.

Charles spent two days at the garrison, mostly sleeping on a cot and voraciously eating all the food put before him. On the third day, an army truck transported him to the regional garrison in Gulu.

Once there, he spent another couple of days answering a battery of questions about LRA activities. As the intelligence officer wrapped up a final series of questions, he mentioned that Charles would be transferred the next day to the World Vision facility.

He knew that name. LRA commanders often told the child soldiers about the wicked spells that World Vision placed on captured rebels. The spirits to whom they pray can infect a child with AIDS, they warned.

Despite his apprehension, Charles's transfer to the World Vision camp turned out to be the happiest day of his life. When he entered the gates, a cadre of boys and girls met him with hugs and slaps on the back. Many he recognized from the LRA; he had assumed they had died in battle. After the hearty greeting, a boy flipped on a boom box, and everyone broke into spontaneous dance. The party was on.

Four years of brutality cannot be danced away magically, unfortunately. For the first few months at the rehabilitation center, Charles had recurring nightmares of the killings he had done.

He spent hours pouring his heart out to Florence. "Every day you watch people around you die, and death loses its grip on you," he told her after many sessions. "My controller told me to climb above my feelings; whether I murdered another or was killed myself, it was always the will of God."

"No," Florence responded, "it is the will of God that you should know love, and it is only love that will set you free."

Idan Lagum Lumoro: Tough Forgiveness

How can the cycle of terror in Uganda ever come to an end?

Idan Lagum Lumoro works hard to address that challenge. She reaches out to the communities out of which the kids have been abducted and against which many have committed atrocities.

She first has to reconcile current events with traditional tribal law. When a murder is committed in the tribal culture, it is a violation against a particular family and an entire clan. A restitution must be paid for the death. If that restitution is not fulfilled, a murderous revenge will be sought against the clan of the killer.

Idan reasons with tribal leaders that it would be impossible in Uganda today to balance the score with traditional restitution. Murder has ruled for decades, and every clan could find a just cause for seeking vengeance. She points them instead to the tribal reconciliation tradition of *mataput*, which literally means "drinking a bitter root from a common cup." To avoid bloodshed, tribal chieftains might bring warring enemies together to put aside their grievances, share a meal, and drink from the bitter cup.

Idan has received support from several tribal leaders. "In our culture, we don't like to punish people," says Collins Opoka, a chief in the Acholi tribe. "It doesn't really get you anywhere."[10]

To illustrate the complexity of reconciliation, Idan refers to the experience of Mary, a Ugandan woman who had her nose, lips, and ears sliced off—a signature torture of the LRA. The rebels use the macabre practice to intimidate the civilian population—a visible threat to those who might share information with the national army about rebel movements.

Mary was tilling soil in a communal garden alongside five other women when a small band of rebels arrived at her village. Mary was eight months pregnant at the time.

A young rebel commander led three boy soldiers to the garden and ordered the women to sit on the ground. He then raised a walkie-talkie to his mouth and delivered a report to his superior on what he had discovered in the village. A voice came back over the walkie-talkie instructing him to assign a boy to guard the women while he took the rest of the soldiers on a raid of the village.

After completing the looting, the commander escorted his band back to the garden. He relieved the boy assigned to guard duty and prepared to depart the village.

As the rebels reached the edge of the village, Mary saw the young commander lift the walkie-talkie to his ear. To her horror, she watched the boys retrace their steps back to the garden and viciously hack away at her friends with machetes.

They killed all five of the other women, but they did not touch Mary. The commander told the boys to spare the life of "the pregnant one."

"We will use her as a sign," he said, and then added, "To kill her might bring us bad luck." Two boys held her down while a third boy sliced up her face.

Several months later, when Mary came to the World Vision center for medical aid, she was horrified to encounter the young commander who had ordered her torture. He had been wounded and captured in a battle with the national army. He, too, now received World Vision's help. Mary wanted justice and complained to Idan: "No help should go to this criminal!"

In his own defense, the ex-commander claimed that he was following the orders of his superior officer to kill all the women. "But I showed mercy by not having this pregnant woman killed," he argued.

The husband of one of the women murdered in the garden massacre confirmed the ex-commander's story. The husband was taken captive in the raid and tied up at the feet of the senior officer. He heard the senior officer order the execution of all the women over his walkie-talkie.

Regardless, one can imagine how difficult it would be for Mary to forgive the young ex-commander. On the office wall at World Vision hangs a picture of Idan leading a reconciliation ceremony. On one side of Idan sits Mary, and on the other sits the ex-commander—all three holding hands in a sign of peace.

A year has passed since the ceremony, and Idan admits that Mary still harbors some bitter feelings toward the ex-commander. *Mataput* never tastes sweet. But Mary has dropped all her demands for tribal vengeance. That is a huge step toward reconciliation in traditional tribal culture.

Nearly every child abducted into the LRA has been forced to participate in some kind of atrocity. For example, the twelve-year-old child soldier who wielded the machete on Mary's face also resided at the World Vision camp when Mary arrived. She did not recognize the boy, however, and the child did not share the truth of his role in the event. Only after he had left the camp and been reunited with his family did he share his secret with Idan.

Idan urges every child soldier who comes to World Vision's camps—victims and torturers alike—to reach a place of forgiveness. It's an extraordinary mountain to climb, but Idan believes that Ugandans have no alternative if they are going to have a future: "Only in unity can we rebuild our land with peace and development. If we do not forgive, our communities will explode."

Margaret: An Army Rescue

After five years of rape, the biological lottery caught up with Margaret. At the age of sixteen, she became pregnant.

Her rebel unit had recently returned to southern Sudan. She was grateful at least that they would settle in one camp for a while. Morning sickness does not go well with a nomadic existence.

Early one morning when she was more than seven months into her pregnancy, rebel advance scouts breathlessly ran into the camp. They had observed Ugandan national troops moving rapidly in their direction. The soldiers would reach their camp in half an hour, the scouts predicted.

The commanding officer ordered preparations for a swift retreat. Just as he finished his command, she heard the first mortar hit. It was followed by a second blast no more than twenty-five yards from where she stood.

Michael appeared from nowhere and yelled for his wives to leave their belongings and start running. He then sprinted off, clearly demonstrating that he would not be waiting around to help them.

LRA commanders had spoken of the terrible things that would happen if national army troops captured them. Soldiers with AIDS would rape the girls, the LRA commanders warned. A pregnant girl had even more to fear. Soldiers would cut open her stomach and tear out the fetus. Due to her advanced pregnancy, Margaret could not move very fast, but she did her best.

A mortar exploded fifteen yards in front of her and put an end to her retreat. A fragment flew into her knee, and she dropped immediately to the ground. Her one attempt to lift up her weight proved fruitless, so she lay still, hoping that the onrushing soldiers would overlook her.

Five minutes later a soldier detected Margaret lying injured on the ground and took her into custody. Two soldiers carried her on a stretcher to a heavily fortified army position no more than a twenty-minute walk away. Another young LRA girl, perhaps two years younger than Margaret, was already sitting on the ground holding a baby when they arrived.

The prisoners were in for a pleasant surprise. At midafternoon, the soldiers brought them a full plate of hot food and as much water as they could drink—two luxuries that they had not enjoyed in years. A medic attended to Margaret's knee, extracting the embedded shrapnel and pouring a red solution over the wound.

The prisoners were then brought one at a time to speak with three men dressed in crisp uniforms. "You are older than the other girl," they said to Margaret. "You have a responsibility to tell us everything you know."

And that's exactly what Margaret did. She divulged everything she knew about where the LRA stashed weapons and how many senior commanders resided in her camp. She also told them what little she knew about Kony's whereabouts: she had heard the other commanders mention that he had moved his camp to the Congo.

The army officers seemed pleased with her information and told her not to be afraid for her life. They transferred her to the army garrison in Gulu the next day. Following a second session of questioning to see if she could recall any additional intelligence, they released her into the care of World Vision.

Florence Lacor met her at the front gate and greeted her with a big embrace. "My sister, you have made it to freedom," she told Margaret with a beaming smile. "The road to reclaiming your life is not as long as you think."

A month later, Margaret gave birth to a strapping son. She named him Daniel, for he had been rescued from the mouths of lions.

"THESE CHILDREN NEED CONCRETE FUTURES"

Ending the enslavement of child soldiers around the globe will require abolitionists to adopt a broad range of strategic initiatives and skill sets.

Heroic individuals like Florence Lacor and Idan Lagum

Lumoro of World Vision are needed to provide material aid and emotional support to slaves who find their way to freedom. And though it may not sound as romantic, we sorely need individuals and organizations that will focus on advocacy and public policy.

In April 2006, World Vision played an instrumental role in persuading members of the U.S. House of Representatives to hold a public hearing on child soldiers in Uganda.

On that occasion, Grace Grall Akallo, an ex-slave, gave her personal testimony. Grace was one of the renowned abductees from Saint Mary's College in Aboke town. She told the House subcommittee, "Unfortunately, my story . . . has become so common that abduction is now a fear that daily defines the lives of children who live in the war-affected areas."[11]

Responding to her testimony, Rep. Diane Watson asked Grace, "Do you feel they'll ever be normal again? You've learned to use a gun to kill. And I'm wondering how we could really impact on that?"

Grace told the congressional representatives exactly what the children of northern Uganda long for: "These children need love. These children need peace. These children need concrete futures. A matter of counseling a child for only six months doesn't help. . . . [We need you to] mobilize the international community . . . to protect children and to end the conflict."

Members of Congress finally acted proactively in 2009 with the introduction of legislation called the Lord's Resistance Army Disarmament and Northern Uganda Recovery Act. Forty-two senators cosponsored the bill. Dozens of representatives signed on to the companion bill in the House. The bill mandates a "regional strategy to support multilateral efforts to successfully protect civilians and eliminate the threat posed by the Lord's Resistance Army."[12]

THE CAMPAIGN: BUILDING A
SCHOOL FOR FORMER SOLDIERS

While the departure of tens of thousands from internal displacement camps is a cause for celebration, the Internal Displacement Monitoring Centre noted in 2007 that many parents were leaving their children in the camps because schools were not functional in many parts of northern Uganda.

For that reason, the Not For Sale Campaign is supporting the Jesuits in northern Uganda in building a top-notch academic high school in Gulu. The school will open with eight classrooms specifically designed for children who have been heavily impacted by the atrocities of war. The Campaign will ensure that the dozens of children attending the school have desks, chalkboards, books, and other necessary supplies.

In a separate initiative with the Jesuits, the Campaign hosts music festivals and concerts to promote reconciliation between returning child soldiers and their home communities. Steve Msele, the Jesuit priest who runs the project, had previously utilized the arts for reconciliation in his native country of Rwanda—to bring reconciliation between the tribes that once had performed untold acts of murder and desecration against one another. The movement has now come to northern Uganda in an effort to heal bitter memories and tender wounds. In 2010, the Campaign contributed to the construction of a music amphitheater in Gulu that will host larger youth concerts and reconciliation gatherings.

Four

Undermining the Sex Syndicate

Europe

San Foca, a fishing village situated at the tip of the boot of southern Italy, seduces you with its charm. The azure waters of the Adriatic Sea perfectly offset the grayish white rocks that dot its shores. In the late afternoon, boats bob lazily in San Foca's harbor while fishermen meticulously mend their nets. Off in the distance—just beyond eyesight—lies the dramatic Albanian coastline and the port town of Vlorë.

Though it may be a romantic vista, it marks one of the most trafficked routes in the modern sex-slave trade. Late each night Albanian mafiosi rev up their motorized rafts and transport refugees across the forty-four nautical miles that stretch between Vlorë and San Foca.

Some of their passengers pay smugglers a hefty price to chase their dreams for a more prosperous life in the West. Many onboard, however, do not choose to make this trip. Crime syndicates in Europe maneuver through an intricate patchwork of routes to move girls across international borders. Originally created to smuggle drugs and weapons, today these routes serve to move human cargo as well.

The so-called Balkan Trail has emerged as the most notorious of these smuggling routes. Each year thousands of young girls from eastern Europe are forcibly trafficked along this channel to brothels all over the globe. A victim typically originates from a country that was once part of the Soviet bloc. From her home country, she will be transported through Romania to Serbia, Montenegro, or Croatia, then to Albania and on into Italy. The final destination for the victim will likely be the European Union, though a significant number of girls will be trafficked to the United States, the Middle East, or the Asia-Pacific region.

On the streets of Bangkok, one sees evidence of just how far these trafficking routes extend. As soon as night falls, a flood of blond girls wearing miniskirts and heavy makeup ambulate the Muslim quarter. It's a bizarre scene—these eastern European women weaving along the sidewalks amid a sea of Muslim women wholly covered in black burkas. The Muslim men, meanwhile, don white pants, white shirts, and white hats: the white is meant to represent purity of intention and action. The fact that sexual exploitation can brazenly thrive in such contradiction to a people's deep religious values indicates the immense challenge abolitionists face in their campaign to end sex slavery.

CESARE LODESERTO: THE CROSSROADS OF POVERTY AND WEALTH

An unlikely abolitionist, Padre Cesare Lodeserto has emerged as a formidable obstacle for the crime syndicates that run the Balkan Trail. A Roman Catholic priest and veteran of work with the poor in Brazil and Rwanda, Padre Cesare established a shelter for refugees in the town of San Foca in 1995.

Born and raised in the south of Italy, Padre Cesare walks where angels fear to tread. Yet he's not exactly an Indiana Jones–type figure. A heavyset, balding man in his mid-fifties, he could pass as a parish priest in a sleepy village. Nonetheless, he must deploy every bit of intellect and guile to navigate the turbulent waters of sex trafficking.

Regina Pacis—"Queen of Peace"—is the name Padre Cesare gave to his shelter in San Foca. The name stands as a symbol against the violence and greed that tear young women from their homes. He created the shelter to accommodate a maximum of 250 people, but the need quickly outpaced the space. At its peak in the late 1990s, more than 600 refugees crammed into its rooms and hallways each night.

In its early phase, the refugees who reached Regina Pacis ran the gamut—extended families, single mothers, teens, and even young children traveling alone. Around 1999, however, Padre Cesare detected a shifting trend in his demographic. A wave of young girls from eastern Europe showed up at his door seeking aid and protection. At the same time, he noticed a dramatic rise in the number of Slavic girls selling their bodies on the streets of San Foca and the nearby coastal towns of Lecce and Brindisi. The girls he encountered shared personal testimonies of abduction, rape, and commercial exploitation.

Padre Cesare dedicated a wing of Regina Pacis to cater to the plight of trafficked women. Little by little, he tracked the trail of the traffickers back to eastern Europe. As he explains, geography gave him a unique vantage point to understand the mechanisms of the modern slave trade: "San Foca is the destination where the poverty and wealth of the world collide."

Nadia: The Offer

Saying good-bye to Stefan turned out to be harder than Nadia had imagined. At the tender age of six, Stefan could not comprehend why his mother had to leave.

"Mommy, are you mad at me?" he asked when she came into the room with her suitcase in hand. The words cut her like a knife.

"No, Mommy's not abandoning you. She loves you," she whispered through sobs. "I'll make some money, and then I'll be back home." She moved hastily to the door before she fell apart completely.

Initially, Nadia did not seriously entertain Katrina's offer to arrange a restaurant job for her in Italy. Nadia knew plenty of girls who had left Chişinău to work in the West. But she did not know how she could manage Stefan on her own in a foreign land. At least here in Moldova, her family could support her and take care of him whenever she found the odd bit of work.

But she had a change of heart the day she failed to get Stefan enrolled in school. Nadia could not afford to pay the school's enrollment fees or buy a school uniform. Her family could not help her. They had no savings; every penny went to put food on the table.

Following that depressing day at the school office, she sought out Katrina at the café. The two had met long ago in grammar school. Though they had never been the best of friends, they continued to bump into each other at the occasional party. When they last met, Katrina had mentioned that she had a connection in Italy who gave jobs to teenage girls. "Let me know if you are ever interested," she had told her.

She found Katrina exactly where she hoped, at the corner table of the café. Following a bit of small talk, Nadia moved the conversation to her agenda: "Hey, remember you told me about jobs in Italy? If they're still available, I'm interested."

"You bet," said Katrina, pleased to help out her friend. "I just talked with my contacts, and a few more jobs just opened up. But they need to fill the positions really fast. Do you think you could be ready to travel a week from tomorrow?"

Now faced with the moment of truth, Nadia had to swallow hard. Could she bear to live apart from Stefan? Maybe she could make enough money in a year's time to come back home with a bit of savings in her pocket. "Okay, count me in," she blurted out.

"Fabulous," Katrina said, beaming. "We'll have such a good time together in Italy."

She told Nadia to arrive at her flat in eight days with her bags packed, ready to travel.

Cesare Lodeserto: Answering the Call

Set on the grounds of a former summer camp, the Regina Pacis facility could be mistaken for a high-security prison. High chain-link fences crowned with barbed wire circle the rectangular building. The few windows that do grace it are covered with iron bars. Only the front entrance conveys the slightest hint of invitation. The security measures have proven necessary: on occasion, traffickers come to Regina Pacis expecting to reclaim their "property."

Each girl who comes to the shelter can relate a unique tale of how she was trafficked. The most fortunate girls escape on the trip across the Adriatic to Italy. The Italian coast guard

monitors smuggling operations and from time to time inter-
cepts a boat full of immigrants. Albanian traffickers will go to
any lengths to avoid capture, however. When hotly pursued,
they've been known to throw young children overboard, forcing the coast guard to give up the chase in order to rescue the
kids from drowning.

Padre Cesare encourages trafficked girls to press criminal
charges against their abductors. Under Italian law, individuals
who have been forced to migrate and agree to testify against
their exploiter can gain legal status to stay in Italy and work.
The law does not treat trafficked individuals as criminals but
as victims of a crime. It is a significant piece of legislation—
similar to the T visa program in the United States—that ought
to be emulated in countries around the globe.

Most of the girls, nevertheless, fear going to the police. The
mafiosi threaten to kill them or harm their families if they
testify against members of the syndicate. Moreover, police officers back in eastern Europe may have played some role in their
abduction. A trafficked girl therefore does not easily place her
trust in the police.

Padre Cesare does not minimize the dangers of pursuing legal action, but he stresses that the traffickers will ruin
the lives of other innocent girls if they are not stopped. A
spontaneous reading of the text messages on Padre Cesare's
cell phone suggests why he feels such a burden to take down
the traffickers. A sixteen-year-old girl from Romania writes,
"Please help me! Only a dog would be treated in this world like
I am. Only you can help me!"

Another message comes in from a girl living in Moldova:
"I'm dying here! Help me! You're my final hope!" Her plea ar-
rives without details.

A Bulgarian girl who reports being enslaved in a massage parlor in Milan sends a third text message: "Padre! I am one of four girls stuck in this pit of hell. We plan to escape soon. I hope you will take us in."

After reading these text messages aloud, Padre Cesare shakes his head sadly and remarks, "I am praying for a new generation of abolitionists who will open up their hearts. Traffickers get away with murder because good people won't answer the calls of these young women crying out for help."

THE PERFECT TRAP

The collapse of the Soviet Union in 1991 did not deliver the lofty benefits that many living in its freed republics envisaged. The early intoxication of self-government and individual liberty gave way to depression once economic realities hit home. The liberalization of the financial markets had promised to open a porthole for new investment. Instead, the reforms turned into convenient escape hatches for a massive flight of capital.

Life under the Communist regime was no bed of roses, of course. But at least jobs—however menial—could be found, and few people starved. While a small elite amassed wealth at an astounding rate in the 1990s, the masses faced skyrocketing unemployment and disappearing social services. Under this pressure, families struggled to stay intact. The dramatic rise in alcoholism among men did not make that task any easier. Orphanages sprang up across the region to support abandoned children.

The disintegration of Moscow's iron rule left a power vacuum in its former republics. Organized crime quickly moved in to seize ripe opportunities. Often the criminals turned out to be former Communist officials who used their powerful connections for personal enrichment. A new breed of crooked capitalists who held no scruples about their business transactions also arose. The rule of law became a sham, for sale to the highest bidder.

Almost immediately in the post-Soviet era, mafiosi turned a huge profit selling guns and drugs. It did not take the syndicates long to realize that the former Soviet republics had another gold mine worth exploiting: educated, healthy young women who suddenly found themselves destitute.

Women got hit with the brunt of unemployment after the fall of the Iron Curtain. In the Ukraine, for instance, females accounted for 80 percent of the population who lost jobs in the 1990s.[1] Unemployment rates for women ranged between 70 and 80 percent in most of the former Soviet republics. Yet despite the difficulty of finding a job, women were often expected to shoulder responsibility for the survival of their family.

Human traffickers had the ideal candidates to trade in the global sex market, and the perfect ruse to recruit them. Eastern European youths have grown up with a fascination for the West. They watch its movies, listen to its music, and crave its consumer luxuries. To be offered a job and an apartment in western Europe would be a dream come true for many young people.

Even the threat of danger would not dissuade them. By the end of the 1990s, sordid tales started leaking back home about what happened to girls who migrated to the West. Despite these red flags, golden dreams of emigration persist. A study conducted in the Ukraine in the late 1990s revealed that three out of four girls between the ages of ten and nineteen expressed a strong desire to work abroad.[2] Some girls fall for the glamour of a luxurious lifestyle, while others hope to become the financial savior of their family. Whatever the allure, traffickers use it for their deception.

Nadia: The Judas Kiss

When she arrived at Katrina's flat, Nadia was surprised to find six additional girls with baggage waiting there. She had assumed that she and Katrina would be traveling alone.

Katrina did not bother to explain the circumstances. After a brief greeting, she asked Nadia in business-like fashion, "Okay, you brought your passport along, right?"

Nadia nodded her head, dug the document out of her purse, and held it up.

"Great," Katrina said. "Let me have it, and I'll give it to the guide for safekeeping."

Once Nadia handed it over, Katrina scurried off to speak with a middle-aged man who paced across the flat. They had a short conversation while the man's eyes fixed on Nadia. He handed Katrina what appeared to be a roll of money.

Uncomfortable with the man's glare, Nadia turned her attention to the other girls. She noted at once that she had at least five or six years on them; none of them had yet reached eighteen, she guessed.

One of the girls wandered over to Nadia and, with a hint of anxiety in her voice, asked, "Do you know where we're going?"

"Katrina found me a job working in a restaurant in Italy," Nadia reported matter-of-factly.

"Oh, she told us that, too," the girl said. "But I was wondering whether you knew exactly where in Italy we would be traveling."

Before Nadia could answer, the man whom Katrina had presented as "the guide" spoke up: "We will be leaving in a few seconds." He paused and then proceeded with instructions: "Outside we have three vehicles waiting. I will assign you to one of the cars. Don't worry which one you end up in, because we're all going to the same place."

Katrina picked up her suitcase and led the way out the door of the flat. Nadia followed and climbed into the backseat of her assigned vehicle. She settled down next to a girl whom she had not yet met. The driver started the engine once the lead car lurched onto the road.

The three cars moved along as a caravan for several hours. Nadia did not speak a word. She passed the time thinking about Stefan. In a panic she second-guessed herself. Shouldn't she be at home raising her son? Who cares if she can't afford all the things that she wanted for him? But what kind of future would he have without an education? With the droning wheels of the car sounding the backbeat, her internal debate rapped on for some time.

As they neared the border with Romania, the caravan came to a sudden halt. It seemed to Nadia as if they were in the middle of nowhere. After ten minutes, she could see three pairs of headlights approach slowly from the other direction. The cars stopped directly across the road from where they were parked. Nadia saw "the guide" swagger over to them and speak into the window of the first car. He then returned to her vehicle and opened the back door.

"Grab your bags, girls," he ordered. "You're shifting cars for the next leg of the journey."

Once Nadia had moved to her newly assigned seat, she peered out the window. Across the road she could see Katrina sitting in the backseat of one of the cars that the girls had just departed. The first whiff of trouble reached Nadia's senses. Why wasn't Katrina coming along with them?

Nadia rolled down her window and waved her arms to get Katrina's attention. Having failed at that, she yelled out her friend's name. Katrina did not flinch, keeping her gaze dead ahead.

A minute later the caravan was driving across the border into Romania.

TRAFFICKING ORPHANS

Orphanages have become one of the few (legal) growth industries in eastern Europe over the past two decades. The collapse of the family led to massive numbers of abandoned children with nowhere to turn.

Imagine the impact of emigration on the family in a country like Moldova, from which an estimated one in four people emigrated between 1991 and 2002.[3] It is not uncommon for parents to leave their children behind when they leave the country. Other children lose parents to alcoholism, death, or outright destitution.

Despite the proliferation of orphanages, the need is still greater. Nearly every orphanage in eastern Europe overflows its capacity and has a line of kids waiting to get in. To deal with overcapacity, the orphanages usually force the older children to leave once they reach the age of seventeen. Few of these kids have savings or vocational training that might lead to a job. Quick to identify their vulnerability, sex-slave recruiters view these children as ripe pickings.

Recruiters have started pursuing children who live inside the orphanages as well. Sadly, the recruiters find willing collaborators inside the orphanages who will betray children for the right price. Human-rights groups report that orphans in the region are sold and trafficked internationally for use in child-pornography rings. For instance, in its 2003 report card on human trafficking, the U.S. State Department exposed orphanage directors in Moldova for selling background information on children to traffickers and in some cases arranging their abduction. The report details similar travesties in Romania, where "many orphanages are complicit in letting girls fall victim to trafficking networks."[4]

Cesare Lodeserto: Infectious Compassion

Like many of San Foca's residents, Enzo can attest to the legend of Padre Cesare. Enzo operates one of the most vibrant sidewalk cafés in the village. On warm summer nights in August—when the whole of Italy seems to be on holiday—the plaza in front of Enzo's café fills with people looking to enjoy musical entertainment and a cold drink. The girls who wait on the tables might speak Romanian or Russian or Moldovan. They were trafficked to San Foca for another kind of labor, but Padre Cesare rescued them.

Enzo relates that one blustery winter day he had gone over to Regina Pacis to lend a hand preparing meals for the refugees. Several young boys burst into the shelter yelling frantically that they had witnessed a small boat capsize not far off the shore. Enzo threw on his coat and reached the shelter's front door at the same moment as Padre Cesare. They jumped into Enzo's car and rushed to the location where the boys indicated they had last seen the boat.

Glancing out at the sea as they drove along, Enzo shuddered. In the off-season—when tourism dies down in San Foca—he works as a fisherman. He knows the sea all too well; once a swell kicks up, the angry waves can easily consume a small craft.

Enzo parked the car off the road, and he and Padre Cesare ran along the beach in opposite directions. A gale blew sheets of rain horizontally, making it difficult to see.

Five minutes of searching yielded nothing. Enzo began to fear that the anonymous passengers might be lost at sea. Suddenly he heard a high-pitched cry over the sound of the crashing waves. At first he mistook the noise for a howling wind, but after a pause he distinguished a baby's wail.

Turning in all directions, he detected movement along the base of the cliffs. He motioned to Padre Cesare far down the beach and then ran for the rocks. He found twenty-five Iraqi refugees of all ages—elderly men and women, young mothers, children, and three babies—huddled in a crevice cut into the cliffs, trying to find shelter from the wind and rain.

Enzo stood motionless ten feet away from the refugees, unable to speak their language and unsure what action to take next. The Iraqis stared back at him equally confused, fretting over whether Enzo might be a friend or a foe.

Padre Cesare broke the stalemate, sprinting past Enzo to approach the huddled mass. Throwing off his coat, he wrapped it tightly around the young children. The priest addressed the Iraqis in Italian; though they did not understand a word of what he was saying, the compassion in his voice expressed his intention. He pointed up the beach and started walking. The Iraqis followed him as one.

A caravan of vehicles from Regina Pacis pulled up just as the ragged assembly reached the road. The refugees piled in and were given safe haven at Regina Pacis.

"It was just another day in the life of Padre Cesare," says Enzo, reflecting on the event, "but for me it became a special memory to cherish."

Behind the bar at his café, Enzo keeps pinned to the wall a photo of Padre Cesare with his arms around two of Enzo's children. The priest is practically a patron saint of the establishment. Enzo honors Padre Cesare's example of embracing the foreigner by providing jobs to trafficked girls.

Padre Cesare has touched many lives in San Foca and has inspired them to acts of extraordinary kindness. Young women who escaped sex slavery work at local restaurants, fruit shops, and bakeries. They have married locals and are raising children. "Padre Cesare's girls"—as they are sometimes called in the village—do not walk the streets in shame.

Nadia: The Crossing

The caravan of cars traveled for several hours across Romania before pulling up behind an old country house. Though Nadia could see the lights of a small village in the distance, she had no clue where they had stopped.

The drivers barked out orders to move swiftly into the house. They ushered the girls into a dimly lit room and locked the door behind them. Three young Romanian girls sitting on dingy sofas already inhabited the room. They stood up expectantly when the door opened, but dejectedly slid back down onto the chairs once they heard the click of the lock.

"Can you tell me where we are?" Nadia asked.

"I really couldn't tell you," replied a blue-eyed girl of exceptional beauty.

"How long have you been here?" Nadia charged on, hungry for information.

"Oh, I'd say two weeks," the blue-eyed girl replied, "but to be honest, it's hard to keep track."

"Two weeks!" Nadia exclaimed. "Has anyone explained to you what's going on?"

"They're having trouble securing tourist visas for us," the Romanian reported.

That's the only explanation Nadia ever received about their incarceration. A man brought them simple meals twice a day but would not let them step outside the room.

"Why are you keeping us here?" Nadia yelled each time the man entered with the food tray. He invariably grunted that she should "shut up," and departed.

After seven days in confinement, a well-dressed man entered the room, trailed by three scary-looking goons. "Good news," the elegant man announced. "We have your travel visas. So we're off to Serbia!"

Almost as an afterthought, he said, "From there we'll put you on a bus that will take you to Italy. Your new employers have secured apartments for you there, so you can start earning money right away."

The rosy announcement lifted Nadia's spirits for the first time since she had left Chişinău. The goons led the girls outside the house, where two white vans waited. The girls stepped up into the vans and immediately hit the road.

For the rest of the day the vans negotiated narrow mountain

roads that cut across desolate wilderness. Late in the evening, the vans veered off the road into a sheltered cove of trees. The goons ordered the girls out of the vehicles.

The elegant man then shared a part of the travel plan that he had conveniently omitted that afternoon: "Girls, we have visas for you to work in Italy, but we failed in our attempts to obtain tourist visas for you to enter Serbia. So you are going to have to sneak across the border under the cover of darkness."

The girls unleashed a cacophony of complaints and queries. The elegant man brusquely cut them off: "I'm sorry. It's the only way we can get you to the bus that will transport you to Italy."

Cars would be waiting for them on the other side of the border, he explained. The drivers would blink their lights three times every two minutes until they all arrived. He went on to warn that if they were captured going across the border, the girls would be thrown into prison, maybe for years. "And trust me," he said, lowering his voice ominously, "you do not want to serve time in a Serbian prison."

The men guided the girls for nearly half a mile until they reached a clearing. They rested until they could see lights flashing amid a line of trees on a ridge in the far distance.

"There, that's it," the elegant man said, pointing his finger. "Go now, and don't stop running until you reach that ridge."

TRAFFICKING AND GLOBALIZATION

Sex trafficking simultaneously exploits both the best and the worst aspects of globalization. The champions of globalization tout the growing ease of conducting business across national borders. Sophisticated communication tools and relaxed banking laws make it possible to exchange assets internationally with ease. Virtual enterprises can operate everywhere and nowhere, making themselves known only when and where they choose.

Organized crime syndicates take advantage of these tools to create more efficient overseas networks. Although most trafficking originates with local operators, they deftly connect to an international sex industry looking to fill slots in brothels, massage parlors, strip joints, and lap-dance bars.

A club owner in Chicago can pick up the phone and "mail-order" three beautiful young girls from eastern Europe. Two weeks later a fresh shipment of three Slavic girls will be dancing in his club. Though a number of quasi-independent traffickers were likely involved in moving the girls, the operation would appear seamless to the Chicago client.

The critics of globalization point out that capital flows wherever it can most easily exploit cheap labor. The owners of capital will abandon a specific location quickly once one of two conditions occurs: (1) the assets it exploits are depleted; or (2) those assets can be obtained more cheaply in other markets.

Sex trafficking also manifests itself in this form. Over the past three decades, the prime area for recruiting sex slaves has shifted rapidly from one zone of economic depression to another. In the 1970s, traffickers targeted girls from Southeast Asia—above all Thailand and Vietnam—as well as the Philippines. After ten years or so of mining in Asia, traffickers shifted their focus to Africa: girls from Nigeria, Uganda, and Ghana flooded the international sex bazaars. In the mid-1980s and spilling over into the early 1990s, girls from Latin America—Brazil, Mexico, the Dominican Republic, and Central America (especially El Salvador and Guatemala)—became the favored pool.

Traffickers move opportunistically to prey on vulnerable populations. In the 1980s, the trafficking of girls out of eastern Europe hardly registered on the radar screen. Following the economic and political collapse of the Soviet Union, that situation changed dramatically. The International Organization for Migration (IOM) estimates that roughly a quarter of a million females were trafficked within Europe alone—from the East to the West—since 1991.[5]

Even within eastern Europe, the prime recruitment zones for trafficking shift rapidly to exploit opportunities. In 1992, the vast majority of trafficked victims came from Poland, Romania, Hungary, and Czechoslovakia. By the mid-1990s girls in those markets had been depleted, so traffickers started targeting Russia, Ukraine, Bulgaria, and Moldova. After the turn of the century, the prime recruitment zone shifted to central Asia— Uzbekistan, Kazakhstan, and Kyrgyzstan—and Georgia.

Which countries these women are destined for is completely determined by a supply line and center of profit. For example, trafficking in Israel has been relatively low-volume in the past, but as of 2008, Israel's Task Force on Human Trafficking noted that Israeli organized crime rings were bringing as many as five thousand women per year into the country from Balkan nations for the purposes of prostitution.[6]

Wherever the greatest profit can be extracted, there the traffickers move. In an impassioned speech delivered in Brussels, EU commissioner Anna Diamantopoulou aptly characterized the "ruthless efficiency" of these modern-day traders in human property: "They know their business inside out and respond to changes in the market with a speed unmatched by even the most competitive corporations. Their expertise and ability to exploit the market are surpassed only by their disregard for human life. Women are bought, sold and hired out like any other product. The bottom line is profit."[7]

A report issued in 2009 by the European Commission brought to light just how viral trafficking has become. The report cites the latest International Labour Organization statistics that several hundred thousand individuals are trafficked into and through Europe per year. Forty-three percent of these are victims enslaved for the purposes of prostitution, while 32 percent are utilized in forced-labor settings. Out of those trafficked for sex, 98 percent were women and girls. Overshadowing all of these statistics in the report was the startling assertion that in Europe, human trafficking has overtaken the commerce in illegal drugs.[8]

Nadia: The Livestock Market

The girls started off across the border in a sprint. The elegant man had not mentioned how hard it would be to cross the terrain. Unable to see their own feet, they repeatedly tripped over sharp rocks and brambles armed with pointy thorns. By the time they reached the ridge, most of the girls had lost at least one shoe. All had bruises and deep cuts up and down their legs. Nonetheless, they managed to track the flashing lights and reached the destination with their entire band intact.

Now safely in Serbia, they piled into three cars and wove their way through a seemingly endless succession of mountain passes. They finally came to a remote stone house that seemed to be planted in the middle of a forest.

Upon entering the house, the girls once again merged with

more trafficked victims. A dozen girls, also battered and blood-ied, sat on the floor in the entry foyer, leaning their exhausted bodies against the walls.

The woman in charge—who appeared to be in her early thirties and blessed with gorgeous blond locks—spoke in flaw-less Russian to the assembly gathered in the foyer. She seemed genuinely concerned with their condition and instructed her staff to bring hot, wet towels so that the girls could clean their cuts.

The Russian woman then divided the girls into groups of five or six and assigned each group to an upstairs bedroom. As it was now well past midnight, she urged the girls to get some sleep. "You need your rest because you have a big day tomor-row," she remarked cryptically.

The depleted girls slept to nearly noon the next day. Care-takers woke them up with loaves of bread, butter and jam, and steeping hot tea. It had been a couple of days since they had eaten a scrap of food, so Nadia and her roommates devoured the bread.

After their meal, the girls lay back down on their mattresses and shared details of their escapades. The Romanian girl with the deep blue eyes, whom Nadia had met at their last stop, was a roommate. Two girls told of their journey together from the Ukraine, and the fifth girl told of her trek from Bulgaria. Like Nadia, they had all been promised jobs in Italy.

The woman with the golden locks opened the door and in-terrupted their peaceful interlude. "Okay, girls, I need you to perform well for me," she sang out. "Downstairs in the parlor an important group of men is waiting to evaluate you. We'll go down together as a team, and before we enter you will take off your shirts."

alone. The Russian Mafia can therefore decentralize its operations while remaining the puppet master.

The Russian syndicate also has a reputation for the ruthless use of violence when it feels threatened or betrayed. Add that intimidation factor to its effective, clandestine networks, and it becomes a daunting foe for abolitionists in eastern Europe.

Cesare Lodeserto: The Danger Zone

Wherever Padre Cesare goes, an armed bodyguard hovers nearby. He does not request such protection. The Italian government unilaterally decided to give him around-the-clock protection whenever he works inside the country. By order of the president of Moldova, he receives the same security measures when he flies into Chişinău.

Their concerns for his safety do not arise from an irrational paranoia. More than a few mafiosi would like to see Padre Cesare six feet under. His commitment to undermining sex trafficking has become costly to their operations.

Early in 2001, two thugs paid Padre Cesare a visit to deliver a warning—or possibly to take more serious action. After dinner, the priest had elected to take a walk on the beach that lies in front of the Regina Pacis property. The mafiosi, who took no pains to hide their identity with masks, were awaiting him on the beach. They calmly suggested that he accompany them to a grove of trees just off the beach. One of the men had a gun tucked into his belt, openly displayed. Under the circumstances, Padre Cesare could not refuse their suggestion.

Once they reached the woods, the thugs turned more menacing: "Padre, you are in deep trouble. Our boss wants you to know how much he dislikes having his property stolen."

At first Nadia thought she must have misunderstood her Russian hostess. "Sorry, but what do you want us to do?" she asked, trying her best to stay calm.

"Undress to your waist, with your breasts bare," the woman said as casually as if she had asked them to kick off their shoes and walk in with bare feet.

"You must be joking!" Nadia said incredulously.

"Don't worry. Nothing will happen to you," the woman said in an effort to reassure her. "It's just a check. Your employers in Italy have sent these men to ensure that you are healthy."

Noting their puzzled expression, she added, "Sometimes recruiters beat their cargo, and the girls are unable to work. We just need to prove to them that you are in good shape."

Despite her misgivings, Nadia went along with the pageant. Her group descended the stairs and halted at the double doors leading into the parlor. They then shed their shirts while the Russian woman clucked, "All right, all right, that's it, that's it. We're ready. Let's go."

Passing through the doors, the girls spotted a dozen or so men seated in a circle around the four walls. The Russian woman asked the girls to stand apart from the pack one at a time, announce their names, and rotate slowly in a full circle. The men eyed them carefully as if they were examining livestock at the county fair.

Once this humiliating exercise ended, the girls returned upstairs to their bedrooms and rested. Within the hour, the Russian woman swept into the room and called out Nadia's name and that of the blue-eyed Romanian. "You two will be leaving with your courier in five minutes," she stated curtly.

The two girls hurriedly arranged their bags, wished their roommates good luck, and scampered downstairs. A slight-framed man with black, greasy hair awaited them at the foot of the stairs.

"You work for me," the man said in halting Russian. "You go with me now."

He led them out the front door to where a car stood idling. He directed the girls to the backseat and addressed the driver in a language that Nadia guessed must be Serbian.

They drove in silence for a couple of hours until they reached Belgrade. Their "courier" delivered them to an apartment located in a residential district. "You wait me here," he instructed them in his broken Russian. "I be back in few minutes."

Half an hour later, the girls heard the apartment door open. It was the courier, accompanied by two portly men, both of whom sported soiled brown leather jackets. The men eyed the girls lustily as they spoke to each other in a thick Serbian dialect. Once they appeared to reach an agreement of some sort, the courier grunted, "Okay, you work now."

"What do you mean?" asked a befuddled Nadia.

"You cost me much money," he replied angrily. "You give good sex to these men."

Both girls took several steps backward, and Nadia spoke strongly: "No way! You have the wrong idea about us!" Desperately searching for a way out of this mess, she offered an alternative. "We will work very hard for you in a restaurant, but we cannot do this kind of work."

The Serbian man had no patience for negotiation. He reached inside the right side of his jacket and pulled out a flat instrument. Nadia could not make out what he was holding until she saw the blade flick out from its shell. He deftly grabbed her by the hair and pressed the blade against her throat.

"You show men good time, or I cut throat," he threatened.

Shaking with fear, the girls went into separate bed[rooms] where the portly men raped them.

Over the next month, this script was played out o[ver many] times. Four simple words—"You go work now"—tra[nsformed] Nadia into a living hell.

THE RUSSIAN MOB

Illicit activity as pervasive and lucrative as sex tra[fficking in] eastern Europe could not happen without the machi[nery of or]ganized crime. The structure of those syndicates an[d how they] work remain somewhat of a mystery. The criminals [work hard] to stay clandestine.

It's clear that the Russian Mafia has its stamp o[n nearly] every facet of the sex-trafficking trade in eastern [Europe. Its] home base within Russia is massive, linking thous[ands of orga]nizations, including otherwise legitimate busines[ses. The] mob's influence goes far beyond the region: Russi[an organized] crime is thought to control sex trafficking in Isr[ael, parts] of western Europe and has a strong presence [in the United] States, Canada, and Southeast Asia.

The Russian Mafia's greatest strength might [be its ability to] forge profitable alliances. For instance, it coo[perates] with autonomous syndicates in both Albania an[d Serbia to trans]port girls into western Europe. For the Russi[ans to] build their own smuggling operation in these [areas—] along with a protection racket of paid police [and customs] officials—would be far too costly. Instead, [the Mafia] outsources the costs of "product distribution." [Each link in the] chain earns its share of the revenues, realizing [there is] more commerce working with others than [...]

Padre Cesare put up a crafty defense: "Gentlemen, you know that I would never take anything that rightfully belongs to another!"

"Don't play coy with us, Padre," one of the men replied in perfect Italian. "If you take one more of our girls off the streets, you will not live to tell the tale."

By this time, the security guards who watch Regina Pacis had grown worried. Padre Cesare had been absent from the compound longer than usual on one of his evening strolls. The guards frantically dispatched a makeshift search party. Their yells for the missing priest sent the thugs scurrying away, and he escaped harm.

Padre Cesare relates the story as if he were recounting the plot of a film that he had watched at the theater. Asked how he can treat this threat so lightly, he replies, "There's nothing these men can do to me that could compare to the suffering that trafficked girls undergo."

Unable to scare Padre Cesare off his mission, the mafiosi have more recently tried to tarnish his reputation. A few young girls—former residents of Regina Pacis—have made formal accusations against him. They presented themselves to the court as "victims of psychological abuse," charging that Padre Cesare runs the shelter like a prison and tries to control every movement of their lives. How ironic—the rescuer charged as an abductor.

The staff who work at Regina Pacis staunchly defend Padre Cesare and are convinced that Mafia chiefs coerced the girls to bring charges. Before a judge's careful questioning, one of the supposed victims recanted her entire testimony, according to the staff.

Padre Cesare, on the other hand, does not care to expend energy defending himself. When asked directly about the accusations, he gives one of his characteristic shrugs and remarks, "I can tell you that I am neither a saint nor a criminal, but beyond that I will let my work speak for itself."

POLITICAL EFFORTS TO CURB TRAFFICKING

For more than a century, sex trafficking has been a concern of international leaders. In 1904 twelve nations, including the United States, ratified a treaty called the International Agreement for the Suppression of the White Slave Trade. Written in response to the widespread abduction of girls for the purposes of sexual exploitation in Europe and Asia, this agreement urged governments to prohibit "procuration of women and girls for immoral purposes abroad."

After World War I, the League of Nations adopted a broad-reaching document against slavery that essentially affirmed the 1904 treaty but added children to the agenda. The League also replaced the term "white slave trade" with the term that enjoys currency today: "trafficking in women and children."

Then, in 1949, the United Nations General Assembly set out to establish a legal framework to stop the traffic. Known formally as the Convention for the Suppression of the Traffic in Persons and of the Exploitation of the Prostitution of Others, it declared that the enslavement of women and children for the purposes of sexual exploitation was a violation of fundamental human rights. It called on governments to adopt procedures for punishing any person who sexually exploits another individual or who runs a commercial enterprise that profits from such activity.

Under the terms of the convention, the consensual contract between two individuals would be honored as a matter of free choice. All the same, the convention deemed prostitution to be unfitting the dignity of a human being and encouraged nations to offer public education and material assistance to persuade individuals not to sell their bodies for sex.

Unfortunately, the convention was ratified by fewer than half of the member states of the United Nations (72 out of a total of 185). Today, nearly half a century later, its translation into policy yields widely divergent legal strategies. As of 2009, there is only one country—Estonia—out of the 39 European nations without a specific codified offense related to human trafficking.[9]

The United States took a very narrow interpretation of the convention. All of the states except Nevada criminalize prostitution and make all parties liable for prosecution—prostitutes, customers, traffickers, and commercial exploiters. In actual application, the U.S. public justice system has addressed the supply side of the equation (prostitutes and brothel owners) much more aggressively than the demand side (johns).

Rather than seek to prohibit sexual commerce, western European nations make a more concerted effort to regulate it. The best policies for accomplishing that goal, and their consequences for sex trafficking, are matters of heated debate.

The Netherlands, for example, has historically maintained an open tolerance for the commercial sale of sex. In October 2000 it went a step further and officially legalized prostitution. The German government followed suit two months later.

The lawmakers of these nations were persuaded that exploitation thrives in environments of illegality. If prostitution will always be with us—and lawmakers in Germany and the Netherlands presume that to be the case—then criminalizing it will create a black market where the mob underworld makes the rules. The fact that 70 percent of prostitution in the United States is linked to organized crime would seem to support that argument.[10]

In Germany and the Netherlands, sex workers are offered legal protection from commercial exploitation and receive social-service benefits. But these laws do not apply to individuals who are not citizens of member nations of the European Union. To the chagrin of lawmakers, a booming underground sex trade has emerged in both countries. A 2003 survey found that foreign-born women make up 65 percent of the sex market in the Netherlands and 50 percent of the market in Germany.[11]

Most abolitionists vehemently argue that legalizing prostitution engenders a broader social acceptance of brothels for sexual entertainment. That kind of cultural environment, in turn, leads to a greater demand for young girls that will be filled by sex traffickers. Ongoing research should be able to determine whether prohibition or legalization does spawn higher levels of sex trafficking into a country.

At the very least, the legalization of the sex trade makes the prosecution of traffickers, pimps, and brothel owners almost impossible. They can use the defense that the girl consented to work as a prostitute, and the burden of proof will be on the girl to prove otherwise. If at any point the girl actually did consent to work as a prostitute, all subsequent forms of coercion will find legal cover.

Sweden has moved in a unique direction. In 1999 the Swedish government became the first in the world to prosecute the buyer of sex, the john, while legally treating the woman as a victim. The Swedish government also established a comprehensive outreach program that encourages sex workers to change their livelihood.

The maximum sentence in Sweden for a convicted john is six months in prison. In the first five years following passage of the law, about 750 men had been charged, and two-thirds were sentenced. As a result, street prostitution in Sweden has dropped dramatically, as has the influx of trafficked women.[12]

"What differentiates us from the Netherlands and Germany . . . is that we link the 'slave trade' with prostitution and pornography," explains Marianne Eriksson, a Swedish member of the European Parliament and a strong proponent of her country's legal strategy on sex trafficking. "Everyone in the European Union is against human trafficking, of course," she clarifies, "but we know that 90 percent of this commerce has to do with sexual exploitation."[13]

Nadia: Passage Through Hell

Just when Nadia concluded that she would never get out of Serbia, the Russian woman with the golden locks turned up in her life again.

"Oh, look at you two. These Serbs are real pigs," the woman remarked as she reached out and caressed the face of the Romanian girl. "Let's get out of here," she added. "Looks like you both could use a hot meal."

Though Nadia had been deceived once before by this woman's faux compassion, she could not help herself from appreciating any warmth that might come her way.

"It's taken a while, but I finally got you visas to work in Italy," she announced once they settled into some seats at a nearby restaurant. "Soon you will be working a normal job in a café in Rome."

She held open Nadia's passport and showed her an official stamp as proof. "Now you'll be protected if the police in Italy ask you for documents. You'll leave in two more days."

From that point forward, Nadia counted the minutes until her departure. The Serb continued to bring a steady flow of paying customers to the apartment. She did not understand the business arrangement the Serb had with the Russian woman, and she feared him too much to ask. But Nadia mouthed a quiet curse on the apartment two days later when she walked out the door for the final time.

Two burly Russian men transported Nadia, along with the blue-eyed Romanian and three young girls from the Ukraine. They stopped in Montenegro for a few days at a place that the Russians called a "safe house."

On the evening of the third day, they left the safe house and drove to the edge of a very large lake. The driver stopped the vehicle but left the headlights beaming out on the water. Before long, a small rubber dinghy appeared in the headlights. The Russians ushered the girls to the lake's edge and instructed them to jump into the boat.

Nadia asked one of her burly escorts if the boat would be taking them to Italy. "No, first you will go to Albania," the man replied. Her heart sank. She wondered whether her trek would ever end. The Russians left the girls in the care of the Albanian pilot.

As soon as they moved away from the shore, he throttled the motor at full bore for well over an hour. He spoke Russian fairly well and tried to strike up a conversation with a few of the girls. None of them felt chatty, though, and they kept their contributions brief.

Eventually they could see a cluster of lights off in the distance. The Albanian indicated that their destination lay just beyond the lights, and then he unexpectedly cut the motor. Nadia initially thought the engine had run out of gas.

"Now I'm going to choose one of you to screw," he said bluntly. "If my selection refuses to cooperate, I will drown all of you right here. I don't give a damn."

The girls exchanged frightened glances. "I can't swim," one of the girls from Kiev said in a small voice. One by one, the girls admitted to being completely helpless in these deep waters.

"Okay, let's give this bastard what he wants," the Romanian girl said in a resigned voice. Saying this, she instinctively grabbed Nadia's hand, and Nadia did the same to the girl next to her, and so on, until the five were all linked together.

They braced themselves for the selection. The pilot squinted and scanned the circle, then pointed at Nadia: "You come here."

Nadia looked at her companions with dread.

"Please, go on," the Kiev girl pleaded. "Don't be ashamed. You'll be doing it for us."

Nadia stood up in the raft and moved toward the pilot. He undressed her and then raped her in front of the other girls. After he finished, he declared, "You were really good. If you didn't perform well, I was going to drown you and your friends." He let out a loud laugh and restarted the engine.

When they floated toward Albanian soil fifteen minutes later, an unexpected welcoming party awaited them. All of the men standing on the shore hoisted machine guns. Nadia was even more surprised that some of the men wore uniforms. Her concern heightened once she lifted her eyes to the road above the beach and saw "POLICE" written on the side panels of two vehicles. How ironic. After getting so close to Italy, it looked as if she would end up languishing in an Albanian prison.

The police took the girls into custody and drove them in their squad cars to the city of Shkodër. But they never reached a police station. The officers brought them to a private home, and before departing each took a turn raping the girl of his choice.

POLICE CORRUPTION

Why don't the police in eastern Europe do something about sex trafficking?

Some do—by opening border crossings for traffickers, by shielding them from arrest at the hands of their more conscientious colleagues, by issuing licenses so that the traffickers can operate as a legitimate business, and by capturing girls who escape and returning them to their "owners." In sum, trafficking syndicates depend heavily on the police to sustain their operations.

Corruption makes a mockery of the concept of public justice in the former Soviet states. The vast majority of girls who were trafficked along the Balkan Trail report encountering at least one police officer who abetted their abductors. In some instances the girls testified that the police raped them—and did not feel the need to hide their identity while doing so.

The strategic location of Albania for the transit of young girls from East to West has been well documented. A country report on Albania by the State Department's Bureau of Democracy, Human Rights, and Labor confirms that police are "often directly or indirectly involved" in these operations.[14] The report also critiques the Albanian Ministry of Public Order, which is the public body charged with oversight of the police. Despite strong evidence of police complicity in high-profile trafficking cases, the ministry failed to take any punitive action against officers. Whenever a law-enforcement group in Albania does muster the courage to confront the traffickers, "local police often tip off the traffickers when raids are scheduled."[15]

Imagine how powerless it must feel to be the target of a crime and have nowhere to turn for justice. Police officers and government officials more than look the other way when a crime occurs: they are apt to be active participants. Citizens in eastern Europe cannot trust public officials and are unlikely to file a complaint against a bogus agency that has abducted one of their family members. This is especially true for girls already involved in the sex trade: the police treat them as if they deserve whatever maltreatment comes their way.

The complicity of law-enforcement authorities in sex trafficking is not peculiar to eastern Europe; it is a worldwide phenomenon. Given the public nature of the industry, it must be so. Narcotics and weapons can be smuggled and sold in a clandestine fashion. The sex trade, however, must be transparent to those who ultimately pay for the freight. It stands to reason, then, that if the johns can find the illicit "product"—openly marketed on a street corner or in a published advertisement—so could law-enforcement authorities. The fact that they do nothing to fight sex trafficking demonstrates apathy to the problem, an ignorance of its prevalence, or a financial stake in its continuation.

All the same, abolitionists will need the help of the police to stem the rising tide of sex trafficking. If the police in eastern Europe—or anywhere else in the world—are written off wholesale as the criminal element, the antislavery campaign will never gain traction. The poor and vulnerable cannot stand alone and survive the onslaught of potent criminals who deploy whatever means are necessary to maximize their profits. Abolitionists must build alliances with honest police officers and support their efforts to establish a credible presence locally.

Cesare Lodeserto: Moving Upstream

Padre Cesare operates like a sage environmentalist who finds poisoned fish at the end of a stream. As concerned as the environmentalist might be for the ill fish, he would go upstream and eliminate the source that pollutes the waters.

Padre Cesare realized that by the time trafficked girls arrived in San Foca seeking safe haven, most had already been incorporated into the commercial sex trade. So he followed the trafficking trail back to eastern Europe and tackled the problem at its font. "I could no longer accept our position; essentially, we were waiting for girls to become victims," he says.

In 2003, he began winding down his refugee service and reformulated the core mission of Regina Pacis. A number of factors contributed to his decision: The war in the Balkans had reached a peaceful resolution, and the gush of refugees from that region had slowed to a mere trickle. A more stable political situation in Afghanistan also cut the flow of refugees. Given these developments, Padre Cesare could focus his attention more exclusively on sex trafficking. From a shelter that had become Italy's largest refugee-processing center, Regina Pacis morphed into an international abolitionist network.

Regina Pacis still operates a modest lodging program in San Foca. The staff aims to find stable solutions so that trafficked girls do not fall into dependence. After an initial period of recovery, girls are, under ideal circumstances, placed with a healthy foster family. Foreigners get help sorting out their immigration status with the government: trafficking victims have rarely kept possession of their passports. The girls may learn a new vocation. If they already possess special skills, the staff helps them find a job that provides a sense of dignity and self-determination.

These days, one is more likely to find Padre Cesare in eastern Europe. He has established Regina Pacis centers in Moldova and Romania to carry out a broad range of antislavery activities. "We address three main enemies in sex trafficking," Padre Cesare explains. "First, poverty; second, the john who drives demand; and finally, the trafficker. We create programs that reduce the influence that these enemies can have on the lives of young girls."

Poverty is the most pervasive and invisible "enemy" of the three and therefore the most difficult to fight. In Moldova, for instance, over half of the population struggles below a subsistence-level income, and only one in four people holds what could be considered a steady job. Though the entire population of the country is less than 5 million, nearly ten thousand girls between the ages of fifteen and twenty-two emigrate each year without any formal guarantee of school or work.[16]

During one of his first visits to Moldova, Padre Cesare met a thirteen-year-old girl who had accepted a "job offer" in Rome.

She was the oldest of three daughters in a destitute family. The girl shared with him stories of how her father beat her mother when she asked him for money to buy milk or bread. She also told him how it tore her insides apart to watch her younger sister fall seriously ill. The girl was determined to earn money to buy medicines for her sister.

She saw a billboard in Chișinău advertising job openings for "teenage models." When she went to the audition and participated in a photo shoot, the recruiter told her, "You would be perfect for an advertising campaign in Italy." He gave her a small cash advance and told her, "There is much more to be made once you go to Rome."

Regina Pacis has launched an education program in the schools in Moldova to warn children of exactly this kind of predatory offer. Fortunately, Padre Cesare met this girl at her school before she departed on her "modeling adventure." He investigated the agency and discovered that, as he suspected, it was a front for a trafficking syndicate. He intervened and saved the girl from a terrible fate. "The girl looked for a radical solution to her family's crisis because she did not have any other options," he explains.

Regina Pacis places prominent billboard ads in Romania and Moldova as another tactic to warn girls and their families that criminals use false promises to lure potential recruits. Its staff scours daily newspapers for suspicious ads announcing overseas jobs. Once they identify a front, they expose it as publicly as possible.

Padre Cesare can attest to the large numbers of girls that these collective efforts have saved. Nonetheless, he admits that poverty all too often holds the upper hand. A girl struggling for her family's survival may suspend her better judgment and assume higher risks. "Prevention. Yes, that's a major goal of our operations in eastern Europe," he says. "But before I can persuade a girl to stay close to home—or, in the case of a girl already in the sex trade, to leave her bondage—I have to appreciate the danger of her family situation." He pauses reflectively for a moment, then adds: "Don't forget, poverty kills, too!"

Some girls willingly elect to become prostitutes or strip-club dancers, assuming that the lifestyle could not be as hard as their current financial strife. More than a few have the image of Julia Roberts in *Pretty Woman* dancing around in their head. Recruiters tell the girl that she can make lots of money, live luxuriously, and perhaps even meet a wealthy man who might marry her. It may not be until the girl is working in a brothel in Paris or Barcelona, being forced to have sex with twelve johns a day, that she sees the folly of that dream.

Now that Padre Cesare has immersed himself deeper into the eastern European scene, he has uncovered how traffickers use young girls for other purposes beyond the brothels. He has met several girls who traveled to western Europe—some forcibly and others willingly—to serve as surrogate mothers for wealthy couples who cannot conceive a child. Prospective parents pay around six thousand dollars for the service. Typically the surrogate will live close by the customers during the course of the pregnancy and the delivery, after which time she may return to her home country. In most cases the paying clients have no clue that the girl might have been coerced to serve as a surrogate mother.

Padre Cesare has recently initiated a few experiments in microenterprises—offering small loans at low interest rates to individuals who want to start their own business—in order to offer young girls more financial options. He also tries to persuade wealthy Italian entrepreneurs to invest in the future of the former Soviet republics. He sees it as a simple formula: "If we create new jobs and stimulate economic development, it will proportionately reduce the risks that girls must take that lead to trafficking."

Regina Pacis works on a parallel track to reduce the demand for sex workers. Padre Cesare happily reports that his group played a key role in shutting down a sex-tourism agency in Chişinău that was supplying fifteen- and sixteen-year-old girls to Turkish men. A well-placed mole tipped his staff off to a stream of older men holding the hands of very young girls as they moved in and out of a downtown hotel. Upon further investigation, Regina Pacis found that the agency was openly promoting, in Turkey, full travel packages for "Moldovan sex holidays."

Padre Cesare delivered the evidence to the vice-director in charge of trafficking in Moldova, who promptly arrested the owners of the travel agency. He does not want to give the impression that the law always stands up to traffickers, however. "If we had taken our evidence to the run-of-the-mill police department, they would have thrown us in cages with bars," he remarks, only partly in jest.

All the same, Padre Cesare does report positive progress in his collaboration with government officials and legal authorities in Moldova to counter sex trafficking. Some police units, in fact, have invited the Regina Pacis staff to run workshops on how to identify girls who may be victims of trafficking.

The most dramatic sign of how far Regina Pacis has come in Moldova occurred in July 2006, when the president of Moldova granted national citizenship to Padre Cesare "in honor of his heroic work against human trafficking in our country."

LEVERAGING INTERNATIONAL DIPLOMACY

In October 2000 the U.S. Congress passed a vital piece of legislation. The Victims of Trafficking and Violence Protection Act commits the U.S. government to using its political and economic influence to impede human trafficking around the globe. Though legislation of this sort often turns out to be just highfalutin rhetoric, this act comes with sharp teeth. More details on the piece of legislation and its contribution to abolitionist work within the United States are provided in chapter 6.

On an international level, the legislation directs the U.S. State Department to issue an annual report evaluating the performance of individual governments as they confront and prosecute human traffickers. The report charts the incidence of trafficking within each country and examines the specific laws, policies, and practices that the government implements to resolve the problem. (Until 2010, the State Department did not evaluate the United States on its own performance toward human trafficking prevention, prosecution, and aftercare.)

A country's performance is ranked by its placement in one of three "tiers":

Tier 1: a country whose government complies fully with the act's minimum standards.

Tier 2: a country whose government does not comply with the act's minimum standards but is making significant efforts to bring itself into compliance with those standards.

Tier 3: a country whose government does not comply fully with the minimum standards and is not making a significant effort to do so.

The "teeth" of the act come into play in two ways. First, the State Department publicly releases the report for the entire world to see. It does so with the hope that inactive or offending governments will be sufficiently embarrassed to change their behavior. Second, those countries ranked as Tier 3 are subject to stiff sanctions, including cuts to foreign aid and U.S. opposition to its applications before the World Bank and the International Monetary Fund.

The State Department released its first *Trafficking in Persons (TIP) Report* in July 2001 to great fanfare and controversy. For utter disregard for trafficking within their borders, twenty-three countries were relegated to Tier 3, including Russia, Israel, South Korea, Romania, Albania, and Greece. Even the most cynical observer had to be pleased that the State Department objectively shamed even some of its closest political allies. It was disappointing, on the other hand, to see perched on Tier 1 several European countries, like the Netherlands and Germany, that have significant trafficking problems.

As might be expected, the countries that received abysmal marks cried foul and engaged in serious political lobbying leading up to the *2002 TIP Report*. Once that report was released, the United States' closest political allies had miraculously improved their performance. Abolitionist and human-rights groups expressed their displeasure that politics had so obviously influenced the report.

The *2009 TIP Report* confirms that bias plays a strong role in the evaluation process. Seventeen nations are relegated to Tier 3; among them can be found Cuba, Burma, North Korea, Sudan, Zimbabwe, Syria, and Iran. These nations just happen to be on not-so-friendly terms with the U.S. government. Meanwhile, countries like Albania, Romania, Serbia, Russia,

India, Israel, Turkey, and Thailand, all of which have abysmal records on trafficking, do not receive a Tier 3 ranking. Several of these countries do appear on a Tier 2 "Watch List," a category established in the *2004 TIP Report*. The countries on the Watch List teeter on the cliff above Tier 3. They show increasing numbers of trafficking victims and fail to demonstrate progress in complying with minimum standards of law enforcement. Again, it is not clear what it would take to tip these U.S. allies over the cliff and into Tier 3.

Despite the uneven application of the *TIP Report*, it nevertheless has the potential to be a very useful tool. The more evidence that abolitionist groups can collect and publicize on the performance of specific nations, the more difficult it will be for the State Department to sanitize the performance of any given country. The overall goal, of course, is to create tangible incentives for government action on trafficking.

Nadia: A Surprise Ending

Nadia considered herself very lucky to spend only a month in the brothel in Shkodër. The Albanian pimps kept the girls moving on a treadmill. On one single day, Nadia counted twenty-five individual encounters with men paying to have sex with her.

It was easy to pick out the girls who had "served a sentence" of more than six months in Shkodër. They looked utterly wasted. If a girl complained or demonstrated the least bit of resistance to her handlers, she would be treated harshly. Even if a girl acted 100 percent docile, the pimps would occasionally throw her a punch or put a gun to her head as a reminder. They beat one girl so badly that they had to remove her from the brothel, and Nadia never saw her again.

Nadia's age turned out to be her salvation; at twenty-two, she was considered over-the-hill. "We have sold you to the Italians," the cruelest of the pimps revealed to her out of the blue one day. "They don't mind old hens in Rome, I guess," he scoffed.

The next night Nadia was sitting in a motorized rubber raft once again. But this boat was at least four times the size of the dinghy that had carried her into Albania. If the dinghy operated like a taxi, this raft was a bus. Nearly forty passengers of all ages—even a mother who cradled a baby in one arm and sat a toddler on her knee—crammed into the boat.

Once they had moved off the shore some distance, the sea turned rough. The boat carried them up and down steep water valleys. Passengers who leaned their heads over the side of the raft to vomit more often than not received a sharp slap of water in the face. The children at first screamed in terror and then whimpered.

Two Albanian goons sat at the front, keeping a watch for any sign of lights from Italian coast-guard crafts. The pilot had his hands full keeping the boat heading straight into the waves lest they get sideswiped.

Even though it was pitch-black out, Nadia kept her eyes tightly shut. She tried to focus on Stefan, wondering how her son might be faring back in Chişinău. Tears streamed down her cheeks as she admitted to herself that she would likely never see him again.

She opened her eyes and saw bright lights on the distant shore ahead. "Italy?" she asked one of the goons positioned in front of her.

"Yes, Italy," he said without looking back at her.

Nadia lost her mind for a moment. "Italy? Italy? Italy?" she kept repeating, now practically screaming.

"Damn it! I already told you! It's Italy over there," growled the goon angrily.

That afternoon before she had boarded the raft, the cruelest of the pimps had handed her a plastic baggie. Inside she could see her passport, a bit of Italian money, and a small card with scribbled text.

"When you reach the beach near San Foca, your new owner will be waiting," he said. "If for some reason you get lost, I have given you his phone number and enough money to make a phone call. He will drive you to Rome, where you will work for him."

Nadia nodded. He took the gun from his belt nonetheless and put it to her head. "If you try to escape, we will hunt you down. There would be no place to hide; we have people on both sides of the sea."

Now, perched in the hull of the raft, she had a more pressing concern. The pilot had taken the boat within twenty yards of shore, and the Albanians were yelling for everyone to jump out before the authorities detected them. Those passengers who did not comply got forcibly tossed into the sea.

Nadia jumped into the sea, and water gushed up her nose. Then, as the waves crested, she lost contact with the sandy floor and took in large gulps of salty water. She floated, stumbled, and fought her way to shore. A number of other passengers washed ashore on the beach at about the same moment. After a pause to gain their bearings, they all made a chaotic rush to get off the beach and avoid detection.

Nadia slept until daylight, nestled in a crevice in the middle of three large rocks. The sound of a loud horn jarred her awake. Peeking over the top of the rocks, she saw a roadway no more than fifty yards in the distance. She reached inside her pants to see if the plastic baggie had survived her ordeal, and she was pleased to discover that all the documents had remained dry.

Now Nadia had to consider her next move. She knew the fate awaiting her if she called her new owner. She could never willingly go back to that hell. If the Mafia wanted to track her down, so be it.

Absent a plan, she started walking in search of food. It did not take her long to reach San Foca. She used her "phone money" to buy a loaf of bread at a small bakery and started eating it greedily as soon as she hit the sidewalk. Propped against the wall of the bakery, she luxuriated as the sun came out brightly to take away the shivers that had troubled her sleep.

During the course of the morning, the owner of the bakery strolled outside her shop and noticed that Nadia had not left. Based on their brief encounter, she realized that Nadia did not understand Italian. Taking a look at her ragged appearance, the woman guessed that Nadia had recently washed ashore from Albania.

"Regina Pacis?" the woman asked.

Nadia shrugged her arms to indicate that she did not understand.

"Regina Pacis?" the woman repeated, saying the words slowly this time. "Padre Cesare?"

Once again, Nadia gave her a puzzled look. The woman smiled and gestured for Nadia to wait on the sidewalk. She went inside and made a call to the shelter.

Nadia did not know it at the time, but her torturous trek had reached its end. Years later—long after she had married a man from the village and Stefan had joined her in San Foca—she would walk by that bakery wall and smile. It was there, at that spot, that the sun had come out brightly to take her shivers away.

THE CAMPAIGN: TRACKING THE SLAVE TRADE IN EUROPE

In 2010 the Not For Sale Campaign opened an office in Herrnhut, located in eastern Germany, near the Czech and Polish borders, a region strategic for monitoring sex trafficking. We are deliberating opening a second office in Amsterdam. In both locales traffickers bring young woman from across the globe—above all from China, Russia, and the former republics of the Soviet Union—to sell as "pleasure" commodities.

I made a visit to Chişinău, Moldova, in late 2009, eager to learn the latest developments in sex trafficking across Europe. When I told local residents that the next stop on my journey would take me to Amsterdam, several responded in a half-joking manner, "Oh, well, you'll meet many of our finest young women there." In the days that followed in Amsterdam, I indeed did encounter an entire shop-window mall dedicated to human merchandise from Moldova and other countries in eastern Europe. The casual acceptance of "legalized exploitation" in Amsterdam and the vaunted "fast-food sex highway" in Herrnhut should shame all Europeans into abolitionist action.

The early mission of the Campaign's European office focuses on training researchers in how to identify and document both victims and survivors in specific regions, and to nurture trusted relationships with law-enforcement agencies willing to pursue intervention when warranted. The data that these investigations yield will be critical in our advocacy for stronger laws to prosecute traffickers and provide enhanced support for the survivors. Individuals wanting to join the Campaign in Europe will find training dates and volunteer opportunities at www .NotForSaleCampaign.org.

Sheltering the Lost Children

Peru

We often look at heroes and think, "I so admire who they are, but I could never do what they do." The truth is that a heroic path usually begins with a humble act that opens a gate into a new universe.

Lucy Borja passed through that portal in 1991. She reached out to help two boys—both around twelve years old—who feared spending the night on the rugged streets of Peru's capital city, Lima.

She had only recently learned of the existence of a subculture of street kids. As part of an HIV/AIDS-prevention program she directed called Generación—literally "generation," as in "youth generation"—Lucy started visiting Peru's prisons for juveniles. The children shared with her their personal stories of life on the streets, where they faced the threat of violence daily. Sex traffickers had moved some of them to Lima from Peru's rural provinces, while others had fallen victim to poverty or sexual abuse at home.

The president of Peru at the time, Alberto Fujimori, declared that his government would "cleanse" the city of street kids. The dead bodies of several children showed up in city parks shortly thereafter; many more went missing. The street kids reported to Lucy that police used brute intimidation against them, putting a gun to their heads and pulling the trigger on an empty chamber.

So when Lucy met two young boys who were too frightened to spend another night on the streets, she invited them to sleep in the Generación office. She told them to extend the offer to any other child who shared their fears. Since Lucy already had plans to attend a family party that evening, she informed the custodian to give entry to any child who arrived at the office.

After her party ended, Lucy decided to check in with her young guests. She hoped that the custodian, upon meeting the ragged vagrants, had not balked at her instructions. She half expected to find the boys sitting on the curb in front of her office, locked out.

Street kids around the world suffer from a cascade of curses. A traumatic incident initially tears them away from their families. Once displaced, they become vulnerable to predators of every stripe: traffickers set traps to ensnare them; the police consider them outlaws; and "decent folk" regard them as less than human. The stigma of rejection brands their tiny bodies.

Lucy, indeed, had a surprise awaiting her that evening when she arrived at the Generación office. Her key unlocked the front door, but try as she might, she could not shove it open. It felt as if a rolled-up carpet had been lodged behind the door to block the entry. With the help of her sons, Lucy finally moved the door to create enough space to squeeze through.

As she reached blindly in the dark in search of the light switch, Lucy tripped over the "carpet roll." She deftly caught her balance and leaned her body against the wall. Her fingers searched the wall until she eventually found the light switch.

Once the light came on, Lucy looked down at her feet and discovered several young kids curled up on the floor sleeping, their bodies jammed against the door. She cast her vision around the room, though it was hard to register what she was seeing. Sleeping children covered every nook and cranny of the office. "I even found young kids snuggled tightly inside the cupboards where we stored our office supplies," Lucy recalls.

Lucy counted more than six hundred children who slept in the office that night. The word had passed like wildfire on the streets of Lima. Found: a safe shelter from the storm.

Lucy did not know all the details that caused these boys and girls to run scared, but she clearly sensed that her life would never be the same. "Stacked one against the other, asleep on the floor of my office, those children seemed so vulnerable," Lucy says in a slow, soft voice. "They had no one to be their advocate, to defend their rights," she adds. "I knew then what path I had to take."

Making a stand against injustice generally requires us to make some painful personal choices. Lucy soon found herself at one of those crossroads. The kids of Lima kept coming back to the office each night for sanctuary. Her Generación staff got fed up with this ongoing invasion. "You can't have both. It's either us or the kids," they told her.

"Okay, then, it's the kids," Lucy calmly answered.

SEX IN THE STREET

Save the Children, an international aid and children's-rights group based in Sweden, sponsored a team of investigative journalists to conduct a study of child sex trafficking in Peru in 2004. Their research was designed originally to focus on the johns—"to find out what goes on in the hearts and minds of human beings capable of violating the rights of [children]."[1] They cast their net wide and delivered one of the best analyses of sex trafficking of minors in a single country.

Due to the difficulty of getting perpetrators to openly admit to their illicit behavior, the journalists established a fictitious child-pornography magazine they called *Sex in the Street*. They placed employment ads—open positions for administrators, lawyers, writers, drivers, janitors, and more—in major Peruvian newspapers. Applicants from across the socioeconomic spectrum spoke openly with undercover investigators in "job interviews" about their background in the child sex industry and their understanding of the needs of that market.

The final report—published under the title *The Client Goes Unnoticed*—describes how traffickers run a sex trade in children that stretches across Peru. A substantial number of these kids eventually end up on the streets of Lima. Sadly, Save the Children investigators found "very few organizations currently assisting prostituted children and adolescents, and it is very disturbing that there is no effective support from the state to incorporate these young people into the country's labor."[2] The research, in fact, confirms that Generación practically stands alone—with only a handful of courageous allies—in its fight to protect sexually exploited children and bring justice to the streets of Lima.

Sandra: Biography of a Sex Trafficker

Sandra does not match the stereotype of a dangerous pimp. She agreed to be interviewed in exchange for a box of diapers for her newborn child. As the baby fed off her breast, Sandra shared her disturbing passage from street urchin to sex trafficker.

A consistent thread emerges in her story: Sandra is a survivor. She never knew her father. Her grandmother and mother raised her with meager resources. When she turned eight, they kicked her out with explicit orders that she not return until she had some money to contribute to the household income. Sandra slept in the streets of Lima for several nights, and it scared her to death. So she returned home, hoping that her mother and grandmother might have missed her and would reconsider their ultimatum.

"So, did you bring any money back with you?" her grandmother asked as soon as Sandra passed through the door.

"Grandma, no one wants to pay an eight-year-old to work," Sandra replied tearfully. "And it is scary out there alone."

"Don't be such a baby," her grandmother replied unsympathetically. "Your mother and I have a hard enough time feeding ourselves."

"But, Grandma, it's dangerous—" Her grandmother's slap across her face cut Sandra off in midsentence.

"Now, get out of here. Come back when you have cash."

Sandra ran out the door, her eyes blurred by a flood of tears.

CHILDREN ARE NOT PROSTITUTES

Young boys and girls in every city on the globe today are forced to serve as sex slaves. Sex traffickers target twelve- to seventeen-year-old children as their choice candidates. The johns who pay regular visits to brothels prefer adolescents above any other age group. Looked at from the cold perspective of a slaveholder, adolescents also have a longer shelf life. Any older and they start to lose their youthful appeal. Any younger and they may draw the attention of law-enforcement authorities.

Because sex trafficking masks itself as prostitution, the general public does not feel outraged. The children are perceived to be criminals or sexual deviants or, at best, victims of their environment: desperate for survival, the kids "choose" to sell their bodies for profit.

The real criminals hide in the shadows. An illicit network of traffickers, pimps, recruiters, brothel owners, and johns prey on vulnerable kids and force them into a life of sexual commerce. Once the inner workings of that criminal network are exposed, common sense prevails. Of course a child would not volunteer for the repeated trauma of ten (or more) grown men penetrating their bodies every evening. We have a word for exploiting minors that way: *rape*.

It should be noted that the same mechanisms of financial bondage and violent intimidation that enslave children are practiced on females of all ages. Adult "prostitutes," too, can recount shocking testimonies of pimps locking them in closets, flogging them with coat hangers, and forcing them to service a staggering number of clients. The pimps quite explicitly refer to these women as "my property" and will attack anyone who acts to compromise their control.

Without a doubt, we need a more nuanced understanding of prostitution. Katherine Chon, cofounder of the Polaris Project, a Washington, D.C.–based service provider and advocacy organization, points to a conversation she had with a Korean woman in her early twenties who she suspected was a victim of sex trafficking. When Katherine asked the woman whether she had been coerced into coming to the United States to work in the sex trade, the woman adamantly denied that was the case.

Katherine decided to change her tack: "Well, on a scale of 0 to 100 percent, how much control do you feel you have over your decisions each day to continue selling your body to men?"

Given the flow of the conversation up to that point, Katherine expected the woman to give a response that might fall close to 90 percent. But after considering for a few seconds, the woman gave Katherine a surprising answer: "Oh, I'd say maybe 5 percent."

Confused by her answer, Katherine started digging a bit deeper: "So why do you feel such loyalty for the owner of the brothel where you work?"

"The owner told me that if I got into trouble, she would bail me out of jail and pay for an attorney," the Korean woman replied. "I am not from here [the United States]; the police can do bad things to you, so I need security." The Korean woman went on to explain that the brothel owner also keeps possession of all her "savings." If she were to leave the brothel, the owner would not give her the money back. Her pimp also provides her protection, though he threatens to beat her if she tries to leave him.

Is she a slave? It would not be much of a stretch to identify her as such, even though she technically does not live under lock and key. Sadly, the woman herself rejects the label. She has come to accept her destiny; the coercion weaves so seamlessly into her surroundings that she no longer recognizes it as a chain.

Coercing children into the sex trade entails much less ambiguity. The actual process of enslavement varies from place to place; the most influential independent variable is the strength of law enforcement in a particular region. Research across five continents uncovers a disturbingly common pattern in child

sex trafficking, regardless of whether international crime networks are involved or the operation runs on a regional level
with ad hoc players. The process of enslavement involves five
predictable elements:

Recruitment. Traffickers target children most commonly
from communities that lack social power, at times with the
consent of the victims' parents.

Extraction. Traffickers remove recruits from their home
community and shift them to a destination where they are
unlikely to get support from law-enforcement bodies or the
general citizenry.

Control. Slaveholders seek control over every aspect of the
child's life so that escape becomes unthinkable.

Violence. Slaveholders exercise violence as a means to reinforce their control and ensure compliance.

Exploitation. Slaveholders show slight regard for the physical or emotional health of the child in their pursuit of financial gain.

Lucy Borja: Dark Alleys and Bright Office Lights

The street kids kept coming back to Lucy's shelter. After one
especially brutal incident in a city square, she had to find medical attention for eighteen kids that the police had shot.

Generación had to evolve into something more than a short-
term crisis shelter—of that Lucy had no doubt. She above all
wanted to bring some normalcy and structure into the lives of
the children.

Lucy has a remarkable gift for connecting with youth in crisis. Despite being a grandmother in her mid-sixties, she builds an easy rapport with them and earns their trust. At almost any minute of the day she can be found surrounded by a cadre of kids. Their high-paced energy does not seem to overwhelm her. In fact, Lucy keeps steadfastly calm: she neither demands attention nor deems it necessary to use a loud voice to bring order. Yet she can exercise a steely determination when the occasion warrants it.

Once the first wave of street kids made Generación their home base, Lucy established a rule: to stay at the shelter, the kids had to attend school. Although the teens could work in the morning hours, they had to attend classes in the after-noons.

Soon after "Lucy's rule" took effect, a group of seven Generación boys—from fourteen to sixteen years old—found work at a hair salon. About a month after they were hired, Lucy asked the boys about their jobs. When they told her that they cleaned dishes and washed bedsheets and towels, she became suspicious: the tasks did not seem like the kind that would be required at a hair salon. Lucy checked her sources and discovered that the hair salon was a front for a brothel. She urged the boys to quit their jobs without delay.

The boys went to the salon the next day to collect their earnings and inform the managers that they would be leav-ing. The women offered to pay them in sex with the young girls whom they controlled. They put a pornographic movie on the television and told the boys to go to the back rooms of the salon and select a girl. When the boys refused and de-manded cash for their wages, the managers locked the doors to the salon and said they could not leave until they performed sex with their girls. The boys became quite upset and began ransacking the premises. The managers called the police and reported that street kids were vandalizing their property. All of the boys were arrested except one, who escaped out a back window and ran back to the Generación office to inform Lucy about what had taken place.

When Lucy arrived at the local police station, the officers in charge claimed that they did not know anything about the incident. In actual fact, they were holding the boys in a cell at the station. So Lucy reported the incident to a judge of the court, Regina Chavez, a woman of high integrity. Judge Chavez made a personal visit to the salon and found a library of homemade pornographic movies featuring minors. The judge found additional evidence to convince her that the salon was, indeed, operating as a brothel.

A few hours after Judge Chavez had completed her investigation, the police showed up at Generación to arrest Lucy on charges of trespassing and impersonating a judge of the court. Judge Chavez promptly exposed the setup and confirmed that she herself had entered the salon.

A subsequent court investigation revealed what motivated the police actions. The salon was located directly across the street from an office building for several important government agencies, including the police headquarters for Lima. Many of the salon's regular clients walked in from their offices across the street.

Bit by bit Lucy began to put together the pieces of the puzzle. "The criminals exploiting children in Peru do not only hang out in dark alleys," she explains. "They also sit comfortably behind desks in the halls of power."

TRAFFICKING CHILDREN: RECRUITMENT AND EXTRACTION

Only on rare occasions will a sex trafficker abduct a child from a neighborhood that enjoys social power. Doing so carries too high a risk. A family from an empowered community is more apt to mobilize legal and political authorities to conduct an extensive search for an abducted child. If caught, recruiters face a higher probability of prosecution and place their entire operation at risk. Why would recruiters take that risk when so many candidates can be found in relatively powerless neighborhoods?

Furthermore, recruiters can deceive destitute families more easily with promises of a better life. The allure of a steady job may cause parents to overlook the risks of sending their child off to a faraway destination. Teenagers might be promised a modeling job in another country, or less glamorous yet high-paying work in a restaurant or a retail store. Parents of young children in rural areas are told that a wealthy family in the big city needs a domestic servant or a nanny. These offers are crafted to extract children from the reaches of those who might care for them. Recruiters have no intention of fulfilling their promises, of course; they intend to sell the children to a brothel owner at their first opportunity. But their game depends on maintaining the illusion of a golden path out of the depressed conditions that the families face.

In that regard, lower-middle-class families with heightened aspirations can be as vulnerable to traffickers as the most impoverished family. A shortcut to upward social mobility holds tremendous appeal.

Consider the case of Lan, a seventeen-year-old Laotian girl living in Bangkok. Her mother migrated to Thailand with Lan and her two siblings when the children were all under the age of ten. The mother worked in a local street market, and the children worked with her in the family business. Years passed, and the family's hard work lifted them out of dire poverty. Lan works today in a luxury tourist hotel in Bangkok as a waitress. She owns her own car and a modest wardrobe of fashionable Western clothes.

Lan has tasted enough of the "good life" to entertain aspirations for an even more glamorous lifestyle. Her best friend met an American visiting Bangkok on a business trip, and he occasionally sends her friend a plane ticket to meet him in some exotic holiday spot. The American recently invited Lan along and sent her a plane ticket, too. Despite the prevalence of sex trafficking in Thailand, this invitation did not raise a red flag for Lan. She, in fact, aspires to find a "friend" who will offer her nice gifts and travel like her friend receives. It will be only a matter of time before a well-heeled trafficker will ensnare Lan unless her naivete changes.

Abolitionists fighting sex trafficking around the globe report that parents at times sell their kids so that they can make an improvement on their home or purchase a vehicle or other consumer item. These stories align with a report in the *New York Times* that parents in Albania sold their children to traffickers so they could buy a color television.[3]

Nonetheless, the sex trafficker who deals in children usually wants to extract recruits from their home region as expeditiously as possible. When kidnapping is involved, the trafficker has more reason to fear arrest. Even if the parents of the abducted child do not get involved, an adult relative or friend may advocate for the child and press the police to take action.

An anonymous individual who bears the stigma of "child

prostitute," on the other hand, is much less likely to have an advocate. Foreign children evoke even less sympathy than those who share the nationality or ethnicity of the mainstream population. For that reason, traffickers typically shift child slaves to the other side of the country or, even more effectively, across an ocean.

In that regard, Save the Children investigators discovered that kids who are trafficked from the rural regions of Peru become invisible to law-enforcement officials in the capital: "It is alarming to view the impunity with which networks trafficking in minors operate in [Lima], in full view of authorities who not only do nothing, but who . . . also do not consider that children and adolescents are people who need to be defended and protected."[4]

The story of nine-year-old Guadalupe in Lima illustrates a more unusual case: how a parent and a trafficker might work together as allies. Guadalupe's mother had made a financial arrangement with a pimp to "employ" her daughter. As a way to introduce very young girls into sex commerce, pimps in Lima commonly place them on the street only to tempt passing clients. Once a john stops and inquires of her availability, the pimp will bring in a slightly older, more experienced girl to turn the trick. This bait-and-switch role does not last long, especially once the pimp has made a tidy sum selling the young girl (usually multiple times) as a virgin.

Fortunately, Guadalupe met a street counselor from Generación before the pimp had the opportunity to sell her off as a virgin. She moved into one of Generación's high-security shelters, where the pimp could not touch her. Guadalupe's mother then visited the shelter and demanded her daughter back. At great institutional risk, Generación denied the mother her request; the staff knew what Guadalupe's fate would be if they relented.

Neither Generación nor any other child-service agency wants to be in a position where it has to wrestle with parents over the well-being of their children. But abolitionists have to deal with an uncomfortable truth: not every parent has come to the firm conviction that a child, their child, is not for sale.

Sandra: The Temporary Gardener

Sandra eventually met up with other street kids who shared her lot. They traveled in packs, finding safety in numbers. After police officers threatened one night to make her gang of friends "disappear," she crashed at a shelter called Generación for the first time. It became her home for the next seven years.

Most of Sandra's friends had given up on the option of going back to their families: those bridges had been burned and would never be rebuilt. But Sandra still hoped that she could prove herself worthy to move back in with her mother and grandmother.

Generación began creating jobs for the kids. Noting that the parks in Lima were poorly maintained, Lucy proposed to city officials that they hire the kids of Generación to be Lima's public gardeners. With characteristic panache, Lucy called it a "landscaping company" in order to leave the door open for future development. As the kids improved their skills, they could shift upmarket and offer landscaping services as well.

Sandra, now twelve years old, was one of the first kids to sign up for gardening work. But after only a couple of weeks of labor, she visited the city contractor and demanded her pay. The supervisor told her that she would be paid at the end of the month along with everyone else. Sandra threw down her rake and quit on the spot.

The city supervisor just scratched his head. He had never met a young kid so eager to get her hands on money.

Lucy Borja: The Dangerous Games Adults Play

Lucy Borja easily qualifies as one of the most controversial living figures in all of Peru. At last count, she has had more than twenty legal denunciations against her in Lima's courts, including charges of kidnapping children, giving false testimony to the police, and "acting against the public interest." On any given day it is not unusual for a political figure to make a disparaging remark about her on the evening news.

To meet Lucy—and track her movements over a substantial period of time—confounds all expectations. She is neither argumentative nor cantankerous; in fact, her gentle spirit and compassion lead some people to call her the Mother Teresa of the streets of Lima.

How can we square this bipolar public image? It's quite simple: Lucy speaks the truth about what she sees around her. That habit can create formidable enemies in Peru.

On Mother's Day in 1992, for example, Lucy received an invitation to participate in a press conference at the juvenile prison, along with the wife of President Fujimori and Ana Kanashiro, the national director for children's welfare. Once the press conference began, Kanashiro proudly announced to a television audience that the national government had set aside $5 million to resolve "the problem of street children." The symbolism of making this pronouncement at the juvenile prison was not lost on anyone.

When the camera turned to the founder of Generación, she proposed that rather than use government funds to punish exploited children, the money should be used to open "healthy homes" for them. Lucy referred to the hundreds of street kids who slept in her office each night. "While children in the prisons are ill treated," she said, "the street kids at Generación study in the classroom and develop life skills that will move them in a new direction."

Kanashiro was livid at being upstaged, and from that day forward she made it known that Lucy was to be banned from visiting the juvenile prison and from providing HIV/AIDS courses in the public schools. A friend of Lucy's in the national congress rose to her defense. She distributed for television broadcast a video of interviews with children testifying to their treatment inside juvenile prison and the trumped-up charges that incarcerated them. A major television personality in Peru, Juan Carlos, watched the interviews and became inspired to produce a series of special reports on the struggles of street kids in Lima.[5]

Overjoyed that a news reporter of his stature would be interested in their cause, Lucy arranged for Carlos to portray the stories of three young boys who lived at Generación. Carlos devoted a considerable amount of time to interviewing the boys and filming their daily activities. Using Generación as a base, the journalist then dove deep into the netherworld of street life. He filmed the story of Alicia, a young girl who for many years dressed as a man so that she would not be raped on the streets. His short documentaries ran on national television and won critical acclaim both inside Peru and internationally, even winning a prestigious cultural award from the United Nations Educational, Scientific, and Cultural Organization (UNESCO).

Lucy, however, could not enjoy watching the documentaries. Just as Carlos was wrapping up production, the kids at Generación berated her for bringing him into their lives. The boys divulged how Carlos had supplied them with drugs and then raped them. One of the more memorable scenes in his documentary shows street kids using drugs and alcohol at a popular street hangout. In actual fact, the boys reported, Carlos had bought the substances and distributed them before he started filming. It was the first time that many of the younger kids had ever used drugs.

The kids also reported to Lucy that Carlos had exploited his connection to Alicia. He paid her to find young children and bring them to his own house for sex; later he had her pimp children to the homes of his friends as well.

It saddens Lucy today to look back and recognize the pivotal role that Juan Carlos played in the buildup of sex trafficking in Lima. Up until that point, the child sex industry was more or less opportunistic: an adult might find a child in desperate circumstances and induce him or her to engage in sex for money. Carlos initiated a more systematic practice of trafficking.

Alicia, for example, began recruiting kids into the sex trade at his urging and went on to become one of the country's most notorious pimps. Yet try as she might, Lucy could not bring Juan Carlos to justice. The courts would never convict a man of his stature based solely on the testimony of street kids, and that was the only hard evidence she had. Nonetheless, Lucy reported his criminal activities to the police and persistently urged them to investigate.

In a vicious retaliation, Carlos produced a television news report on Generación that he called *The House of Terror: Where Children Go to Contract AIDS*. But his assault on the shelter's reputation backfired. When a judge ordered that the kids at Generación undergo HIV testing, not one of the kids tested positive.

The kids actually turned the tables and testified to the judge about Carlos's sexual crimes with minors. Worried about a possible arrest, Carlos fled the country and worked for many years as a journalist in the United States. Years later, however, he returned to Peru and resumed his successful television career.

TRAFFICKING CHILDREN: CONTROL AND VIOLENCE

Once traffickers extract victims from their home community, they typically sell the children to slaveholders who deal in commercial sex—for example, pimps or the owners of strip clubs, sex bars, brothels, karaoke clubs, or massage parlors. Most traffickers have a steady relationship in place with the slaveholder; hence, they know who the buyer will be before they recruit the child. Although it is more rare, some traffickers act as both recruiter and operator of their own "retail" sex shop.

The slaveholder acts swiftly to take complete control of the child's life. Passports, birth certificates, national identity cards, and any other documents of citizenship are stripped from the child's possession. The child is kept closely guarded and locked in a room when not accompanied. Even if escape were possible, the child has no money, probably does not speak the local language, and does not know to whom he or she could turn for help. Given their past experience, slave children would not instinctively trust public officials or the police.

The slaveholder also generally manipulates a relationship of financial dependence with the child. Basic life necessities like food, clothing, and shelter are charged to the child's "account." Until that money is repaid, the child is obligated to continue in the slaveholder's service.

Slaveholders will buttress these social controls with the constant threat of violence. Almost all trafficked children will testify that they were victims of an extreme act of violence within the first forty-eight hours of their abduction. Whether through rape or brutal beatings, slaveholders use violence to imprint their dominance. In the logic of the trafficking world, a terrified child is a compliant child. The slaveholder, therefore, will never let the child slip out of a state of terror.

Cowboys refer to "breaking the spirit of a wild horse"; in a macabre sense, that is how slaveholders approach child sex slaves. The sex slaves will have to learn to comply happily with whatever sexual act a client requests. The liberal application of violence early on will crack the resistance they will inevitably mount. If a client ever complains that the sex slave was less than accommodating, swift and brutal punishment will be meted out.

The threat of violence becomes a ubiquitous force in the life of a sex slave. The child knows that a failed escape attempt would result in a severe beating. Moreover, the slaveholder may threaten to harm the child's family even if the child does manage to get away. To remind the child of that fact, the slaveholder may occasionally drop some piece of current news about family members, whether real or fabricated, as if to say, "Yes, I am watching them, so don't do anything stupid."

Dina, a sixteen-year-old girl who currently finds refuge at Generación's center for rescued sex slaves, relates how she spent four years under the control of a pimp because she feared for her family's welfare. She has three younger sisters and a brother. The pimp threatened to pursue them as replacements if she ever left him. He would taunt Dina with a diet of comments: "Hey, I saw your sister on the bus in Lima this afternoon. Geez, *chica,* she is turning out to be as pretty as you."

Many mornings Dina would wake up and tell herself that she could not spend one more day in her hell. But then she would see a mental image of her sisters, and she would steel herself to endure whatever might come her way.

Sandra: Pimping for a Living

After Juan Carlos initiated Alicia into pimping, she evolved a lucrative trafficking operation. Her strategy to train a network of pimps to serve as her agents on the streets turned into a big success.

Alicia convinced Sandra that she could make a ton of money trafficking young children. As a recruiter, Sandra would earn a piece of the action every time the child engaged a paying client. As the queen pimp, Alicia also would earn a share off of Sandra's recruits. Their third financial partner would be a *mami* who would give the child a place to live, usually in a hotel, though sometimes in a private residence.

Sandra, then fifteen and no longer living at Generación, quickly earned a reputation as one of the toughest pimps on the street. Her style of recruitment was not very sophisticated. She would spot a child walking alone in the streets—whether day or night, it made no difference. Acting quickly, she dialed any one of a number of taxi drivers who formed part of the trafficking network. After informing the driver of her location, she would move in on her target and concoct some excuse to start a conversation. Then, once the cab pulled up along the curb, she would force the child inside the car, using violence if necessary. Sometimes the taxi drivers would rape the child; other times they would sell the "virgin rights" to a client.

The taxi driver would return the child to Sandra after the rape. He would be sure to give the child a dollar or two for "the service." As soon as the shell-shocked victim stepped out of the cab, Sandra shifted into psychological coercion. "Now that you have lost your virginity, you might as well keep making money with me," she would say matter-of-factly. "Face it. You're now a tramp."

The victim at this stage is wholly disoriented and traumatized, so Sandra delivers the child to the *mami*. At the first meeting, the *mami* shows motherly warmth and sympathy. She offers the child secure accommodations and provides a hot meal and maybe new clothes. Each of these "expressions of sympathy" gets the tab running on the debt the child will owe the *mami*.

Though the child does not yet realize it, she (or he) has just become a sex slave.

Lucy Borja: Extending the Family

It does not feel right to call Generación an "agency" or an "orphanage" or even a "shelter." It does fulfill all of these important roles for the children who go there for help. But none of these labels conveys the sense of extended family that permeates the place.

Certainly it starts with Lucy, who makes a personal connection with every child who walks through Generación's doors. Mention a particular resident's name, and she can rattle off the child's history, habits, passions, strengths, and weaknesses.

Thousands of youths have run to Generación over the past two decades, and Lucy is mother to them all.

Lucy forgives all failures and betrayals, of which there are many. One mention of Sandra, and Lucy's face fills with pain. She knows full well what has become of the little girl who first came to Generación when she was eight years old. Ironically, Lucy now strives to rescue the children whom Sandra seeks to enslave. "I really do believe that down deep she wants to change, to be a different person," Lucy says, refusing to give up on her "prodigal daughter." Then, as if speaking to herself, she adds softly, "One day she will find her way."

The family atmosphere at Generación extends to Lucy's husband, Juan Enrique, and their five grown children, who also embrace the street kids as their own. Lucy's children grew up with a constant stream of visitors invading their home, so it would be understandable if they felt some bitterness about having had to share their mother. If they harbor such sentiments, it does not show. Now that they are adults, the children still chip in passionately to help their mother.

One of Generación's most dynamic programs revolves around surfing. Lucy's own children are avid surfers, and they infuse the younger street kids with their love for riding waves. Generación now runs a house in a coastal town about an hour from Lima, and fifteen to eighteen kids live there full-time. It is a remarkable scene to head down to the beach late in the afternoon and watch a pack of ex–street kids mixing in with the local surf bums. Some of Generación's kids are now entering surfing competitions and performing at a high level.

Juan Enrique, Lucy's husband, has partnered with Save the Children programs in Latin America for twenty-five years. An erudite and reflective man, he has helped to establish graduate programs for children's-rights advocates at major universities around the world. Juan Enrique and Lucy offer the perfect complement of academic and activist, all in the service of abolition.

Save the Children, in turn, has been a good friend to Generación. The children's-rights agency bought an enormous house in 1994 that Lucy used rent free to house the street kids. The office was never a suitable place to shelter so many children, but Lucy did not have the finances to fund an alternative. In the ensuing years, Generación set up more-specialized shelters for teen mothers with children and females of all ages recently rescued from sex trafficking.

Generación approaches its mission like a family that has suddenly adopted hundreds of children. First off, it aims to rescue children in crisis and offer them a safe living environment. Next, it aims to equip the children with the education and work skills they will need to be self-sufficient young adults. Lucy aims to get the kids involved in school as soon as they are emotionally able to handle it. She often has to negotiate with public school principals who do not want to accept street kids into their classrooms. Finally, Generación wants to give its youth, as they move into adolescence, meaningful jobs that offer a positive work experience.

The landscaping company evolved into a true success story despite government interference. During the decade after it was launched, more than three hundred former street kids were provided with daily labor for wages in Lima's parks. The managers of the company grew up in Generación and developed into responsible leaders.

All the same, Lucy has a good laugh at her own expense whenever she speaks about Generación's business ventures.

She spawns microenterprises not because she has a passion for business; in fact, she considers herself an inept entrepreneur. But when she sees a critical need, she rolls up her sleeves and figures out a solution. She dreams of the day when a skilled business professional will roll into town and offer to build companies that transform the lives of the employees. "Work," Lucy stresses, "is both therapy and empowerment for former sex slaves."

TRAFFICKING CHILDREN: AN INDUSTRY OF EXPLOITATION

The classic concept of prostitution invokes the image of a client who pays a sole individual for sexual activity. Most johns like to maintain this illusion because they do not like to think of their "date" as a sex slave. As Save the Children investigators exposed, "[The clients] say that because they do not use violence to force the child or adolescent to have sex, the situation does not violate the minor's human rights. They do not identify the children and adolescents as victims of sexual exploitation."[6]

Most people are vaguely aware, however, that women and children who sell their bodies for sex rarely operate independently. Even in the movies, pimps control the activities of the prostitutes.

But the tentacles of the sex industry go much deeper. An entire underground economy is built around sex slaves. Whether it's Munich or Phnom Penh or Lima, similar economic sectors profit from exploitation.

The conference industry serves as a useful analogy. Major cities hire an entire staff to persuade professional associations and trade groups to host an annual convention or other big event in their city. Not only does the city's convention facility benefit from a successful bid; so do the city's hotels, restaurants, night clubs, taxis, airports, and so on. In other words, a major conference delivers a financial bonanza across the city's commercial sector.

In like manner, the growth of the sex industry in a city like Lima benefits many parties, but much of the money flows through underground channels. Nevertheless, it is safe to say that a substantial number of Lima's hotels could not survive without the sex trade. The financial interdependence that the sex trade spins can be observed even when scaled down to the micro-level. A single child trafficked into the center of Lima brings a significant bonanza to the owner of the hotel where the victim is lodged. The food vendors and bars in the immediate vicinity will benefit from the daily visits of a dozen johns. They will, in fact, negotiate deals with sex slaves to bring the johns into their place in exchange for a free meal. Multiply these connections thousands of times over, and a lucrative industry begins to take shape.

The only people who do not reap financial benefits from the sex industry are the ones upon whom the whole network depends: the slaves.

Sandra: The Long Road Back

The last person in the world that the Generación staff expected to find knocking at the door of their shelter for rescued sex workers was Sandra, and she was holding the hand of a tiny eight-year-old girl. The child had bloodstains on her face and severe scrapes and bruises on her limbs. "Please take this girl in," Sandra told the director of the shelter. "She was badly treated by a john today, and she won't survive another day on the streets." Once the director agreed to help, Sandra turned and walked away.

The news of this good deed certainly brought a smile to Lucy's face. She hoped Sandra had started to "find her way," as she has hoped for so long. But even Lucy knows that the road back is a long one.

Sandra, now twenty-four years old, has given birth to two children. In many respects, she feels trapped in the same dilemma that has long cursed her life: how to make the money she needs to go "back home." The father of her kids is currently in jail. It pains him to see Sandra work in sex trafficking, so he twice has tried to steal a big chunk of money that would allow her to walk away from that life. On each occasion he landed in jail, and Sandra's cycle of desperation continues.

Lucy paid a visit to Sandra after her good deed with the little girl. She delivered a message that Sandra had heard many times before but that has never lost its power to move her: "I am always here for you, my Sandra, but I cannot walk the path for you."

Lucy Borja: Justice at the Center

Lucy dedicates herself wholly to the children who live on the fringes of her society. She does not view a single relationship as a waste of her time. But no matter how many kids she rescues from the gutter, more arrive to take their place. "Nothing will change for street kids until we put justice at the center of our society," she declares. "At the moment, we are ruled by corruption and greed."

To make her point, she tells the story of a failed mission to rescue an eleven-year-old Generación girl who had fallen into sex slavery. The girl just disappeared one day, and no one knew where she went. A few weeks passed, and then Lucy received a phone call from a former street kid who had sighted the missing girl. She had entered a known brothel in the company of an older man.

Despite the prevalence of the child sex trade in Peru, the law states that sex with a minor is a crime. So Lucy was able to persuade three members of the local police force to go with her to the hotel and intervene on the girl's behalf. While two police officers waited outside with Lucy, one officer went inside and found the john with the little girl. But instead of arresting the john, he led him out a back door and allowed him to escape. One can only guess that he received a bribe for his favor. The little girl, on the other hand, was arrested and taken to the police station.

Outrageous, certainly, but not out of the ordinary in the streets of the poor. "We need a police force and a judicial system that are incorruptible and will defend the rights of every citizen," Lucy stresses. "To say that the poor have rights means to accept that street children hold the exact same value as our own children. Our society is not yet ready to affirm this truth."

THE CAMPAIGN:
HELPING LUCY AND THE CHILDREN OF PERU

Proving the cherished value of abandoned kids has been the hallmark of Lucy's work. Sadly, she has received scant financial support from the United States in the past. So there was no doubt that the Not For Sale Campaign would help her build shelters, launch business opportunities, and engage in the lives of her ever-increasing extended family. After all, one of the

Campaign's cofounders is Luis Enrique "Kique" Bazan, one of Lucy's sons. I guess you could say we know of Lucy's effectiveness firsthand.

In 2009, the Campaign built Veronica's House, a facility dedicated to the memory of a young Peruvian girl who was strangled to death by her john. The house provides a safe haven for young "Veronicas" who have been trafficked for sex. It's a place where they can live, learn, and be loved. The property is also home to a vocational center where the girls who come to Veronica's House can learn trade skills geared toward reducing their vulnerability to being trafficked a second time.

The Campaign has created opportunities for the children to pursue surfing, music lessons, or paid work, or to catch up in school. Be it riding a surfboard across Peru's emerald waves or learning a trade at the new vocational center, Generación's youth show their potential: they can flourish in a family environment where they feel loved, protected, and free.

Sex trafficking in children can be a heavy scene and leave the abolitionist in despair. Constantly at odds with government corruption, Lucy has had three homes for the children closed. In many cases, she retains ownership of the house but is not allowed to set foot on the grounds. Yet the children provide constant inspiration for Lucy, and her calling is one that comes from a personal commitment. "Every child deserves a mother who will look out for them, who will protect them and love them. I've raised five children of my own, yet I feel like God has given me hundreds more," she says.

Six

Building a New Underground Railroad

The United States

Louis Etongwe, aged fifty-five, liberates slaves from the homes of wealthy families in the states of Virginia, Maryland, and New Jersey.

No, that's not a news bulletin from pre–Civil War America. Louis lives in modern-day Williamsburg, Virginia, and in seven separate incidents since 1999 he has rescued teenage African girls from domestic servitude and sexual bondage. Remarkably, Louis has no training in immigration law, has no social-services organization standing behind him, and funds his activities with the modest salary he earns working for the telephone company. "I act out of principle," Louis says without a trace of hubris. "I can't sit by passively when predators take advantage of the defenseless."

His odyssey toward abolition began over a Thanksgiving meal at his cousin's home in Richmond, Virginia. His cousin was helping out a family friend by giving shelter to a teen-ager from Cameroon—located just south of Nigeria in West Africa—who was "fleeing captivity." The term *captivity* piqued

Louis's curiosity. He thought maybe the girl had run into political problems back in the country where he himself had been born. So after the meal ended, he asked the teenager directly about her troubles.

His jaw dropped as she detailed her enslavement in the home of a wealthy family in the Richmond area. Her "masters" had promised her parents in Cameroon that, in exchange for work in their home, the fourteen-year-old girl would receive an education. Moreover, they offered to send her wages back to Cameroon on a regular basis. The American couple used their own daughter's passport—fabricated with a photo of their new recruit—to bring the girl into the United States.

Once the girl arrived in Virginia, the slaveholders forced her to work at domestic chores from dawn to dusk. She never attended school; for that matter, she could not leave the house unless accompanied by the husband or the wife. The slaveholders prohibited her from having any communication with her family back in Africa, though they assured her that they were sending them regular payments. As if that were not awful enough, the man frequently violated her sexually.

While relating her story to Louis, the girl dropped a hint that she was not the only girl from her tribe in Africa who had been trafficked to the United States. Louis seized on that reference. "What do you mean when you say there are 'others that have fallen into the same trap'?" he asked.

"Several of us from our region were brought here," she replied.

"Do you know their names and where they went?" Louis asked.

"Certainly, I can provide you with names and locations," she said softly. "I cannot feel totally free while they stay in captivity. You must help them."

At that moment, Louis knew he had been called to a noble cause. He had no choice; he had always stood up for the defenseless. As a young boy in grammar school in Cameroon, he never allowed the playground bullies to take advantage of the weakest kids. "Even when the fight was none of my business," Louis recalls, "I would step in and defend a kid before he got pummeled."

Now, as he heard the testimony of this frightened adolescent, a familiar wave of responsibility welled up inside of him. When his cousin confessed that he could not offer refuge to the girl for more than a few days, Louis and his wife agreed to take her into their own home. The following day Louis called an FBI hotline to report an incident of international abduction and forced labor. As strange as it felt for him to say it, he told the FBI that he was harboring an escaped slave in his home.

SLAVERY IN MODERN-DAY AMERICA

Between January 1998 and December 2003, the anti-trafficking organization Free the Slaves conducted a research project in collaboration with the Human Rights Center at the University of California at Berkeley. The final report, published under the title *Hidden Slaves: Forced Labor in the United States,* documents the nature and scope of slavery inside American borders.[1] The investigation exposed a number of noteworthy trends:

- Foreigners are trafficked into the United States from at least thirty-five countries. Most victims originate in China, followed by Mexico and then Vietnam.

- Those states with the largest incidence of slavery are California, Florida, Texas, and New York.

- Mexican, eastern European, and Asian crime syndicates run extensive trafficking rings inside the United States. They particularly target migrant groups.

- U.S. citizens and permanent residents import thousands of domestic servants into this country as slaves.

- Seventy-five percent of all New York apparel-manufacturing firms operate as sweatshops, often using forced labor or paying workers below minimum wage.

- Forced labor is most prevalent in five sectors of the U.S. economy: prostitution and sex services (46 percent); domestic service (27 percent); agriculture (10 percent); sweatshop/factory work (5 percent); and restaurant and hotel work (4 percent).

It is hard for many Americans to believe that slavery still exists on a grand scale in the world, let alone that it may have a foothold in their community. Yet there is no denying the fact that tens of thousands of people labor each day in the United States without pay and under the threat of violence. Because forced labor is often hidden in unregulated work environments or where cheap labor is the norm, most Americans will walk by an incidence of slavery and pay it no notice.

Given a widely held misconception, it must be emphasized that not all incidences of slavery involve undocumented immigrants. For instance, the *Detroit Free Press* reported in 2003 that Michigan police had uncovered a multistate sex-trafficking ring involving midwestern females, some as young as thirteen years old. The criminal network was exposed when a seventeen-year-old girl fled into a store in a Detroit strip mall and pleaded with a security guard for assistance. Soon thereafter, her traffickers burst into the store in pursuit. The security guard noted that the girl was battered and terrified, so he thwarted the predators and called in the local police.

The girl informed the police that she had been kidnapped while waiting at a bus stop in downtown Cleveland. Her captors drove her to Detroit, where she was forced to engage in commercial sex.

The girl subsequently led the police to the house in Detroit where she had been held, and they arrested the leader of the trafficking ring. Upon further investigation, the police learned that the perpetrators had been kidnapping teenage girls for eight years and trafficking them to cities around the Midwest.

The mother of the girl whose escape triggered the bust declared, "The whole thing is unreal—it's like slavery. They lure and coerce these girls into doing whatever they want. It's a sick game they are playing with our children."[2]

THE PROSECUTOR AND THE WRESTLER

Susan Coppedge joined the U.S. Attorney's office in the Northern District of Georgia not long after graduating from Stanford Law School. Burning with a passion to stand up for the victims of involuntary servitude, she first prosecuted traffickers on a case involving multiple (fourteen) pimps. She quickly became the office expert on human trafficking when subsequent cases landed in the office of the United States District Court. This background prepared her well for a unique case—a legal "bout" with a former professional wrestler, Harrison "Hardbody" Norris.

In the late 1990s, Harrison Norris was a rising star in the World Championship Wrestling organization. A quick-witted and charismatic figure, Norris was likely to succeed in whatever business he chose to pursue. His stint in the U.S. Army had given him self-discipline and a worldly air.

Norris was married and had a young teenage daughter. He and his family lived in Cartersville, about thirty miles north of Atlanta, Georgia. He owned two homes, one equipped with a large exercise training facility. In April 2004, Norris determined to begin training the next generation of wrestling stars. Not just any wrestlers: he would train female wrestlers.

Wherever he went, Norris sought out women down on their luck and offered them a chance at a new life and future stardom. He assigned the women wrestling "personas" and would frequently call them only by the new wrestling name that he had bestowed upon them. He assigned each to a team and rewarded them military-style with "ranks" of achievement. The women adhered to a staunch training regimen that included daily workouts and a strict diet. Norris demanded that they stop smoking and drinking alcohol, and forbade any drug use whatsoever. The women became leaner, more toned, and healthier each day.

The Polaris Project: A Star Shall Guide Them

After two commercial airliners crashed into the World Trade Center in New York City on September 11, 2001, Katherine Chon was not the only university student who grew concerned about the world's future. In the days that followed the attack, the dinner conversations she shared with her Brown University friends regularly turned to global social issues.

"So, what do you think: is religion a tool that people use to justify acts of terror and human oppression?" asked Brown senior Derek Ellerman. "Look at U.S. history," he continued. "Christians used the Bible to sanctify the practice of slavery."

"True," Katherine acknowledged, "but that same Bible inspired other Christians to become the prime movers in the abolitionist movement."

The conversation took off from there as the handful of students around the table argued over what social forces "really" ended the African slave trade in the nineteenth century. Then Derek suddenly shifted the topic: "Well, what do you think it will take to end slavery today?"

Katherine gave him a confused look. "What are you talking about?" she asked.

"Women and children all over the world are being abducted or sold and forced into the sex industry," Derek informed his stunned peers. "And millions of people of all ages have fallen into forced labor in India, Nepal, and Pakistan."

Surely Derek must be exaggerating, Katherine thought to herself; otherwise she would have heard about it in her classes at Brown. Still, when she sat down to study that evening, she could not get the idea out of her head. So she put aside her books and searched the Internet for information about human trafficking. Up popped a human-rights report that detailed the millions of people caught in modern slavery.

Katherine looks back now and recalls her reaction: "Here I was in my senior year at an Ivy League university, and I didn't even know that this huge problem exists!" The following day she sought out the most politically aware students and professors she knew and pumped them for information about the global slave trade. They, too, confessed their ignorance.

Katherine decided to pursue her own line of research. She stumbled across a newspaper article recounting a police raid on an Asian massage parlor located only a few miles from her campus. Someone had tipped off the police that the establishment operated as a brothel, and their raid recovered six South Korean women. Traffickers had brought the women to the United States under false pretenses, taken away their passports once they arrived inside its borders, and forced them to sell their bodies for sex. Despite the corroborating testimonies of the women and obvious signs of torture, the police arrested all six women on charges of prostitution.

Katherine was shocked that this could be happening in her own backyard. But it got even more personal: she herself had been born in South Korea and was about the same age as these trafficked women. Under different circumstances, she might have fallen prey to the traffickers herself.

As she learned more about the modern slave trade, a fire grew inside her. When she told Derek of her desire to become an active abolitionist, he did not skip a beat: "I'm in. We can't let this go on without a fight."

To their consternation, they struggled to find any meaningful volunteer opportunities. The few abolitionist groups that did exist were looking for highly qualified professionals. The only viable options for students came down to organizing a fund-raiser or showing a film on campus. The duo desired a deeper engagement, but they realized that they first had to better understand the mechanisms of the modern slave trade. So they persuaded two of their Brown professors to alter their standard curriculum in the coming semester and require students to carry out original research on human trafficking.

Brown offers an annual competition for entrepreneurs to develop a business plan for a start-up company. Though it is geared toward applicants starting a for-profit enterprise, Derek and Katherine saw themselves as entrepreneurs as well, even if their bottom line was social justice. So they wrote up a business plan to launch an agency that would utilize communication technologies and organizational ingenuity to resist the slave trade. Despite their unorthodox approach, they won second place and received a cash prize of $12,500, enough to launch a new antislavery agency. They named it the Polaris Project, referring to the North Star, which guided slaves toward freedom along the Underground Railroad.

Louis Etongwe: Never Waste a Perfect Opportunity

The FBI was slow in responding to the report Louis had made about finding slavery in Richmond, so he tried engaging the INS and the local police. They showed polite interest, too, but no one made his houseguest's case a priority, nor would they pursue his leads on other girls from Cameroon who might be enslaved.

"I realized that if I didn't take action, no one else would," Louis says. So he dialed the home phone number of a New Jersey family on the list of names that his houseguest had provided. In hopes that the enslaved girl might be in the house alone, he called in the middle of the day. The scheme worked: a seventeen-year-old Cameroon girl picked up the phone and confirmed that she had spent three years in captivity, subject to the same abuses as the first victim Louis had met. The girl on the phone confessed that she had resigned herself to a lifetime of slavery, and so this call out of the blue felt like a miracle.

When Louis asked the whereabouts of her home village in Cameroon, he was mildly surprised that she named a place only two miles from his own childhood home. The real shocker came when he inquired about her family background. She blurted out the name of his first cousin; he had known this girl's mother for most of his life. The daughter had been a toddler when Louis had immigrated to the United States. And here they were, making a first contact in a foreign land at the worst of times.

Then again, perhaps their paths had crossed at the best of times. The girl now had no doubts that a miracle was unfolding. Before she had left Cameroon, her mother had urged her to contact Mr. Louis Etongwe if she ran into trouble in America. She had lost his phone number, but here was Louis on the phone, offering to rescue her. "Please, Mr. Etongwe," she pleaded, "free me from this prison!"

Louis subscribes to the theory that a perfect opportunity should never be wasted; the window may never open again. "The masters of the house have left you at home alone," he noted, "so we must seize this chance to get you out."

They hatched an impromptu escape plan. The girl explained that she was tending three young children and did not feel right simply abandoning them without a caretaker. The mother arrived home promptly at four each afternoon, and the girl could see her car approaching up a long driveway. As soon as her car entered the driveway, the girl could sneak out the back door and run to a side street. Louis has a brother-in-law who lives in New Jersey, and he would call in a favor: the brother-in-law would be waiting in the side street with the car running.

He would take the girl back to his home, and there they would wait for Louis, who would be driving up to New Jersey that evening after he got off work in Virginia.

The plan came off without a hitch, and the girl was rescued. On the long trip back to Virginia, she filled Louis in on the details of her captivity. She had not had contact with her family for three years. On one occasion, she had caught a glimpse of a letter from Cameroon with her mother's handwriting on the envelope, but the letter had disappeared. She assumed that other letters had been confiscated as well.

By 2002, Louis had rescued two additional girls from domestic slavery. So now four young girls lived with him and his exceedingly generous wife. But try as he might, Louis had trouble lighting a fire under the justice system to offer the girls protection. Investigation into a trafficking crime generally moves at a snail's pace, even in cases like these, where the testimonies of the victims are solid. As commonly happens, the slaveholders claimed that the girls' parents back in Cameroon had consented to an employment contract; and they had signed documents to prove it. Neither local nor federal law-enforcement agents were likely to send an investigator over to Africa to unravel the truth.

Louis therefore bought a plane ticket and a video camera and headed over to Cameroon on his own. He visited the families of each girl now living in his home and filmed their testimonies detailing how the traffickers had promised an education and a well-paying job for their daughters. None of the families had heard directly from their daughters from the moment they arrived in the United States, and their "employers" had not sent any money.

Louis particularly relished a visit to his home village. When he arrived, his cousin was in mourning, dressed completely in black. "Dear cousin," she spoke tearfully to him upon his arrival, "I wish it were with joy that I could mark your visit from America. But I have received sad news that my daughter went missing in your new homeland and is presumed dead."

His news that her daughter was alive and safely sharing his own home became a cause for great celebration. He then played for them a video message from the girl to her family and friends. There was not a dry eye in the village.

The Prosecutor and the Wrestler: Down for the Count

Because human-trafficking crimes can be so hidden, trafficking activity can persist for years with unsuspecting neighbors living right next door. What makes for a criminal case today in the United States may begin simply with a lucky break. It was one such random happenstance that brought Hardbody Norris to the attention of the FBI.

Norris often took his trainees shopping for wrestling outfits that would accentuate their feminine features and garner attention. He told the women that they needed to be comfortable with turning heads in public.

On one such trip to a strip mall in August 2004, events took an unusual turn for Norris when one of his trainees slipped away and approached police. The woman told the officers startling information: she and two other women in her company were held against their will by Norris and were being forced to work as prostitutes.

Once the officers investigated, Norris and women he had designated team leaders denied the allegations, saying that the renegade woman simply did not enjoy life in the wrestling troupe. Police took the three victims, pretending to place them in custody to get them from Norris. This incident led to a yearlong investigation into Norris and his activities, conducted by officers of the police department in Smyrna, a northwest suburb of Atlanta, and by FBI agents.

Initially, officers thought they had all the victims in protective custody. Nearly a year later, however, Norris had recruited two other victims with false promises of wrestling stardom. In early August 2005, another victim cut a screen and crawled out of a bathroom window to make a daring escape. She alerted authorities to another woman whom Norris and his five accomplices were holding captive. Ultimately, nine victims were identified in the case, some of whom did not come forward until the case became public.

"Cases like these are often full of unexpected turns," Susan Coppedge notes. "We were closing in on indictments for Norris and his coconspirators but had no idea of the true breadth of his operation. Once he was arrested, it was like a floodgate opened, and a river of evidence came our way."

What followed was the discovery of an intricate world of dominance and control. The government charged Norris with twenty-eight counts of criminal activity, including conspiracy, sex trafficking, peonage, and witness tampering. Under the pretense of training athletes, Norris had developed a ring of prostitutes who both loved and despised him.

He kept detailed records of his rules for the women, referring to them as his "Ten Commandments." He had designated "team leaders"—almost all of whom professed romantic love for Norris and with whom he had sexual relations—to control his other victims. He utilized an extensive system of fines and privileges along with a quota system to keep the women in line. Talking back earned a fifty-dollar fine. Exceeding the daily quota of sex clients could earn a night in the "General's Quarters," a bedroom that Norris would share with the woman who "earned" it.

Hardbody's attention to detail and discipline only made the government's case against him that much stronger. His accounting of all the money "owed" was extensive. Although they couldn't leave the residence without a team leader as an escort, for example, they were charged rent each month. He charged them for food, clothes, training, and every other expense he could invent.

How does a woman whose every move is controlled pay back this large debt she's accumulating? Norris had the answer: forced prostitution. He would pile the women into a van each weekend and transport them to a friend's night club catering to Hispanic men, where they were forced to dance and service clients. All the money went to "the General," who kept it in a safe for which only he had the key.

At trial, Norris chose to defend himself. He pleaded not guilty: the women under his care turned clean thanks to him— healthy, fit, and off substances.

Coppedge admits that Norris's charisma provided a bit of a challenge for the prosecution. "While we were confident in the investigation and evidence we had against him, judges tend to give people who defend themselves more latitude than a professional attorney. We told the victims they would be questioned by Norris on cross-examination, a fact that was unnerving for many of them," she says.

Despite his charm, Norris failed to win his case, and the federal court handed down the harshest sentence delivered to a trafficker prior to 2005—life in prison. The verdict has been upheld on appeal, but the case has been remanded and Norris is awaiting re-sentencing. The judge in the case noted Norris's intelligence and business acumen. In fact, it was partially because of those attributes that the judge told Norris he was getting such a harsh punishment. He could have been successful in any legitimate enterprise he undertook, the judge declared, and yet he chose to become a predator.

All of Norris's victims were adult American citizens—American slaves—freed by a uniquely American justice system.

The Zambian A Cappella Choir: Slavery in the Church

Sandy Shepherd presumed she was doing God's work. The mother of three daughters in Colleyville, Texas—a suburb of Dallas—she had taken an active role in bringing the Zambian A Cappella Choir to her Baptist church. The choir's members came from impoverished families in Zambia, a country that borders Angola and Zimbabwe in the center of Africa.

A pastor from Texas, Keith Grimes, had formed his TTT (Teaching Teachers to Teach) ministry to bless constituencies on both sides of the Atlantic. Church audiences in the United States would be moved to hear young African boys sing songs of Christian praise—so deeply touched, in fact, that they would open up their wallets to fund education projects back in Zambia.

When he was recruiting boys for the choir, Pastor Grimes told the boys' parents that American donations would fund the construction of local Zambian schools. Moreover, their boys would receive cash stipends that they could send back home. While on tour, he would add, his staff would provide tutoring for the boys, and upon their return to Zambia they would be the first students in a newly built schoolhouse.

Pastor Grimes brought his first boys' choir to the United States in 2003 and scheduled a tour that would last three months. Over that period, revenue from donations and CD sales of the boys' performances totaled nearly $250,000. The cash receipts exceeded the pastor's wildest dreams, and so he unilaterally extended the tour for an additional half year without the consent of the boys or their parents. The financial success of the tour continued to soar.

After the first tour group returned to Zambia, Pastor Grimes set out to recruit another choir. Between 1993 and 2000, the pastor formed five boys' choirs from Zambia and one from Liberia. The Liberian choir featured blind children. During a tour, families from the churches where the choir performed provided the boys with hospitality. Between tour dates, the boys stayed at the TTT headquarters, located on a property in rural Texas.

Sandy signed up to host some of the boys when the choir gave its first performance at the Colleyville Baptist Church. The total experience—the beautiful a cappella songs, Pastor Grimes's graphic description of their impoverished lives back in Zambia, and a shared meal with the boys in her home—made Sandy ache for Africa. She enthusiastically joined a church delegation to visit Zambia and see firsthand the region that the boys came from and the site planned for the new school.

On that trip, Sandy witnessed Pastor Grimes in action. Being a white preacher with a freshly pressed shirt and tie gave him credibility, while his kind, personable way won over the hearts of Zambian villagers. Sandy noted how proud the parents were that Pastor Grimes had selected one of their sons to join the boys' choir. They signed contracts written in English that they could not read, but they trusted that the pastor would take good care of their sons. "I sympathize with the Zambian families," Sandy says. "I could not imagine that a pastor, in the guise of Christian ministry, could enslave young kids just so that he could put money into his own donation plate."

On the choir's first visit to Colleyville, the boys who stayed at Sandy's home kept very quiet. Their behavior did not seem especially unusual for young kids who had landed in a wholly foreign culture.

Behind the scenes, the TTT staff had threatened the boys to keep quiet about their life in the choir. If a host family gave them a gift, the boys were required to hand it over to the leaders. Even phone numbers and addresses of host families were treated like contraband. The leaders directed them to "be polite yet stay silent whenever possible."

After Sandy returned from Zambia, the boys' choir made a number of return engagements to her church. The boys opened up slowly and began sharing tidbits of information that alarmed their hosts. The TTT staff screened their letters to and from Zambia, the boys claimed, and forbade phone calls home. The choir averaged four concerts a day, performing in shopping malls, churches, and schools. On heavily scheduled days they might put on as many as eight separate performances. If any boy fell ill or became exhausted, Pastor Grimes threatened to send him back to Zambia, subjecting him to utter shame in the eyes of his parents. Finally, the boys revealed to their hosts that they lived in squalor here in America because TTT did not pay them stipends as they had been promised.

When Sandy called Keith Grimes and voiced her concerns, he lashed back with red-hot fury. She never saw this side of his personality on the mission field in Zambia. His heated denial only fanned her suspicions, so she called federal law-enforcement agencies to request an investigation. "At that time I did not know much about human trafficking," she admits, "so I spoke to the federal agents about a cut-and-dried case of child exploitation."

FBI agents did investigate TTT, but they dismissed accusations of forced labor and bondage because they did not uncover any signs of shackles or bruises on the boys' bodies. Pastor Grimes explained to agents the mission of the boys' choir, and they accepted his motives at face value. The pastor even produced contracts that the Zambian families had signed that proved his rightful guardianship over the choir members within the United States.

Despite this setback, Sandy persisted. She contacted state law-enforcement officials in Texas, the INS, and the office of Attorney General Janet Reno. Unfortunately, her efforts yielded very few tangible results.

In 1998, the boys' choir to which Sandy had grown close returned to Africa. She heard reports that Pastor Grimes had recruited a new choir of sixty-seven Zambian kids. But she could no longer bear fretting daily about TTT's control over the boys, and her campaign to pursue legal justice waned.

For its part, TTT sought to avoid the Colleyville Baptist Church. Pastor Grimes warned his new crop of boys that an "evil church" existed in Texas and that they should reject any invitation to visit families there. "If you go to that church," the pastor warned, "they will deceive you, and you will end up in terrible conditions of abuse." It was the voice of a wolf warning the sheep to watch out for the hens.

CAST: Bringing Slavery out of the Closet

In August 1995, federal agents swooped in on an eight-unit apartment complex hidden behind a barbed-wire fence in El

Monte, California, a municipality of metropolitan Los Angeles. Seventy-two garment workers had been kept captive inside the compound for as long as seven years. The slaveholders recruited females from poor, rural communities in Thailand and promised to give them high-paying sewing jobs in the United States. Once the workers arrived in Los Angeles, the slaveholders took away their passports and informed them that they had to pay back the expenses of their trip.

The garage of the apartment complex served as the sewing factory. Industrial machines stood side by side in a space so cramped that the workers could barely walk between stations. The garage offered no ventilation, and the windows were covered wholly with posters.

The roach-infested bedrooms in the apartment complex held no furniture—just mattresses lying on the floor. No light could get through the covered windows. A typical American family would find the bedroom space tight for two people, yet ten Thai women shared a single bedroom in El Monte.

The slaveholders operated two additional sewing factories in the bustling garment district of Los Angeles. While some of the Thai women sewed in the El Monte garage, others were shuttled back and forth each day to the other factories. The women labored sixteen-hour shifts while armed guards monitored their movements around the clock.

The slaveholders paid the workers about seventy cents an hour and then recouped that money immediately as a debt repayment. Because they did not allow the workers to leave the compound unguarded, the slaveholders established a commissary for toiletries and essential food. A bar of soap sold for twenty dollars; a bag of rice went for ten dollars.

After the intervention at El Monte, Secretary of Labor

Robert Reich called it "the worst case of slavery in America's recent history."[3] Nevertheless, the multiagency strike force that raided the compound treated the victims like illegal aliens. Having survived seven years of enslavement, the women now had to endure another form of captivity—behind bars and forced to wear prison uniforms. Their treatment sent a horrible message to slaves held anywhere in the United States, supporting the slaveholders' warning: "Report us to the authorities, and you will be the ones thrown in jail."

A loose network of human-rights and Asian community groups based in Los Angeles fought the detention of the survivors and raised funds to post their bail. Once the women were released, the groups quickly realized that no single organization could handle medical care, legal representation, immigration issues, and the daily livelihood needs of the trafficked women. In the months to follow, the Thai Community Development Center and Little Tokyo Service Center, academics, and legal-aid groups marshaled their resources to form CAST—the Coalition to Abolish Slavery and Trafficking. The group functioned informally in the aftermath of the El Monte case and then became an independent organization in 1998.

THE U.S. CONGRESS GETS IN ON THE ACT

The shocking revelation of the El Monte case—that more than seventy women could be held in slavery in a Los Angeles residential neighborhood for seven years and not be detected—and the high-profile trial that followed raised the alarm in political and legal circles that the United States lacked effective legislation to combat human trafficking. Foreign nationals who were trafficked into the country were typically classified as violators of immigration law. As "illegal immigrants," they were detained and deported back to potentially dangerous situations.

CAST and other nationally active NGOs pressed federal lawmakers to engineer comprehensive legislation that would protect the rights of trafficking victims and shift the focus of law enforcement onto the real criminals. They also encouraged the U.S. government to provide measures for the physical, psychological, and social recovery of victims of trafficking.

The U.S. Congress passed a major piece of legislation, the Trafficking Victims Protection Act (TVPA), in late 2000 with an express purpose: "to ensure just and effective punishment of traffickers, and to protect their victims." Most important, the law recognized that human trafficking is simultaneously a domestic U.S. problem and an international crisis.

The TVPA gave law enforcement better tools to prosecute criminals who engage in involuntary servitude, sex trafficking, and forced labor. Under the new law, trafficking in human beings for any of these reasons became a felony with penalties of up to twenty years in prison, and sentencing could be increased to life imprisonment in cases involving severe sexual abuse, kidnapping, or murder.

The TVPA also created a new category of visa, the "T visa," especially important for trafficking victims who were brought across the border illegally or were forced to overstay their admission. The statute allows them to remain in the United States if it is determined that they could suffer "extreme hardship involving unusual and severe harm" if they were returned to their home countries. Another requirement for eligibility: victims must be willing to cooperate with law enforcement against those responsible for their enslavement. After three years in "T status," qualified candidates may apply for permanent residency. The regulation allows them to apply for nonimmigrant status for their spouses and children. Victims under the age of twenty-one may apply for nonimmigrant status for their parents as well.

Under the auspices of the TVPA, the Congress further mandated specific government departments to launch new mechanisms to combat trafficking. As noted in chapter 4, the U.S. State Department was tasked with establishing an office to monitor international trafficking activity and to submit an annual report to Congress detailing how effectively individual national governments had performed in confronting trafficking within their own borders. The Department of Health and Human Services (HHS) was charged with increasing the American public's awareness of trafficking and with extending the range of services available to trafficking survivors.

The TVPA went a long way toward creating a new legal environment so that trafficking survivors would feel safer identifying themselves to law-enforcement authorities, would be confident that they would not be criminalized, and would benefit from social programs specifically designed to help them. Despite this strong legal framework, anti-trafficking enforcement since the TVPA's passage in 2000 has been tepid at best. Fewer than one thousand victims of trafficking have either received a T visa or been granted "continued presence" in the United States. Those figures are anemic when put next to the tens of thousands of people who have been trafficked into the United States since 2000.

The data on successful prosecution against traffickers also pale in comparison with the level of criminal activity. In 2005, the U.S. Attorneys' offices nationwide initiated prosecutions against ninety-five defendants, 87 percent of whom were charged with violations under the TVPA. The good news: that's more than twice the number of defendants who were prosecuted in 2004.[4]

In the last couple of years, agencies at the federal and local levels have reached the right conclusion—that they cannot fight the slave trade alone. A plethora of community partnerships (or "task forces") are springing up around the country to link NGOs that specialize in trafficking; social-service and health-care providers; and local police departments.

Anna Rodriguez: Breaking a Curse

When U.S. Attorney General John Ashcroft signed the TVPA legislation at a major press conference in Washington, D.C., Anna Rodriguez and Chica Garcia stood behind him in prominent positions. Ironically, less than two years earlier neither Anna nor Chica was even remotely aware that a modern slave trade existed. Now they had front-row seats for the most important piece of antislavery legislation in more than a century.

A twist of fate drew the two Hispanic women close together in 1999. Anna was working with the sheriff's office of Collier County, Florida—which includes the fertile agricultural region of Immokalee—as an advocate for victims of crime. She was frequently called in to help with cases of domestic violence.

The sheriff's office alerted Anna one morning to an assault in a neighborhood heavily populated with migrant workers. Its officers had responded to a 911 call the previous day. At the premises a battered Guatemalan woman told of how she had come home and found her husband in bed with their "domestic helper." When the wife protested bitterly, he violently assaulted her. No one from the sheriff's office bothered to interview the "domestic helper," and rather than try to untangle a complex marital spat, the sheriff's office passed the case along to Anna for evaluation.

When Anna visited the home, she interviewed the couple separately and then asked to speak to the "domestic helper." The husband became very nervous, but he could not refuse her request. Her suspicions raised, Anna made sure to find a private space to talk to the young girl. The girl introduced herself as Chica and said she was fifteen years old. Six months earlier, the master of the house had kidnapped her from a rural village in Guatemala, where her abductor's brother was mayor. The man brought her through the U.S.–Mexico border on a bus, and then across the southern United States to Florida. She now lived with her slaveholder, his wife, and their children.

Over a six-month span, she was a field slave during the day and a sex slave at night. The slaveholder forced Chica to work in the tomato fields, always hovering close by to ensure that she did not talk to other field laborers. He claimed that it cost him two thousand dollars to bring her to the United States, and so he would keep her wages until he had recouped his expenses. The man's wife worked in the evening, and that is when the master violated her sexually.

Anna was stunned. She had dealt with many cases of sexual abuse and domestic violence, but this was blatant slavery. She nevertheless kept her composure and gave comfort to Chica, telling her that she could find immediate shelter for her. To Anna's surprise, the girl strenuously resisted the option of leaving the home.

Anna alerted the sheriff's office to the man's crime, and that afternoon he was arrested and put in jail. Over the next week, Anna returned several times to the home and tried to convince Chica to move out and get into a shelter. Each time the girl refused.

As the trust in their relationship grew, Anna began to unravel the mystery. First off, she learned that Chica was really nineteen years old. The man had instructed her to say that she was fifteen so other people might think she was his niece. Then Anna learned why the man had such a hold over Chica. Witchcraft carries tremendous sway in many parts of rural Latin America. The slaveholder had taken a lock of the girl's hair and had told her that he had gone to a witch doctor to bind her to him. If she tried to escape, she and her family would face a calamity. As long as the slaveholder held the lock of hair, Chica was terrified to leave the property and unleash the curse.

When the police checked the man's wallet, they found the lock of hair exactly where Chica had said it would be. On Anna's next visit, she used her own deception to get help for the girl. Anna told Chica that she had just come back from visiting the slaveholder at the county jail and that he had forfeited the lock of hair and had forgiven the money she owed him.

Freed from her psychological chains, Chica happily left the property and within a year became the first recipient of a T visa in the United States. Chica has since married and with her husband is raising three children, among whom is a daughter named Anna.

Louis Etongwe: Passing a Test

After gathering crime evidence in Cameroon, Louis faced tribulations of his own back in the United States. The slaveholders had discovered who had facilitated the escape of "their property," and they began making threatening phone calls to his home. Louis received angry phone calls as well from other Cameroon foreign nationals living in the United States who believed that his activities had tainted the reputation of their entire community. "Why don't you just leave good enough alone?" they told him bitterly. "You know as well as I do that these girls were as poor as dirt back home; they are much better off here."

Meanwhile, Louis's wife had tired of the constant drama that the rescued slaves had brought to their lives, not to mention the mounting costs of meals, medical care, and legal aid. On one of the many long trips that Louis made to the INS district office, his car broke down and he did not have the money to fix it. Louis's wife wanted it all to end—and soon.

His troubles reached an apex in mid-2002 when he came home from work and saw several police cars parked in his driveway. The police had been tipped off that Louis was harboring illegal aliens and running a brothel out of his home. The "tips" had come from the slaveholders, who wrote slanderous letters to local social-service agencies and the police. The police now threatened to throw Louis and the girls into jail.

Fortunately, Louis had kept meticulous documentation of his work on behalf of the girls. He also had kept the business cards of those immigration attorneys and law-enforcement agents who had invited him to call anytime he might need help. That moment had arrived, and he passed the cards on to the police. Once the police called his references, they received confirmation that Louis was "one of the good guys."

Following the raid on his home, the local newspaper published a feature story on Louis's activities and lauded his sacrifice to liberate enslaved teens. Neighbors stopped by to congratulate him and to sheepishly acknowledge that they had been asked to monitor his activities. "Now we understand why so many investigators were coming to our homes and asking about you," they told him.

Almost as if he had passed his test, everything started to fall into place following the police raid on his home. The attorney general's office arrested the slaveholders and brought them to trial. Once juries had watched Louis's videotape of the parents and heard the testimonies of the girls, they convicted the perpetrators of abduction and sexual assault. The girls obtained residency in the United States, found boyfriends and jobs, and now maintain regular contact with their families in Cameroon.

For his part, Louis has rescued three additional girls enslaved in domestic labor and is working covertly on a few other, unresolved cases. He is reticent to talk about his work, mostly because he wants to deflect attention from himself. He desires no greater reward than what he has already gained. "I've never felt so much strength and passion in my life as I have liberating these girls," he explains. "I feel like I tapped into a gold mine of meaning for my own life."

Asked from where he draws his strength, Louis points to his grandparents. When he was a young boy, his village had the good fortune to land one of the first schoolhouses in all of Cameroon. Families from distant regions hoped against hope that their children might attend the school, but they did not know how they could manage the logistics. Louis's grandparents offered to take in as many as a dozen kids at a time so that they could attend school. Walking into his grandparent's home felt like entering a dormitory.

"But they did not treat it like a sacrifice," Louis recalls. "To help someone in need felt like a gift." Louis ponders that comment for a moment, and then adds, "I think my grandparents would be very proud of what I am doing today."

Indeed, the Etongwe legacy has crossed an ocean but has lost none of its power to move mountains.

Slavery in the Shadows of the White House

Polaris cut its teeth on dozens of cases in the metropolitan Washington, D.C., area. Human slavery, Derek and Katherine came to realize, is a serious crisis not only in China, Thailand, Nepal, Ukraine, and other poor nations. Strong trafficking networks operate covertly within U.S. borders as well and even reach to massage parlors within a few blocks of the White House.

About half of the sex slaves that Polaris assists in the metropolitan Washington, D.C., region are foreign nationals, and the other half are internally trafficked U.S. citizens. At some point, they all end up in deep gratitude to Tina Frundt, the woman who pulled them through their darkest night.

Tina has been rescuing sex slaves from the streets of Washington for years, first as the Polaris outreach coordinator and now as director of Courtney's House, a survivor aftercare organization also located in Washington. It troubles Tina that Americans still think sex trafficking happens only to women and children overseas. "We run into a foreign victim of sex trafficking, and we instantaneously sympathize with her coerced passage into the sex industry," Tina says. "But when we encounter an American girl on the street, we think, 'Why did she make this choice? Surely she can walk away anytime she wants.'"

Tina explains that most domestic trafficking victims are between twelve and fourteen years old. They do not sell their bodies willingly. "How many girls at that age do you know who would choose to be sexually assaulted a dozen times a night?" she asks pointedly.

A domestic trafficking episode can begin with any number of scenarios. Traffickers sometimes kidnap children and transport them to another region of the United States, or they might buy a child from parents addicted to drugs. Pimps may court young teens as if they were looking for girlfriends and then coerce them into sex slavery. The pimps also troll strip clubs and juvenile jails, which they consider target-rich environments.

Tina recounts "a typical case" that took place in early 2006. Two young women—one eighteen years old and the other nineteen—called her hotline number from the bathroom of a Washington hotel. They had turned on the shower so that the pimp and his "bottom," who shared their hotel room, could not hear them make the phone call.

Pimps often select one of the women whom they control to be their "bottom," or go-to girl, for recruiting new sex slaves. The bottom may be the woman who has been with him the longest, or his favorite, or the most trusted. Regardless, the bottom will carry out much of the dirty work that the pimp could probably not do as effectively alone.

Tina instructed the frightened girls to stay in the bathroom while she made an emergency call to the local police. By the time the police arrived at the hotel, Tina was there waiting for them. She called the girls back on their cell phone and told them to ask the pimp if they could buy a soda from the vending machines outside the hotel room. After the girls emerged, the police rushed inside and arrested their abductors.

Once they were free, Tina learned more about their story. The two girls live in the Midwest. The bottom had been a longtime acquaintance of theirs, and she asked them for a favor. She and her boyfriend needed to get to Washington, D.C., where they had landed new jobs, but their car had broken down. She offered to pay the girls to drive them out east.

The girls considered it a great deal to be paid to take a road trip and visit Washington. But once they arrived in the nation's capital, the man bluntly informed them that they were his property. He invited several friends over to the hotel their first night in town, and the men took turns raping the women. "You might as well get used to it, because this is what you will be doing from now on," he said matter-of-factly.

Luckily, he never thought to search the girls to see if they possessed a cell phone. The night before, during their orientation to local street life, a community advocate was handing out Polaris hotline cards. The girls grabbed one and kept it hidden, waiting for the right moment. Their hotline call passed to Tina's cell phone.

Tina knows intimately about the trauma of being trafficked. When she was fourteen years old, growing up in Chicago, a man coerced her into sexual commerce. Ten years her senior, he pretended that he had fallen in love with her—a classic recruitment technique called "the lover boy." After several months of courtship, he suggested that they run away from her "meddling parents." They ended up in Cleveland, where he said they were going to visit his relatives. That evening, several of his friends came by the hotel where they were staying, and her "boyfriend" told her to have sex with them. She refused, and the men raped her. After they left, her boyfriend simply said, "That wouldn't have happened to you if you had just listened to me in the first place."

Tina today tells clients, "You don't have to explain to me

everything that happened to you, because I have been in your situation." At that point the client typically breaks down in tears, the dam released simply because someone else knows the deep pain she has endured. "What happened to me twenty years ago is still going on today," Tina notes sadly.

Tina realizes that slaveholders will not surrender their trade easily because they make so much money off of it. She reports crossing paths with a Washington, D.C.–based trafficker who held three young girls in his "stable," each of whom was bringing in about $1,500 a day. Multiply those figures out and this one slaveholder was making about $45,000 a month, or $540,000 a year, tax-free, selling these girls every night.

"The pimps are cocky now, not afraid of the police, not afraid of the judicial system, because they feel like they are untouchable," Tina informed a House committee that was seeking to understand the criminal syndicates behind the sex trade. "We, as Americans, have made them untouchable by not recognizing the problem and solving it."[5]

The Zambian A Cappella Choir: Smile and Sing

When Pastor Grimes recruited him to join his choir in 1998, Given Kachepa was an eleven-year-old orphan. His mother had died when he was in the second grade, and his father passed away two years later. Given and his five siblings moved in with their Aunt Margret, who already had six children of her own.

The promises that Pastor Grimes made to Given and Aunt Margret seemed like a dream come true. The boy could earn some money for his destitute family and gain a top-drawer education in the United States. Pastor Grimes also pledged that the boys would be baptized once they reached the United

States, which to a Christian convert in Zambia means a great deal. "When you are from a poor country, and you have someone from a rich country tell you that they can provide all the things that you are missing in your life, you treat it like a gift from God," Given explains.

It is almost impossible for a poor Zambian to obtain a visa to visit the United States. But a senior officer in the Zambian national police collaborated with Pastor Grimes to facilitate the visa process for hundreds of choirboys. Other government officials must have been on TTT's payroll as well, for the American pastor had the birth dates on the boys' passports altered. Once he learned that U.S. audiences would donate more generously to help small children, Pastor Grimes fabricated the image of a choir of extraordinarily young boys.

Not one of the pastor's promises to Given came to fruition in the United States. Each day at TTT headquarters in Texas, the staff woke the boys up at the crack of dawn and forced them to dig, by hand, a deep hole to build a swimming pool. After hours of hard physical labor in the blazing summer sun, they would rehearse songs in the afternoon and into the evening.

Despite the exhaustion they felt at the end of a day at TTT headquarters, it was nothing compared with the pace they kept on tour: eighteen-hour days, seven days a week, for perhaps a month at a time. The boys would travel from one location to the next crammed into an overcrowded van. Once they arrived at a venue, they set up the stage for the performance, and then dismantled it after the concert was finished. They repeated this drill multiple times each day. "I felt like a puppet on a string being moved around," Given says. "I was told to smile and sing with an expression of joy for my God, but eventually singing to the Lord lost its meaning for me."

Given had his heart set on an education, and so three months into his U.S. stay he asked Pastor Grimes and his daughter, Barbara Grimes Martens, when the boys' tutoring might begin. Father and daughter passed into an angry frenzy, screaming at Given, even swearing at him, for being so ungrateful for the opportunity to live in America. It was the last time he inquired about study. The boys' baptism in a church also turned out to be an empty promise. Given concluded that the TTT leadership spoke only in lies.

Pastor Grimes died in 1999, and his daughter and her husband, Gary Martens, picked up where he had left off. The couple had been involved in "the ministry" from the start. Barbara kept track of the finances, and Gary handled the tour schedule. Not much changed in the daily lives of the boys after the pastor's death. Given and his peers kept up with the grueling pace.

Barbara and Gary Martens lacked the pastor's smooth diplomacy and shrewdness. At one point they determined that two of the boys had become a negative influence on the choir, and so they called the INS to pick the boys up and deport them back to Zambia. On the way to the airport, the boys divulged to the INS agent the truth of what went on behind closed doors in the Zambian A Cappella Choir. The agent found their stories credible and took the boys to a safe house instead of to the airport.

The agent then launched an in-depth investigation into TTT. Given recounts the day that INS agents came to TTT headquarters to conduct interviews. Barbara and Gary Martens had scripted how the boys should answer questions and had warned the boys that the agents would throw them in jail and torture them if they felt that something was amiss. "We believed that no one would help us," Given explains. "In our country, government officials take bribes every day. We do not trust men in uniforms."

Because the boys refused to come forward, the INS investigation did not yield immediate results; in fact, it lasted another seven months. Finally, in January 2000, the INS rescued the boys from the grasp of TTT. Given was thirteen years old, an orphan cut off from his siblings, left in limbo in a foreign land.

That's about the time Sandy Shepherd received an unexpected call from the pastor of her church. The INS had just contacted the pastor with a report that a group of boys from the Zambian A Cappella Choir had been rescued from TTT, and they needed safe houses. If the church could not accommodate the boys, the agent would have to detain them in an INS holding cell.

Sandy was not about to let that happen. She jumped on the phone and found some good Samaritans in her community who were willing to help out on short notice. Given stayed with Sandy, and she walked him through the endless hoops of health screenings, depositions, work permits, and visa applications.

In 2001, Sandy and her husband, Deetz, gained legal custody of Given and enrolled him in the seventh grade. He excelled in high school and graduated from a Texas university. He has worked part-time jobs at a grocery store and a landscaping business and sent most of the money back to his siblings in Zambia. He even helped three of his brothers start a small business.

Given has worked with Texas state representative Lon Burnam to pass a statute on human trafficking. He is also doing something that TTT promised but never delivered: he is raising funds to build schools in his native Zambia.

Given and Sandy remain devoted to putting an end to human trafficking. Given speaks nationally to groups about his experience and what it feels like to be a victim. "Look beneath the surface," he tells audiences. "People who are trafficked usually are hidden, so pay attention to signs that seem out of the ordinary."

CAST-ING A BROAD NET

Kay Buck became executive director of the Coalition to Abolish Slavery and Trafficking in 2003. The Canadian-born visionary has an extensive international background in antislavery work. From 1990 to 1996, Kay lived in Asia and supported the efforts of abolitionists in Thailand and Japan to design strategies that would reduce the incidence of trafficking in rural communities. Although creative economic and social interventions helped build stronger communities, Kay could not help ignoring the fact that a destructive cultural pattern persisted: society tolerates violence against women.

An objective analysis of the global slave trade supports her conclusion. Select a random sample of five people who have fallen victim to trafficking, and four will be females. The statistics do not change radically even if sex slavery is separated out from forced labor. Though females certainly are the prime targets for sex traffickers, they also dominate the ranks of coerced factory workers, rug and loom weavers, and domestic servants, just to name a few major categories of forced labor. Research further shows that regardless of her form of slavery, a female in most cases will be subject to sexual violence as part of her domination.

When Kay left Asia, she returned to North America and joined a Canadian NGO that focused on societal violence against women. Though the semantics changed—from human trafficking to gender violence—she felt as if she continued to address many of the same issues that she confronted in Asia. When the top post at CAST opened up, she jumped back over the fence into the dynamics of human trafficking.

The Women's Foundation of California became the first private foundation to support CAST's work. They appreciated what Kay and a growing number of abolitionists have seen. The tidal wave that could sweep over trafficking networks worldwide will begin to crest when women organize internationally to empower other women.

It would not do CAST justice, however, to categorize it as a "women's organization." The agency has pioneered community-based models that bring help to trafficking survivors and grief to traffickers. CAST has distinguished itself in the area of training the police in how to identify and rescue potential victims and how to usher them into victim aftercare.

Imelda Buncab once headed up the training programs at CAST, and today she serves as the national constituency director for the Not For Sale Campaign. Imelda trains police units in regions far beyond California—in the Virgin Islands, Arizona, Texas, Washington, Kansas, Alaska, and Hawaii. Imelda admits that she can never quite predict what response she will get from police officers.

When she led a training workshop for the police in Tucson, Arizona, in 2005, the controversy over border patrols was at its height. A self-styled vigilante group called the Minutemen had taken it upon themselves to stop immigrants from crossing into the United States. So when Imelda began talking about trafficking, the Tucson police were adamant that they were not responsible for enforcing immigration laws. Smuggling, which is what they interpreted trafficking to be, was a federal issue, not a state matter. Eventually Imelda enabled them to see the distinction between smuggling (a crime in which individuals aid migrants to cross borders without proper documents or official approval) and human trafficking (a crime in which individuals are coerced or deceived into entering the United States and then forced to work against their will).

Captain Kyle Jackson, the commanding officer at the Los Angeles Police Department who oversees human-trafficking cases, heralds community-partnership training as invaluable for his officers. "Trafficking usually is so underground, we had to shift our mind-set to notice the signs," he says. "In the past we would focus solely on the crime at hand. In a domestic-violence case, for instance, we did not ask a victim what country she was from or how she might have fallen under the control of the owner of the house."

Captain Jackson also underscores the importance of partnering with NGOs to obtain the trust of victims and potential witnesses in a trafficking case. Foreign nationals particularly may fear to speak to a police officer. A community NGO can help assure victims that the police are on their side and will help to stop their predator. At the same time, the NGO can help the police understand the unspoken cultural assumptions that the victim or witness is bringing to the case. Captain Jackson notes that law enforcement has to approach human trafficking with a fresh pair of eyes: "Local police work changes dramatically in a global village."

Anna Rodriguez:
Community Action Against Trafficking

Anna began helping victims of violent crimes as a second career. Born in San Juan, Puerto Rico, she came to Florida at the age of eighteen when her father's company transferred him to the Citrus State. She married young and, together with her husband, raised a family. After her children had grown up, Anna explored how she might help her local community. The director of a domestic-violence program invited her to volunteer a few days each week at its shelter.

Anna loved working at the shelter and discovered that she had a knack for treating crises with a cool head. People quickly came to believe that she could help them resolve their problems. That's due in part to the fact that she is blessed with a unique mix of personal qualities. On the one hand, she radiates compassion in such an affable way that crime victims do not feel pitied. Yet she conducts herself with a hard-nosed, let's-do-whatever-it-takes-to-get-this-job-done demeanor. In sum, she's someone you definitely want on your side, not battling against you.

At the shelter, Anna teamed up with the public justice system to bring domestic-violence cases to trial. Previously, county crime investigators and prosecutors could not coax abused women to talk about what their boyfriends or husbands had done to them. Furthermore, most migrant workers in her county do not trust the police. They fear being deported if they so much as report a crime. As a result, the justice system in her county had lots of open cases that never came to trial.

In 1995 Anna joined the county sheriff's office to act as a bridge to the community. She aimed to be available. Because most farm laborers start their day at four in the morning and finish at dusk, she worked evening shifts several times a week. Once the migrant community viewed her as a trusted advocate, the sheriff's office filled up like a doctor's waiting room. The county saw a sharp increase in the number of cases flowing through the court system.

After her first slavery case, with Chica, Anna detected an increasing number of human-trafficking incidents. But the scarcity of services geared to trafficked victims exasperated her. In a single incident, the sheriff's office rescued seven children who had been trafficked to the county as sex slaves. Anna could not find even one place that could give them shelter; the justice system was set up to send runaways and minority offenders to juvenile prisons. But jail was no place to send victims of a crime.

Anna also became frustrated that so many trafficking cases would languish and never come to trial. Prosecuting a trafficking case demands extraordinary dedication because it is so costly and time-consuming. Many times an investigator needs to travel to a foreign country to check out the original scene of the abduction. Moreover, victims are often slow to cooperate because they have been psychologically terrorized or told not to testify under threat of death. Sex traffickers might videotape a victim being violated and threaten to show the tape to the victim's family and neighbors in the home village if she testifies.

Observing firsthand all the reasons a slavery case might fall through the cracks, Anna resigned from the sheriff's office to establish the Florida Coalition Against Human Trafficking. Her primary goal as executive director was to create an agency linking law-enforcement bodies, social-service agencies, and trafficking victims. She secured funding from several government agencies—above all, the federal Department of Health and Human Services—and a few individual donors. In addition, Anna serves as a trainer on human trafficking for the Organization of American States.

Anna is convinced that it will take community-wide action to shut down the slave trade and has worked closely with local law enforcement to ensure that officers are trained to handle human trafficking cases. So she runs workshops for any group that is likely to have contact with people in their homes or at their places of work. For example, she teams up with the utilities company to train the workers who read the meters in residential neighborhoods. She also delivers workshops for home-care nurses and social workers who are likely to make home visits. "The more people who know about the indicators to look for, the more trafficking victims we can save," she notes. With each seminar she conducts, she moves one step closer to locating more victims, and this key strategy has resulted in her finding more than 250 victims in the state of Florida in the year 2009 alone.

In her workshops, Anna identifies hot spots where slaves turn up time and time again:

Housecleaning services

Landscape and gardening businesses

Households in which domestic (home) workers are present

Large-scale agricultural labor

Construction sites

Casinos

Garment factories

Hotels (housekeeping)

Nail salons

Migrant or transitional communities

Zones known for prostitution

Strip clubs / massage parlors

Domestic-violence cases

After reviewing common destination sites with her workshop participants, Anna suggests a series of questions to evaluate a potential case of slavery:

- Does the suspected victim have freedom of movement?

- Is the suspected victim allowed to socialize with other people or attend community events and religious services without accompaniment?

- Does a minor appear to be under the control of an adult who is not his or her parent?

- Does the residence have doors with locks on the outside, or is it surrounded with a barbed-wire fence directed internally to keep people inside the property from getting out?

- Are the windows at the residence boarded up?

- Does a steady flow of males pass in and out of the residence?

- Do male guardians appear to be constantly monitoring women who come in and out of the residence?

- Has the suspected victim been threatened with deportation or law-enforcement action?

- Has the suspected victim, or a relative, been threatened with harm if the victim attempts to leave?

- Is the suspected victim in possession of identification documents (like a passport); if not, who has control of the documents?

- Does it seem that the suspected victim was coached on what to say when questioned by law-enforcement officers?

- Is the suspected victim coerced to engage in some kind of work?

- Is the suspected victim forced to perform sexual acts?

- Has the suspected victim been deprived of food, water, sleep, medical care, or life necessities?

Anna's experience proves time and time again that good things happen once people learn the warning signs of slavery and feel confident about taking action. For example, in April 2005, a social worker approached Anna after a training workshop and told her that she had a client in the fast-growing resort town of Cape Coral who fit her profile of a trafficking victim.

A few days later, Anna accompanied local police on a raid of the property. They rescued a fourteen-year-old Guatemalan girl who had been enslaved for almost three years. The slaveholder owned a landscaping business and forced the girl to make meals for his workers. When the landscaping team went out to work, he locked her inside the house. The slaveholder also sexually abused her and pimped her out to workers and suppliers to whom he owed money.

"Finally, someone believes my story": that's the first thing the girl said to Anna after the raid. A year earlier, when she was six months pregnant, her slaveholder had beaten her badly. A neighbor rushed her to the hospital, and she gave birth to a one-pound baby who survived. The neighbor reported the crime, but the police never responded. They treated it like a family dispute.

Anna tells this story to highlight the difference that a community coalition makes. At her insistence, the police did finally intervene and arrest the perpetrator, who pleaded guilty to child sex trafficking. The girl was not treated like a criminal, and she received her T visa. Not only did the trafficker go to jail, but his sister, who lived in the house, was convicted for aiding and abetting a crime. One of the associates who accepted sex as payment for a debt was also convicted for rape of a minor.

Anna stresses how much has changed in the last decade, and much of it has to do with creating a united community front that can deal a blow to trafficking networks. In her experience, the smallest action can make a difference. "Human trafficking can work only if the victims remain invisible to the public eye," Anna says. "We have to remove the veil of ignorance."

Ending the Slave Trade in Our Time

I believe in the power of individuals to save the world. Social movements take root and blossom when enough individuals take personal action. When you tell yourself that there is nothing you can do to arrest the global slave trade, you underestimate your own potential and abandon hope for those trapped in captivity.

I speak from experience. In the early 1980s I went to the country of El Salvador to visit grassroots organizations that provided food and medical aid to impoverished communities. I had no grand plan in mind beyond seeing whether there was anything I could do to support their work.

At the time a military government terrorized the civilian El Salvadoran population. The generals, especially, did not like groups that preached democracy and social development for the poor. Two years before I arrived, the archbishop of the Roman Catholic Church in El Salvador, Oscar Romero, was shot in the heart in the middle of mass as he stood behind the altar. During his sermons Romero had boldly addressed military atrocities against civilians.

A year later military death squads savagely violated and murdered four U.S. religious women who worked in El Salvadoran
refugee camps. The response from the United States was quick.
President Jimmy Carter induced Congress to cut off tens of
millions of dollars in economic aid to the government of El
Salvador. That act certainly got the attention of the generals.

Up until that moment, military death squads had acted with
near impunity. They would conduct intelligence on people
working for social change and then take off their uniforms at
night to visit the suspects' homes. In the morning neighbors
would find their mangled bodies with a note attached: "This is
what happens to subversives."

During my first visit, my new El Salvadoran friends implored
me to start a human-rights program that would protect them
from the death squads. I had no background in this type of
work. In fact, I had never been involved in any kind of political
work or international diplomacy. I was a fairly recent graduate
of Westmont College, a small liberal-arts college in Santa Barbara, California, where I had earned a degree in psychology.

After about nine months the U.S. Congress restored economic and military aid to El Salvador, but the generals had
learned a lesson: it was fine to kill El Salvadorans but not U.S.
citizens. I, too, took note of the skewed rules of international
politics, so I decided to leverage the value of a U.S. citizen to
save an El Salvadoran life. I recruited friends and acquaintances
to go to El Salvador as unarmed bodyguards, telling them their
only shield would be their U.S. passports.

The initial plan was simple. A team of six U.S. citizens
would pass a month in El Salvador on twenty-four-hour alert.
One member of the team would accompany any El Salvadoran
health-care worker, pastor, or literacy worker who received a

death threat. Two more of my "bodyguards" would stay at the family home of the individual at risk. I assigned an additional two bodyguards to stay full-time at the threatened individual's agency office; the death squads would, at times, bomb the offices of grassroots organizations that they sought to destroy. The final member of the six-person team would visit the chief of the military police as well as a senior El Salvadoran government official and the U.S. ambassador. These authorities would be informed that U.S. citizens had aligned their fate with the targeted community leader.

I participated in the first team of six that went to El Salvador in 1984. We had been in the country for only a few days when the leader for all the Baptist churches in El Salvador, the Reverend Carlos Sanchez, contacted us. He held in his hand a note from one of the more notorious death squads. The message was clear: "Unless you leave the country within 48 hours, you and your family will be killed."

Sanchez had received similar death threats on two different occasions and had taken his family out of the country for a year at a time. But now that he was responsible for all the Baptist churches in his country, he did not want to leave. If a high-profile church leader fled when he received a death threat, how would the parish pastor in a rural village feel? What motivation would that give a health-care educator teaching peasants community medical models? So Sanchez asked if we could help him and his family stay in the country and continue their work.

We swiftly put our plan into action. A university graduate student from Las Vegas, Nevada, accompanied Sanchez around the clock. Two members of the team went to his house to stay with his wife and four children, and two others camped out at the Baptist national headquarters. I took on the role of visiting the authorities, essentially warning them of a major international incident if they did not take quick action to stop the death squad. Each authority I visited denied knowing the identity of these "shadowy groups," the death squads. I politely responded that it was in their power to stop this assassination. I relayed our commitment to stay by the side of our El Salvadoran friends.

Fortunately, the gambit paid off. Sanchez and his family survived and continued their valuable work in local communities. Over the months that followed, our project sent a new team of six U.S. citizens to El Salvador every month to play a similar role. The life of an El Salvadoran was protected on each occasion by the presence of U.S. citizens.

The El Salvadoran authorities eventually discovered the leadership behind our human-rights work. I was banned from entering the country, and many of our team members had trouble securing visas. Quickly shifting to plan B, we decided to launch an economic-development agency as a front for our human-rights group. I still get a chuckle when I recall the phone call I made to one of my Westmont College friends, Jim Morgan, asking him to go to El Salvador and become our first agronomist. Jim had graduated with a degree in religious studies and, at the time of my call, was driving a forklift at a yogurt factory. His initial response was reasonable: "But I know hardly anything about agriculture." I explained that it did not matter, since his primary role was to serve as a human-rights presence; he had only to pretend to be an agronomist. I made similar calls to other friends asking them to take on other roles—a nutritionist, a health-care worker, and so on—in our new "economic development agency." Every one of us was under twenty-six and lacked experience for the job we set out to do.

A long story could follow, for we stayed in El Salvador for more than a decade, until a peace treaty ended the violent civil war. I'll cut to the chase. Not only did we continue to carry out human-rights work and rescue the lives of many El Salvadorans; we also evolved into a proficient economic-development agency. Jim Morgan became one of the more highly respected agronomists in El Salvador. He initiated an experimental farm where he introduced peasants to new ways of farming on steep, poor land. Our other staff also developed excellent skills in areas for which they had no formal training. What we did have going for us was an education, a compassion for the defenseless, and the courage to stand up for what is right. We did not listen to family, friends, and politicians who told us that this international problem was too big for us, that making a difference was beyond our means.

That's why today I am convinced that every individual can make a valuable contribution to arresting the global slave trade. If you doubt that fact, it is probably because you underestimate the power of your personal resources. Twenty years ago all it took for a U.S. citizen to save the life of an El Salvadoran was to hold up a passport. Sometimes it is simply who you are, and not only what you can do, that can make a difference.

Truly, the hardest step to take is the first one—the commitment to take action. The ensuing steps have a way of revealing themselves.

THE ABOLITIONIST'S VOCATION

As a university professor, I frequently challenge my students about their obsession with a career beyond college. I tell them they will be far more fulfilled if they seek a vocation instead.

To build a career they will stitch together jobs into a valuable résumé. To build a vocation they will design and pursue meaningful endeavors. Those two paths may take an individual in divergent directions.

How do you find your vocation? You identify where your passion meets the needs of the world. The first part of that equation is to engage yourself in those activities that you feel you were put on this earth to do. The second part of the equation is to carry out those activities so as to benefit others. The world is filled with unhappy people who are doing work that they do not care about, all for the sake of making more money or because they are trying to fulfill someone else's dreams.

A new Underground Railroad is emerging that aims to put an end to human slavery once and for all. It desperately needs reinforcements—a new wave of abolitionists—to join in the struggle. Lawyers are needed to protect the rights of victims and prosecute their predators. Business entrepreneurs are needed to launch enterprises for freshly liberated slaves. Students are needed to carry out research and influence policy. Health-care workers and mental-health professionals are needed to pick up the pieces of broken lives. Construction workers are needed to build shelters. Employers are needed to offer jobs. Owners of two blankets are needed to donate one. On the list goes: mention a resource, and the abolitionist movement needs it. The movement needs your time, talent, and money.

THE CAMPAIGN LAUNCHES

I wrote the first edition of this book motivated by a deep conviction that the movement needs our talents. I am a writer, so when I learned of modern-day slavery in my own neighborhood I decided to use my natural curiosity and communication skills to educate those who were unaware of the millions held captive.

When I set out to investigate across six continents in 2006, I did not intend to create a new organization. I simply hoped to encourage people to join the Lucy Borjas, Florence Lacors, Padre Cesares, Anna Rodriguezes, and Kru Nams of the world in standing up for justice while celebrating the work of these amazing modern-day heroes. That seemed simple enough: investigate and tell the truth, and then pat myself on the back as the book was published, people got educated and inspired, and I moved on to my next writing project.

Then came the phone calls from Kru Nam. When we met initially, I had promised her that I would raise funds to build permanent housing for the twenty-five or so kids that she had rescued. How much could construction cost for one house in northern Thailand?

She was determined, however, to keep rescuing children before traffickers ensnared them, and she was quite successful. She would call every month or so to give me an update and inform me of the number of children now under her care. After the third phone call I realized that one house would not be large enough for the number of kids who were now safe with Kru Nam. Okay, I thought, I'll find the money for two houses.

I'll never forget the call in October 2006. The book was almost done. Kru Nam called to say she had now rescued eighty-eight children, and she would need something like a village rather than one or two homes to provide shelter and support for them. It was a moment of decision for me. Would I turn my back on her and tell her that there was only so much I could do as a professor, writer, and business entrepreneur? Or would I do whatever it would take to help her and the children she had saved from slavery?

I talked with my family and two friends, Kique Bazan and Mark Wexler. It didn't take long for us to decide to take a leap of faith, just as I had done when I traveled to El Salvador two decades earlier. Kique, Mark, and I spent a lot of time in coffee shops that winter planning and dreaming—and preparing to launch the Not For Sale Campaign.

People sometimes ask me why we started an organization rather than join an existing group. When we began to analyze the antislavery movement within the United States, we found that most NGOs were driven by professionals and operated primarily as single-issue groups: direct aftercare providers, advocacy groups focused on legislation change, or research centers. We aimed to fill a gap: mobilize a grassroots constituency that could work locally, nationally, and internationally.

We officially launched the Not For Sale Campaign in February 2007. We had a book, a documentary that introduced viewers to the abolitionists featured in the book, a lot of excitement, and—truth be told—a healthy dose of apprehension. The Campaign's launch coincided with the two hundredth anniversary of the British parliament's historic vote to ban the transatlantic slave trade. The film *Amazing Grace*, about William Wilberforce and Britain's abolitionists, was released during the same month, and Walden Media adopted the first edition of this text as the "official book" of the Amazing Change Campaign. We were on our way.

SMART ACTIVISM

Even as we focused on developing the Not For Sale Campaign through 2007, we saw no need to replicate the tremendous work being done by the other organizations mentioned throughout this book. Instead, we wanted to design innovative technologies and educate passionate individuals about the roles they could play in eradicating human trafficking in their own backyards. In short, we wanted to engage a constituency of "smart activists."

The Campaign aims to mobilize students, entrepreneurs, artists, people of faith, athletes, law-enforcement officers, politicians, social workers, skilled professionals, and all justice seekers to fight the global slave trade. As I jokingly tell audiences, there are enough "dumb activists" in every social movement! To confront the complexity of the global slave trade demands a highly skilled and trained army of abolitionists.

In 2007 we began the process of galvanizing a constituency via a sixty-city road show that we took to college campuses, faith communities, and business conferences. We introduced the concept of "open-source activism," one of the central tenets of the Campaign.

Open-source activism encourages—even mandates—that individual abolitionists develop their own creative solutions wherever they live. This decentralized approach invites Campaign members to identify what slavery looks like in their city, state, or province, addressing these essential questions: What laws are in place? Do law-enforcement agents and prosecutors make good use of those laws? What anti-trafficking organizations are already working on the issue in the area? Who is generating primary research about possible trafficking sites? Where are the gaps?

Open-source activism catalyzes individuals and small groups armed with that information to exercise social power while collaborating with others to exchange ideas and share resources.

Living out that mantra, when the Campaign started I used my role as a professor to mobilize a group of students at the University of San Francisco to do what the local police department at the time did not make a priority: systematically track questionable businesses that could be fronts for involuntary servitude.

Working along with my USF colleague Mike Duffy, we developed research strategies that formed the foundation for the techniques that we now teach at the Not For Sale Academy. I am still amazed by that first group of intrepid students who could have—and probably should have—bolted for the door when I told them the focus of the course but who instead dug in and uncovered slavery in their own community.

After months of tracking potential trafficking situations, that first group of students uncovered a massage parlor in the financial district of San Francisco (not in the Tenderloin, our red light district) that was quite suspicious and troubling. The establishment promised, over the Internet, "hot Asian girls fresh off the boat each week," just as an importer of fresh fruit from, say, Chile might claim of its product.

The students really wanted to do undercover surveillance, but I responded firmly that they were not expendable. Using one's talents and passion for the cause of abolition is one thing; getting hurt is something else entirely. I could not help but ponder the screaming headlines that would appear were I to let a student waltz into a potential trafficking scenario and get hurt, or worse. The program would not be replicated elsewhere—and that is not smart activism.

Nonetheless, the students were correct on one count: someone needed to go into the massage parlor with a hidden camera and find out what was happening behind the door with the bars; local police had no interest in doing so. So, posing as out-of-town businessmen, Kique, Mark, and I got the evidence we needed. Then, armed with the students' months of work, public records, surveillance video, and our hidden-camera footage, we took our collective evidence to the San Francisco District Attorney's office. The San Francisco police eventually acted to shut down the massage parlor.

Each fall I walk into class on the first day and calmly explain to students that the "Justice Studies 101," the title of my course, is shorthand for "Investigating and Mapping Human Trafficking in San Francisco." No one has run from the room yet, but they do still seem surprised.

MANY PLATFORMS, ONE MOVEMENT

When I map out everything that the Not For Sale Campaign does and how fast it has grown in just a few years, I still cannot believe that it started simply as a response to Kru Nam's need for shelter. Partnering with international abolitionists remains a central focus of the Campaign—and always will be. We look specifically to partner with indigenous agencies to implement projects that meet three criteria: being innovative, replicable, and financially sustainable. These agencies are our feet on the ground, and we are reminded of that fact each time they introduce us to a child who has been freed from a brothel or a young woman rescued at a border crossing. They are why we push forward.

Our international projects are just one of many platforms of the Campaign, however. Here's a quick summary of other key initiatives:

SlaveryMap

In our zeal to make the invisible visible and to answer the refrain "Slavery may happen 'over there' but not where I live," we built a visual representation of exactly where slavery occurs, and we equip researchers to help us populate it. The result is a Google-based tool we call SlaveryMap (www.SlaveryMap.org).

In a short period of time we have featured more than fifteen hundred cases on SlaveryMap, and the numbers steadily increase. The tool offers a public rendering of documented cases, which allows law-enforcement officials, academics, politicians, and the common citizen to see that, indeed, slavery does occur in their jurisdictions and local communities. SlaveryMap does not publish suspected "live" or unresolved cases; for those, the Campaign provides the relevant evidence to law enforcement for potential intervention.

SlaveryMap enables us to understand the types of slavery most prevalent in a particular region, and the country of origin of the victims. It also provides us with a rich source of data on the number of victims, the number of traffickers, the role of law enforcement, the penalties delivered in the cases that are prosecuted, and trends within various states, provinces, and regions. At the moment, the majority of SlaveryMap cases are located specifically in the United States. As more people contribute globally, we will get an even more accurate picture of slavery around the world.

Each accurate entry brings us one step closer to talking in real numbers, not estimates or hyperbole, about how many slaves are in a given place and provides us with valuable intelligence about how to stop the slave traders. Advocates also find the data useful to persuade local officials that the prevalence of cases in their region calls for a higher priority of attention and commitment of resources to confront human trafficking.

Free2Work

We launched Free2Work (www.Free2Work.org) in 2009 to provide consumers with easy access to information that they need to make informed, ethical purchasing decisions. In partnership with the International Labor Rights Forum (ILRF), we created a sophisticated rating system that scores companies on the way that labor was used in the raw-material sourcing and manufacturing of their products. We aim to equip "smart consumers" with all the tools they need, placed conveniently at their fingertips. Free2Work will be a primary focus in the coming years for the Campaign, because we understand the role that consumers play as they "vote" with their purchases.

Free2Work nudges companies toward progressively more responsible supply chains. We especially want to reward companies that do not utilize forced labor anywhere in their acquisition, production, and distribution process. We designed a training course for leaders who want to lead supply-chain responsibility efforts inside their companies, and we partner with Manpower, Inc., the world's largest private employer, to offer this course to hundreds of thousands of companies internationally.

Consider what a single advocate inside a company can achieve. David Arkless runs government and corporate affairs for Manpower. Susan Mubarak, wife of the head of state of Egypt, asked David in January 2006 what he and his company were doing about human slavery. David admitted that he had no idea what she was talking about. Once he started investigating the prevalence of human trafficking, he was appalled. He decided to test how a Manpower office in southern Europe would screen to ensure that a slave would not be deployed for a work assignment. To his surprise, the office did not even check into an individual's background or otherwise check out whether he or she might be forced to perform the job.

David subsequently persuaded his own company to declare a zero tolerance for slavery worldwide, and the company's worldwide offices are now required to screen for forced labor and possible cases of human trafficking. Manpower has become a key strategic partner in the Not For Sale Campaign. Though some social activists may be cynical about the tangible benefits of a company's signing a policy declaration, the act has a key strategic purpose. Subsequent monitoring can help identify the practice of slavery in any corporation's supply chain. When the company has already made a public commitment to a standard of behavior, the obligation to address the violation becomes all the stronger.

The Not For Sale Academy

A burgeoning social movement sorely needs research and training, so we formed the Not For Sale Academy to offer experiential educational programs. We piloted the first of these programs, the Investigator Academy, to train researchers in ways to discover cases of trafficking in their region and publish those findings on SlaveryMap. We filled all the summer sessions and had to create a waiting list due to excessive demand.

In 2010, therefore, we secured facilities that would enable us to offer Investigator Academies throughout the year. We also offer academy courses on supply-chain tracking, social-venture entrepreneurship, advanced investigation in partnership with law enforcement, and training for health-care providers. In collaboration with an innovative service provider in Northern California, MISSSEY (Motivating, Inspiring, Supporting, and Serving Sexually Exploited Youth), we offer an Aftercare Academy to promote best practices among those organizations across the country that are working directly with victims and survivors.

Justice League

Traffickers commonly show up in unlikely places where law-enforcement officers do not have dedicated personnel or possess the proper training and financial resources to effectively pursue a case of involuntary servitude. There does exist, however, a growing number of experienced officers, federal agents, and prosecutors who work together to pursue intervention and prosecution of human trafficking crimes. The Not For Sale Campaign designed the Justice League to facilitate cooperation among law-enforcement agencies and trained community investigators.

In a single month, April 2010, the Justice League network demonstrated its potential. An NFS Academy graduate who directs our South Africa office played an instrumental role in turning evidence over to local police officers that led to the raid and closure of a brothel holding five teenage women, all victims of trafficking. That same week, in the United States, private investigators (with no previous connection to the Campaign) working on a marriage infidelity case stumbled onto a ring linking at least eleven massage parlors located in various cities in Northern California. The private investigators contacted NFS headquarters in San Francisco and delivered evidence that we in turn shared with federal law enforcement agents. The final outcome of this investigation is still pending. Finally, we learned in the month of April 2010 that an Academy graduate who lives near Edmonton, Alberta, provided Royal Canadian Mountie Police with a tip that led to the arrest of three traffickers who held Chinese women against their will and forced them to perform sexual services to paying customers. The Not For Sale Canada volunteer reported, "The training at the NFS Academy showed me red flags to look for and it ended up in assisting in the first trafficking charges laid in the province of Alberta."

All of these arrests became possible due to the close collaboration of trained civilian investigators who turn qualified leads over to the appropriate law agencies. The Justice League continues to be a dynamic network of federal agents, local police detectives, financial transaction and money-laundering investigators, tax specialists, prosecutors, and civilian investigators who are bent on seeing that criminals who trade in human lives are brought to justice.

Abolitionist Faith Communities

The faith community played a vital role in the American and British abolitionist movements of the 1800s, and the Campaign understands the key role it could play in the modern-day abolitionist movement. Therefore, we develop tools and initiatives specifically geared to an abolitionist faith network. We produced an eight-week Bible study as a companion to this book (it can be downloaded at www.NotForSaleCampaign .org), and the Campaign Web site offers additional resources geared specifically to faith communities.

Each year we celebrate Freedom Sunday (the first Sunday of Lent for Christians) and Freedom Shabbat (the first day of Passover for Jews) to galvanize thousands of churches and synagogues, respectively. Congregations that participate make a commitment that they will pray/preach/sing/act for freedom for the captives and stand beside any child of God who is for sale in their neighborhood. What an extraordinary opportunity for people of faith all around the world to unite against slavery.

Free2Play

Athletes can link their love for sports in a way that ensures that all kids are free to play. The program began when my son Caelin and his sixth-grade boys' basketball team committed ten cents for every basket they made during their season. The program has now expanded to high school and college athletic teams across the country, and even to professional athletes, who tie their personal or team achievement to a funding commitment. I am proud of the school where I teach, the University of San Francisco, where the athletic director has mandated that every sports team participate in a Free2Play activity during the course of its season.

Jeremy Affeldt, the star middle reliever for the San Francisco Giants, has become the face of Free2Play. At the beginning of the 2009 baseball season, he committed one hundred dollars for every strikeout he threw. He then recruited his friend Matt Holliday, the St. Louis Cardinals slugger, to commit five hundred dollars for every home run he hits. When I watch the Giants play the Cardinals, and Jeremy pitch against Matt, I admit to torn feelings. My love for the hometown Giants sway me toward a strikeout, however.

The funds we raise via the Free2Play program go toward funding sports programs for kids rescued out of trafficking. For instance, we run a dynamic surfing team for kids in Lima, Peru, built a basketball court at Kru Nam's project in northern Thailand, and created an in-line skating club for young girls in Oakland, California. Indeed, all kids should be Free2Play.

Freedom Store

The Freedom Store began as an online merchandising wing of the Campaign. Essentially, the Freedom Store sells goods produced out of our international project or from partner organizations. In late 2008, the Campaign made it possible for individuals to create "Freedom Store Outposts," or franchises. While the Freedom Store is an effective tool in itself, the Outpost program makes it that much more so by providing new venues for the sale of Campaign merchandise. In May 2010, the Campaign launched its first bricks-and-mortar retail store, in Half Moon Bay, California. Thus the story behind the product comes to life rather than simply being featured on a national e-commerce platform.

The Freedom Store sets four key priorities: (1) generate jobs/income for survivors and vulnerable populations; (2) create a viable marketplace and distribution center that makes priority one all the more feasible; (3) provide tangible "handles" that enable the Campaign to share the story of modern slavery and innovative means to fight it; and (4) offer distributors a means to generate revenue for their local antislavery efforts.

If women's groups in every professional association, religious community, and funding network would get behind abolition, they alone would fuel an international movement that could eradicate slavery.

That's a strategic proposal, not a normative one: Women obviously have no more ethical burden to end slavery than men. But it's an educated guess that women will carry the abolitionist movement forward. John Miller, former ambassador of the TIP office, passed along an idea that he received from a government minister in South Korea. The minister has initiated a national campaign in her country asking every business run by women to hire at least one freed slave for a legitimate job. Miller was inspired to consider how that kind of initiative might take root in the United States and Europe. The aggregate impact of such an employment scheme would be far-reaching.

In like manner women could give a tremendous lift to microenterprises around the globe with their consumer dollars. Annie Dieselberg's NightLight jewelry is sold through the Freedom Store because we are cognizant that every sale provides economic stability for women in Bangkok who are desperate to avoid returning to the sex industry. A shift of consumer dollars to fair-trade items and survivor-made goods could make an enormous difference for NightLight and the many agencies we support that are engaged in the financial-sustainability aspect of rescue and restoration.

Global Advocacy Days

Global Advocacy Days is a multicountry effort spearheaded by key Campaign personnel in each nation. Once a year hundreds of constituents gather in their nation's capital to advocate in favor of legislation that increases the efficacy of prosecution of trafficking, the solidity of protection from trafficking, and the rights of trafficking victims. This activity is the keystone event in a year-round effort to revise and strengthen anti-trafficking laws passed by national, state, provincial, and local governments.

The Global Forum

Once a year the Campaign gathers influential leaders across the social spectrum and our own grassroots in a "think tank" environment. The Global Forum has become a focused time for international anti-trafficking advocates—a beehive of intelligence—to design creative solutions to thorny problems. New legislation proposals and enterprise projects often emerge from the gathering as well as fresh alliances across the private and public sectors.

TIME TO TAKE ACTION

The moment to become an abolitionist is now. Waiting until "after I graduate," "after I retire," "when I have free time," and so on feels like an empty excuse. There are so many ways to get involved, to put your talents, abilities, and passions to use in the Campaign—just like my students do.

To begin, check out the "I Am . . ." menu at our online headquarters, www.NotForSaleCampaign.org. Pick the description that fits you best ("A Person of Faith," "A Student," etc.). You'll find tangible ideas for action, such as the following:

- Find a local leader at the "Regional Director Map" on the Web site. Directors can help you plug into local events and activities. We have forty regional directors across the United States and Canada, and Campaign operations on every continent.

- Use the Free2Work tool to inform your shopping choices. Or be more proactive and launch a Freedom Store Outpost through which you can increase the demand for products that bring enrichment to the producers, most of whom are former slaves.

- Make your exercise/sports pledge. By running, swimming, shooting hoops, or kicking field goals, your support will help to build recreational facilities for children rescued from slavery. Whole teams can sign up, so develop a Free2Play tournament in your Little League association or at your favorite golf course.

- Take part in Advocacy Days in your country's capital. If your country does not have an advocacy program, start one!

- If you are a person of faith, persuade your congregation to take part in Freedom Sunday or its equivalents in the other faith communities.

- Host a screening. The Not For Sale documentary, "Backyard Abolitionist," provides a great introduction to the issue of modern-day slavery and a primer on the role each of us can play in ending it. Get a few friends, family members, and colleagues together to host a screening. Get creative. Could you set up a large screen and host an outdoor screening? What about using a free meeting room at the local library or community center? Know a civic group that would like to sponsor the screening? Remember to have fair-trade chocolate on hand. Your guests will want treats!

- Ready to go deep into the movement? Attend an Abolitionist Academy and hone your skills. Better yet, apply to be a Not For Sale Campaign Fellow. You can work directly with the national staff on important initiatives while learning more about how your actions ripple through the abolitionist movement and bring freedom.

TEARS OF THE OPPRESSED

The book of Ecclesiastes is one of the most extraordinary pieces of ancient wisdom literature. The author beautifully expressed the desperation of the powerless: "I saw all the oppressions that are practiced under the sun. Look, the tears of the oppressed—with no one to comfort them! On the side of their oppressors there was power" (Eccles. 4:1).

In our world today, more than 30 million people live as slaves. Frankly, the power is on the side of the oppressors at the moment, but the number of abolitionists is on the rise. They will wipe away the tears of the oppressed and deliver justice to the oppressors. The movement gains momentum each time a new individual joins. It's your time. We need you.

I am not for sale.
You are not for sale.
No one should be for sale.

Notes

INTRODUCTION

1. U.S. Department of State press conference, June 16, 2009.
2. In the first edition of this book, I indicated that 27 million slaves exist in the world today. That figure is widely cited and traces back to research done by Kevin Bales in *Disposable People: New Slavery in the Global Economy* (Berkeley: Univ. of California Press, 2004). Siddarth Kara estimates a figure of 28.2 million for "contemporary slaves" in *Sex Trafficking: Inside the Business of Modern-Day Slavery* (New York: Columbia Univ. Press, 2008). Precise numbers for slaves are hard to come by because the slave trade operates in the shadows. Consider that the Dalit population in India is estimated at more than 160 million, and human-rights advocates persuade me that nearly 20 percent of the Dalit population are victims of forced labor. My conversations with Nanci Ricks, cofounder of the Dalit Freedom Network, have been particularly informative. See her book, *To Love the Slumdog: My Journey Serving the "Untouchables"—the Dalit,* self-published, 2009; www.loveslumdog.com. In its 2010 report on child labor, the International Labour Organization (ILO) estimates that there are 215 million children at work around the globe today; of these, 115 million are trapped in the worst forms of labor, such as the sex trade, military service, heavy mining and manufacturing, and drug trafficking (the *International Labour Organization 2010 Report on Child Labor,* Geneva, 2010). Based on my global advocacy, I am convinced that well over 30 million people live in slavery around the globe. Nonetheless, though I carefully document statistics in this book, I hold no illusion of their 100 percent accuracy. The anti-trafficking movement must set a priority on better data sourcing and investigation. In the conclusion of this book I explain how the Not For Sale Campaign makes that effort one of its priorities.
3. The "over one hundred thousand" figure comes from my own best-guess projection based on existing data and documentation by the Not For Sale Campaign. See also Richard J. Estes and Neil Alan Weiner, *The Commercial Exploitation of Children in the United States, Canada, and Mexico* (Philadelphia: Univ. of Pennsylvania School of Social Work, 2001), a three-year study funded in part by the U.S. Department of Justice.

4. George W. Bush, speech to the United Nations General Assembly (New York, September 23, 2003).

5. International Labour Organization, *The Cost of Coercion* (Geneva, Switzerland, May 2009).

6. U.S. Department of State, *2009 Trafficking in Persons Report* (Washington, D.C., 2010).

7. Miron Varouhakis, "Trafficked Women Are Victims," *Global Outlook* (Centre for Research on Globalization), July 26, 2002.

8. Benita Ferrero-Waldner, speech at the conference Combatting Trafficking in Human Beings (Vienna, Austria, March 17, 2006).

9. United Nations, *Ten Million Children Exploited for Domestic Labor* (New York: June 14, 2004).

10. International Labour Organization, *Combatting Child Labour in Cocoa Growing* (Geneva, Switzerland, 2005).

11. Kim Meston gave her testimony to Risa Medrick. I met with Meston and Medrick in Newton Center, Massachusetts, in September 2006.

12. U.S. Department of State, *2005 Trafficking in Persons Report* (Washington, D.C., 2006).

13. Bales, *Disposable People,* pp. 3–4.

14. Sam Brownback, press conference (U.S. Capitol, Washington, D.C., September 23, 2003).

15. Bales, *Disposable People.*

CHAPTER ONE

1. U.S. Department of State, *2009 Trafficking in Persons Report* (Washington, D.C., 2010), p. 279.

2. Alex Perry, "The Shame," *Time Asia,* February 2, 2002, http://www.time.com/time/asia/features/slavery/cover.html.

3. Deena Dudzer, "Child Sex Boom in Thailand Fueled by Poverty," *MinnPost.com,* October 29, 2009, http://www.minnpost.com/globalpost/2009/10/29/12961/child_sex_boom_in_thailand_fueled_by_poverty.

4. United Nations Development Program, *Human Development Report 2009—Cambodia* (New York, 2010), http://hdrstats.undp.org/en/countries/country_fact_sheets/cty_fs_KHM.html.

5. Sirirat Pusurinkham, "Child Prostitution in Thailand," *Witness,* December 19, 2001, p. 5.

6. UN Refugee Agency, "Burma: Conflict Children in Forced Labor," September 14, 2009, http://www.unhcr.org/refworld/docid/4ab9c9df2.html.

7. "Children for Sale," *MSNBC.com,* January 9, 2005, http://www.msnbc.msn.com/id/4038249.

8. Mikel Flamm, "Trafficking of Women and Children in South East Asia," *UN Chronicle,* no. 2 (2003): 1.

9. J. K. Reimer, *At What Price Honour? Research into Domestic Trafficking of Vietnamese (Girl) Children for Sexual Exploitation* (Phnom Penh: Chab Dai Coalition, 2006), p. 4.

10. Pusurinkham, "Child Prostitution in Thailand," p. 6.

11. Janejinda Pawadee (staff worker for the International Justice Mission, Chiang Mai, Thailand), in discussion with the author, June 17, 2006.

12. UNICEF, *State of the World's Children,* special ed. (New York, 2009), pp. 40–43.

13. International Labour Organization, *Give Girls a Chance: Tackling Child Labour, a Key to the Future* (Geneva, Switzerland, June 12, 2009).

14. International Labour Organization, *Give Girls a Chance,* p. 39.

15. International Labour Organization, *Give Girls a Chance,* p. 38.

16. Anne Gallagher, "Human Rights and Human Trafficking in Thailand: A Shadow TIP Report," in *Trafficking and the Global Sex Industry,* ed. Karen Beeks and Delila Amib (Oxford: Lexington, 2006), p. 145.

17. U.S. Department of State, *2009 Trafficking in Persons Report* (Washington, D.C., 2010), p. 280.

18. Dudzer, "Child Sex Boom," p. 5.

19. Center for the Protection of Children's Rights, *Case Study Report on Commercial Exploitation of Children in Thailand* (Bangkok, November 2003), p. 37.

20. World Vision, *Report on Sex Tourism* (Washington, D.C., May 2002).

21. Nicholas Kristof, "If This Isn't Slavery, What Is?" *New York Times,* January 4, 2009, p. WK8.

22. Andrew Perrin, "Special Report: Child Slavery," *Time Asia,* August 26, 2002, p. 25.

23. "Unwanted Visitors," *Economist,* August 23, 2008, p. 36.

24. Bales, *Disposable People,* p. 45.

CHAPTER THREE

1. World Vision Resources, http://www.worldvision.org/content.nsf/learn/globalissues-uganda\.

2. World Vision Resources, http://www.worldvision.org/content.nsf/learn/globalissues-uganda\.

3. Jan Egeland, interview on the BBC, November 10, 2003.

4. Florence Lacor, Gulu, Uganda, May 2006.

5. Grace Grall Akallo, "The Endangered Children of Northern Uganda" (testimony before the House Subcommittee on Africa, Global Human Rights, and International Relations, April 26, 2006).

6. Library of Congress, "A Country Study: Uganda," http://hdl.loc.gov/loc.gdc/cntrystd.ug.

7. "'Both Sides' Violate Uganda Truce," BBC News, October 15, 2006.

8. International Red Cross, "Uganda: Water and Sanitation Project Restores Hope in IDP Camps," http://www.icrc.org/web/eng/siteeng0.nsf/htmlall/uganda-feature–280907.

9. World Vision, *Pawns of Politics: Children, Conflict and Peace in Northern Uganda* (Washington, D.C., 2005), p. 26.

10. Jeffrey Gettleman, "Uganda Peace Hinges on Amnesty for Brutality," *New York Times,* September 15, 2006, p. A6.

11. Akallo, "The Endangered Children."
12. The Lord's Resistance Army Disarmament and Northern Uganda Recovery Act is referred to in Congress as S. 1067.

CHAPTER FOUR

1. Donna M. Hughes, "The 'Natasha' Trade: The Transnational Shadow Trade of Trafficking in Women," *Journal of International Affairs* 53, no. 2 (Spring 2000): 8–15.
2. MiraMed Institute, *Preliminary Survey Report on Sexual Trafficking from the CIS Countries* (Moscow, June 1999).
3. Moldovan Intelligence and Security Agency, cited in United States Aid and International Development Agency, *USAID Anti-Trafficking Assessment: Critical Gaps in and Recommendations for Anti-Trafficking Activities* (Washington, D.C., 2002).
4. U.S. Department of State, *2003 Trafficking in Persons Report* (Washington, D.C., 2004).
5. International Organization for Migration Counter-Trafficking Center, *Changing Patterns and Trends of Trafficking in Persons, the Balkan Region* (Geneva, Switzerland, July 2004). See also Martti Lehti, *Trafficking in Women and Children in Europe,* European Institute for Crime Prevention and Control, paper no. 18 (Helsinki, 2003).
6. Yedida Wolfe (executive director of Israel's Task Force on Human Trafficking), in discussion with Not For Sale Campaign staff, June 2008.
7. Anna Diamantopoulou, "Trafficking in Women: Prevention and Protection" (speech, Second Conference on Women in Democracy, Vilnius, Lithuania, June 16, 2001).
8. Ekaterina Popova and Ivailo Anguelov, "Human Trafficking in Europe Outweighs Drug Smuggling," *The Epoch Times,* April 14, 2009.
9. United Nations Office on Drugs and Crime, *Trafficking in Persons: Analysis on Europe* (Vienna, Austria, 2009).
10. Donna M. Hughes and Janice G. Raymond, *Sex Trafficking of Women in the United States: International and Domestic Trends* (New York: Coalition Against Trafficking in Women, March 2001).
11. Lehti, *Trafficking in Women and Children in Europe.*
12. Karin Alfredsson, *No to Prostitution and Trafficking* (Stockholm: Swedish Institute, 2005).
13. Alfredsson, *No to Prostitution and Trafficking.*
14. U.S. Department of State, Bureau of Democracy, Human Rights, and Labor, *Country Report on Human Rights Practices* (Washington, D.C., 2004 and 2005).
15. Department of State, *Country Report on Human Rights Practices.*
16. Regina Pacis, *Focus Moldova* (San Foca, Italy, 2005).

CHAPTER FIVE

1. Verushka Villavicencio et al., *The Client Goes Unnoticed* (Stockholm: Save the Children Sweden, 2004), p. 7.
2. Villavicencio, *The Client Goes Unnoticed*, p. 40.
3. Nicholas Wood, "For Albanians, It's Come to This: A Son for a TV," *New York Times,* November 13, 2003, p. A3.
4. Villavicencio, *The Client Goes Unnoticed*, p. 40.
5. "Juan Carlos" is a pseudonym for an actual television personality in Peru who acted in the way described in this chapter.
6. Villavicencio, *The Client Goes Unnoticed*, p. 40.

CHAPTER SIX

1. Free the Slaves, Washington, D.C., and Human Rights Center, University of California, Berkeley, *Hidden Slaves: Forced Labor in the United States* (September 2004), http://hrc.berkeley.edu/hiddenslaves.html.
2. Ben Schmitt and Suzette Hackney, "Sex Ring Busted by Kidnapped Girl's Tip," *Detroit Free Press,* January 15, 2003; Suzette Hackney, "Abducted Teen's Mother Describes House of Horrors," *Detroit Pree Press,* January 16, 2003; Suzette Hackney, "More Sex Ring Arrests Likely Today," February 4, 2003; Ben Schmitt, "More Charges in Sex Ring," *Detroit Free Press,* February 4, 2003; Suzette Hackney, "Man Sentences in Sex-Ring Case," *Detroit Free Press,* September 16, 2003.
3. Robert Reich, press release, U.S. Department of Labor, Office of Public Affairs (September 15, 1995).
4. U.S. Department of Justice, *Assessment of U.S. Government Efforts to Combat Human Trafficking* (Washington, D.C., 1996), p. 3.
5. Tina Frundt, statement made at a public hearing before the Subcommittee on Domestic and International Monetary Policy, Trade, and Technology, Committee on Financial Services, U.S. House of Representatives (Washington, D.C., April 29, 2005).

Acknowledgments

This book project began over a casual lunch with Mark Tauber, a longtime friend and deputy publisher at HarperOne. I owe Mark a tremendous debt for recognizing how my background uniquely qualified me to investigate the global slave trade and the emerging movement to resist it. Once the writing started, my editor at HarperOne, Mickey Maudlin, got involved. I came to treasure his friendship and advice during this project. My thanks to Mark and Keisha Hoerrner, who made major contributions to this second edition of the book.

Mark Wexler and Kique Bazan launched the Not For Sale Campaign with me and have proven themselves to be visionary, talented, and irrepressible—qualities essential for building a movement out of a molehill. Over the past three years we have been joined by extraordinary companions who act as conductors of the Campaign: Laura Aguirre, Kevin Austin, Don Batstone, Ethan Batstone, Brad Berky, Imelda Buncab, John Carson, Greg Galle, Stephen Goode, Christina Hebets, Cathy and Roger Hoesterey, Erik Lammerding, Dennis Mark, Hugh Marquis, Brant Menswar, Kilian Moote, Keturah Scott, Allison Trowbridge, and Stephanie Voorkamp. I wish I could list each regional director and international project leader of the Campaign by name as well, since each of them has given so deeply and achieved so much. A special recognition goes to David Arkless (Manpower), Jo Lawson (Apple), Jack Dorsey (Twitter; Square Up), Bernita McTernan (Catholic Healthcare West), and Shervin Pishevar (SGN) for their dynamic support in so many ways.

My admiration goes out to Steve Privett, S.J.; Jennifer Turpin; and Claudio Chiuchiarelli for their unyielding support and inspiring leadership at the University of San Francisco. My professorial life changed radically the day I teamed up with Mike Duffy at USF. Teaching the Erasmus Program with Mike has helped me to find my vocation as an educator of justice. My heartfelt thanks go out to all the Erasmus students with whom I have shared wonderful classroom dramas and global investigative trips.

A number of people played significant roles in helping me find my way through the invisible world of trafficking. I am deeply indebted to Bama Athreya, Tim Newman, Branka Minic, Pamela Livingston, Joe Mettimano, Margaret Larson, Nola Brantley, Justin Dillon, Ambassador John Miller, Ambassador Mark Lagon, Ambassador Louis CdeBaca, Pierre Tami, Lucy Borja, Kru Nam, Gary Haugen, Sean Litton, Blair Burns, Michael Kane, Kay Buck, Kru Nam, and Annie Dieselberg.

Randy Newcomb and I turned a coffee chat in a San Francisco café into an impromptu planning session for a movement that has become the Not For Sale Campaign. Randy's entrepreneurial spirit is a real gift. I owe a great debt to the rest of the Humanity United team as well, above all Lori Bishop and Saadiya Zaki. Special thanks go out to T-Bone Burnett, Callie Khouri, Ed Solomon, Bono, Ricky Ross, Lorraine McIntosh, Dan Russell, the Costello clan in Australia, Jim Wallis and the Sojourners staff, Michael and Frannie Kieschnick, Robert and

Joyce Marcarelli, Martin and Meg Wroe, Simon and Hilary Mayo, Laryn Bakker, Todd Sheffield, Steve Crisman, Erik Lokkesmoe, Mark Foreman, Bob McKenzie, Jon Foreman, and the fearless threesome of the Black Rebel Motorcycle Club.

Words alone cannot convey my love and appreciation for Wendy, Jade, Zachary, Jesse, and Caelin. Each family member made real sacrifices to bring this book and the Campaign to fruition. Wendy showed a remarkable ability to hold our chaotic family life together while I sank deep into this book and the subsequent Campaign. Beyond that, her photographic contribution to the Peru trip was stunning. You are a jewel, Wendy. I thank Caelin for being an amazing travel companion to Uganda. His journal entries from that trip inspired me beyond belief. I also will forever value my trip with Zak to Vietnam, with Jesse to South Africa, and with the entire family to Europe and Latin America as we investigated social injustice and human trafficking there. I reckon that we all became committed abolitionists during the process of putting this book together.

About the Author

David Batstone is professor of business and social responsibility at the University of San Francisco and is the author of *Saving the Corporate Soul & (Who Knows?) Maybe Your Own,* which won the Nautilus Award for 2004 Best Business Book. Batstone also serves as managing partner of Right Reality, a firm that invests in profitable ventures to benefit the world's "bottom billion" and the environment. He was a member of the founding team of *Business 2.0* magazine, served for five years as executive editor of *Sojourners* magazine, and has written regularly for the *New York Times,* the *Chicago Tribune, Wired, Spin,* and *USA Today.* He is a cofounder and president of the Not For Sale Campaign. Visit www.NotForSaleCampaign.org to join the cause.

JOIN THE
NOT FOR SALE CAMPAIGN

www.NotForSaleCampaign.org

✠ ✠ ✠

- Get updated research and breaking news on fighting slavery around the world

- Locate Not For Sale regional directors near your hometown

- Register for the Not For Sale Academy and take courses in citizen investigation, consumer fair-trade advocacy, social entrepreneurialism, innovative after-care, and vigilance for health care professionals

- Check out how athletes—major leaguers and joggers alike—are using their love for sports to ensure that all kids are free to play

- Learn how your company can be part of the Free-2Work movement

- Find out how you can start a Not For Sale Club on your college or high school campus and link with other abolitionist students around the globe

- Make a difference

I am not for sale
You are not for sale
No one should be for sale

www.NotForSaleCampaign.org